Integrative Sex & Couples Therapy

A Therapist's Guide to New and Innovative Approaches

Edited by **Tammy Nelson**, PhD

World-renowned expert in relationships and sex therapy

Copyright © 2020 Tammy Nelson

Published by
PESI Publishing & Media
PESI, Inc.
3839 White Ave
Eau Claire, WI 54703

Cover: Amy Rubenzer
Editing: Jenessa Jackson, Marietta Whittlesey
Layout: Amy Rubenzer & Bookmasters

ISBN: 9781683732570
Library of Congress Control Number: 2020934733
Printed in the United States of America

PESI
Publishing
& Media
pesipublishing.com

Acknowledgments

This book could not have been written without the authors' contributions. Thank you to authors Gail Guttman, Daniel Rosen, Pebble Kranz, Wendy Miller, Pamela Finnerty, James Wadley, Malika O'Neill, Neil Cannon, Amanda Holmberg-Sasek, Deborah Fox, Janet Brito, Einat Metzl, and Stephanie King. Thank you also to contributors Sylvia Rosenfeld, Sophie Slade, Orli Wahrman, and Jen Gunsaullus. With special thanks and great appreciation to Linda Jackson, Marietta Whittlesey, and Jenessa Jackson at PESI Publishing.

To my program assistant Scarlett Ross and to all my students and faculty at the Integrative Sex Therapy Institute, who trusted me when I began the program and believed me when I said everyone wants to and should be a certified sex and couples therapist. To all of the certified sex and couples therapists out there: You are ahead of the pack. Keep up the great work. To those who are just discovering this work and are still on the path: Good luck, keep going, and know that you are doing important work in changing the world.

Table of Contents

Introduction

Integrative Sex and Couples Therapy: A New Field

Tammy Nelson, PhD

"We are sexual beings, and our sexuality is part of the pulsating
energy of life which we express through mind, body, and psyche."
—Harville Hendrix

For many years, the field of psychotherapy has focused on the treatment of the individual. It has focused on the gestalt of the person, including object relations from their past, their family history, and the analysis of their deeper desires, dreams, and fears. Although family therapy and couples therapy have recently been added as an adjunct treatment modality, sexuality is still considered only a small piece of the treatment process as it relates to a whole person's life span.

However, in today's society, sexuality and relationships are primary to the experience of a person's life. Our sexual development and education around sexual identity, orientation, and sexual relationships are a complex narrative of eroticism, trauma, guilt, and pleasure. Much like any other lifelong practice, such as a commitment to yoga or meditation, our sexuality can be fraught with difficulty and also contain untold thrills and joys along the way. Contemporary therapists must be able to hear these narratives and sit with the stories, experiences, and struggles. They must have the tools, interventions, and magic, if you will, to bring to light the cause of sexual dysfunction, help repair relationships, and create states of safety and trust wherein clients can find pleasure and joy in their life, both physically and emotionally. There has never been a time in our profession when integrative sex and couples therapy is more needed.

When I initially sought training as a psychotherapist, I was interested in relationships—not only with regard to relationships between couples but also with regard to partnerships of all kinds. It seemed the most interesting part of psychology. I thought counseling was meaningless if it didn't focus on what I believed to be the most fundamental part of a person's life: one's connections to other people. Although my graduate and postgraduate program focused on the complexities of human relations, they never talked about sex. I found this odd. Adult marriages and committed partnerships are not simply roommate relationships. However, my program did not train me to deal with what is simply a primary part of existence: sexuality.

Therefore, I subsequently pursued a PhD in sexology and became certified as a sex therapist. I made it my mission to train therapists to talk to their clients about sexuality and wrote a book integrating sexuality with Imago Relationship Therapy (IRT) techniques called *Getting the Sex You Want*. I worked with thousands of couples to improve their relationships and their sex lives. More and more couples came to therapy not just to improve their sexual lives but to repair their erotic relationships. Affairs, betrayals, and disconnection of all kinds led me to write *The New Monogamy: Redefining Your Relationship After Infidelity*. I spoke around the world to couples and clinicians about how to heal their erotic lives, repair their intimacy, and move forward into a new vision of hope.

Through my work, it has become readily apparent that therapists are continuing to miss a vital part of training: the integration of couples *and* sex therapy. While greater numbers of therapists are being trained as sex therapists, they are not receiving training in relationship systems. They are being trained to work with sexual dysfunction, sexual inadequacy, and performance disorders—but they are *not* being trained to work with couples. Similar to the lack of sexuality taught in old family therapy courses, few relationship skills are taught in current sex therapy programs.

Psychotherapy is going to have to focus on relationships and sexuality in order for us to continue to help people. For our profession to support the growth of humanity, we can no longer avoid the conversation around sexual intimacy; we have to train clinicians in the skills necessary to teach individuals and couples how to have healthy relationships. Although integrating sex and couples therapy can be a challenge in sessions, the combination of these skills is the only way to treat people who long for healthy, connected, and intimate partnerships.

In this book, I have gathered the best experts in the field of integrative sex and couples therapy, which is a new field of psychotherapy. In each chapter, the authors describe the techniques and strategies they use to combine their unique and contemporary psychotherapeutic work. Because sex therapists have traditionally been taught little about couples therapy and relationship systems—and couples therapists have had little education in sex therapy—this book introduces a myriad of ways that clinicians can bring this combined skill set into their practice. In these chapters, you will find step-by-step instructions and case examples that will help beginning practitioners expand their field of knowledge and allow even the most advanced clinicians to incorporate new skills immediately into their work.

Chapter One describes the **foundations of sex therapy and its roots in cognitive behavioral therapy.** The chapter explores how sexual issues in relationships and intrapsychic factors can affect self-esteem and the capacity for connection in the couple. This chapter reviews how therapists can attune with each partner in couples work and intervene with regard to specific sexual dysfunctions. The chapter unravels the "dance" between the couple and gives specific suggestions to help couples communicate about their relational space. These interventions create a path toward positive, healthy sexuality.

Chapter Two is written by a married couple, a certified sex therapist and a sexual medicine physician. Together they have created a **Collaborative Sexual Wellness Model** that combines the treatment of sexual dysfunctions, sexual disorders, anxiety, and relationship problems by integrating medical, social, cultural, and psychodynamic aspects within a couples counseling framework. Their collaborative model incorporates couples counseling, sex therapy, and sexual medicine in order to provide comprehensive, whole-person-centered care for couples with sexual concerns.

Chapter Three discusses how to integrate **Emotionally Focused Therapy (EFT) when treating couples who are in a no-sex partnership.** Grounded in attachment theory, the goal of EFT is to help couples develop a secure bond with each other that can form the basis from which sexuality and erotic playfulness can emerge. However, the relationship between sexuality and attachment is multifaceted, and there is often more to this complex relationship work than just the use of attachment theory to treat sexual issues. For some couples, increasing attachment security and emotional connection can facilitate the awakening of positive sexual involvement, but for others, attachment and sexuality seem to exist on opposing dimensions. Therefore, therapists must consider multiple possibilities and avenues to help couples create a satisfying sexual life that is in accordance with their specific needs and history.

Chapter Four focuses on **Imago Relationship Therapy (IRT) and sex.** IRT was created by Harville Hendrix and Helen Hunt, who wrote the book *Getting the Love You Want.* The basic premise of IRT is the notion that partners have the potential to heal each other from their childhood wounds by communicating with each other through the process of active listening, mirroring, empathy, and validation. This chapter describes how sex therapy combined with IRT can encourage fantasy and lead to an increase in erotic desire in couples where passion has waned—facilitating what I call "erotic recovery." Additional contributors to this chapter remind readers that sex therapy is more than just providing couples with mechanical or physical interventions. It is about helping couples create romance, increase play, and create a positive sexual mood.

Chapter Five looks at integrating **Internal Family Systems (IFS) therapy with sex therapy,** which involves working with different parts of the person, including those that are defined as exiles, protectors, and firefighters. Unblending these parts can help individuals move toward more fulfilling sexual relationships. This chapter also discusses a technique called "courageous communication," which involves helping individuals speak on behalf of their protective and vulnerable internal parts to create connection and empathy.

Chapter Six discusses how to conduct **group therapy with couples to help heal sexual trauma.** In couples group therapy, the couple is considered the primary client, and the community of the group functions as a therapeutic environment in which couples learn how to hold each other accountable with firmness and compassion, as well as how to hold difficult and traumatic content. The group atmosphere provides an opportunity for individuals to observe and facilitate the work of other couples, which evolves into a vehicle that creates healthier relationships for all. As group members identify with and participate in the healing of other couples, they develop a healthy mutual interdependence and emotional connection.

Chapter Seven takes a look at the concept of **intersectionality and how it affects clients in minority groups.** In the field of sex and couples therapy, there is a lack of understanding when it comes to intersectionality, as therapists rarely receive intersectionality training and have learned to work only with clients who are traditionally considered part of the dominant culture (e.g., those who are White, able-bodied, middle class, male, heterosexual). The lack of inclusiveness and limited, narrow scope of treatment models can negatively affect those who seek out treatment. In order to conduct competent integrative sex and couples therapy, practitioners need to be aware of their own multicultural background and gender roles, including how these factors may or may not affect treatment.

Chapter Eight focuses on **sex and couples therapy with kinky clients.** This coauthored chapter describes how to conduct effective treatment with couples who fall outside the spectrum of "vanilla." Clients often do not share their kinky interests out of fear their therapist will judge them. For therapists to be kink competent, they must make clients feel heard, safe, and accepted, both in the therapy room and by their partner. This chapter reviews the basics of creating a therapeutic alliance with kinky clients and provides a framework for kink-competent treatment.

Chapter Nine discusses **somatic-focused interventions for sex and couples therapy.** This chapter focuses on helping couples communicate without words, and sex therapy is used to unpack the inherent stress in the postures and gestures in the space between the couple. The integration of somatic therapy with sex and couples therapy involves interventions and directive techniques that release tension and resolve past childhood trauma. It also engages the body as a resource to facilitate growth. The words used in session between partners about what is happening in the body create an access point to guide couples from disconnection to connection.

Chapter Ten discusses the **Nutri-Sexual Health Model.** This treatment model integrates the role of nutrition with sex and couples counseling to treat relationship and sexual difficulties, recognizing that individuals' eating and lifestyle habits impact their sexuality. The model asks that clients increase awareness of foods that promote energy and inspire joy, with suggestions for health-promoting foods. The chapter promotes a way for sexual health providers to bring up the topic of nutrition and review its correlation with sexual functioning.

Chapter Eleven focuses on **art and sex therapy-informed interventions.** This chapter explores how to work with couples from a creative and integrative framework. Using art therapy tools combined with sex therapy assessments and psychoeducation decreases sexual conflicts by allowing couples to explore their physical, sexual, emotional, spiritual, and cognitive experiences. Clients are invited to explore and witness their partner's experiences and express intimacy as their issues and conflicts arise and heal through creative expression. Through the use of art, couples can connect and explore themselves both separately as individuals and together as a couple.

Chapter Twelve discusses how to take a **gender-affirmative approach in working with LGB(Trans)QIA couples.** Transgender clients can have varying sexual orientations and their partners may also be part of the LGB(Trans)QIA community or could identify as cisgender and heterosexual. Given their history of discrimination and marginalization, transgender clients' experience in therapy is often stressful, and their sexual issues are misunderstood. The overall intent of this chapter is to offer clinicians a better understanding of transgender people's needs and discuss more effective ways to intervene in sex and couples therapy.

Chapter Thirteen explores **mindfulness as a treatment intervention for anxiety and avoidance in the context of sexual relationships.** Using this author's six-week erotic recovery protocol, couples use sex therapy, couples therapy, mindfulness techniques, and sensate focus to increase connectedness, arousal, intimacy, and desire in their relationship. When couples improve their sexual functioning while practicing mindfulness and being present, it can ultimately lead to an increase in passion and better sexual performance.

Chapter Fourteen explores the role of **polyamory and technology on how we view monogamy.** It also includes a short discussion on robots and their impact on the future of sex. It is important for therapists to consider these new models of sexuality and relationships when talking about contemporary treatment and what is next for psychotherapy. Polyamory and sexually open relationships are changing how we practice sex and couples therapy, and artificial intelligence and virtual reality will impact clients in the near future as well.

In conclusion, the future of the field of psychotherapy is the integration of sex and couples therapy. All therapists, whether they are marriage and family therapists, social workers, psychologists, or sex therapists, will at some point in their work be confronted with their own limitations. Within this book, they will find the tools, techniques, and knowledge they need to work with the modern couple and go forward into the future.

Chapter 1

Sex and Couples Therapy: Biopsychosocial and Relationship Therapy

Gail Guttman, LCSW

Traditionally, there has been a disconnect between the fields of couples therapy and sex therapy in that therapists trained in one field are generally not trained in the other. This division may be due to the fact that couples therapy and sex therapy are not easy to integrate. Most couples therapy is focused on *process*—that is, helping couples look at their patterns of relating to each other and guiding them to change their interactions. The process of a couple's conflict is the focus of the session, instead of the content, as the process is the root of the problem. Sex therapy, however, is primarily focused on *content*. The content of sex therapy consists of the physiology of sexual functioning, psychoeducation about healthy sexuality, and tools to change sexual performance and interaction. Sex therapists need to have this body of knowledge at their fingertips at all times.

However, knowing content alone will not help clients if there are underlying intrapsychic difficulties or issues in the relationship. Sex and couples therapists must be attuned to each partner in the relationship, as well as to the quality of the relationship, to effectively move from focusing on sexual dysfunction to helping the couple develop a positive, healthy sexual relationship. Another essential factor in providing integrative sex and couples therapy is the ability to help individuals in a relationship understand the various influences that have contributed to their sexual self-esteem and their beliefs about sexuality. Often, an individual's sexual self-esteem needs healing in the context of the relationship and within themselves. It takes skill on the therapist's part to distinguish when to focus on the process of a session versus the content.

This chapter explores the theory and practice of the integration of sex and couples therapy through these three lenses: (1) basic knowledge of sexuality, (2) relationship systems, and (3) intrapsychic factors affecting sexual self-esteem, identity, and connection. It also provides methods to intervene in these three important areas.

SEX THERAPY AS COGNITIVE BEHAVIORAL THERAPY

There is a body of basic knowledge about sexual functioning that is essential in helping couples address sexuality problems. Much of this original knowledge and practice was developed through the research and work of Alfred Kinsey, William H. Masters, Virginia E. Johnson, and Helen Singer Kaplan from the late 1940s until the 1960s (Kaplan, 1974; Kinsey, 1948, 1953; Masters & Johnson, 1966, 1970). From this work, we have come to understand that sexuality is a natural physiological process in the body, as is eating, sleeping, and drinking. When people try to control their sexuality by attempting to change it, direct it, or make it happen in a certain way, they interfere with this natural body function and can experience physiological anxiety. In fact, underlying almost every sexual dysfunction, such as anorgasmia, erectile dysfunction, premature ejaculation, and hypoactive sexual desire, is anxiety. *For the most part, anxiety is a physiological response that is incompatible with sexual responsivity.*

When people are anxious, their blood vessels contract and thus constrict the flow of blood throughout the body. In sexuality, genital and pelvic floor responsivity, such as lubrication in the female and erection in the male, occurs when blood flows into these regions in the body. When a person is anxious about sexuality or their performance and tries to control their response, the blood flow does not occur or stops; this can happen in the beginning, middle, or later stages of the sexual encounter.

Using this body of knowledge regarding the human sexual response, one of the earliest interventions for sexual dysfunction—the PLISSIT model (Annon, 1976)—was operationalized through the practice of cognitive behavioral therapy (CBT). Given that CBT is considered the gold standard of treatment for anxiety disorders, it makes sense that the original treatment of sexual dysfunctions was based on this modality. Broadly speaking, the PLISSIT model provides an approach to addressing sexual dysfunction that is based on the following acronyms: P for Permission Giving, LI for Limited Information, SS for Specific Suggestions, and IT for Intensive Therapy. Understanding each of these components provides a framework to practice sex therapy in a way that addresses anxiety and can improve sexual functioning.

PERMISSION GIVING

Permission Giving is the process of creating safety and acceptance in order for clients to discuss the most vulnerable parts of themselves: their sexuality, sexual beliefs, and sexual self-esteem. Although maintaining a nonjudgmental attitude often comes easily to therapists, helping clients be open about sexuality requires that therapists be comfortable discussing sexuality as well. For therapists who are not comfortable, it is helpful for them to receive supervision or attend a Sexual Attitude Restructuring (SAR) workshop. These workshops can easily be found at the website for the American Association of Sexuality Educators, Counselors, and Therapists (AASECT). The ability to discuss sex in a natural, open way is the most essential skill in giving clients permission to share their sexual concerns.

From my experience, about 50 percent of couples have seen other therapists prior to coming to me for sex and couples therapy. These couples have sometimes experienced previous therapists who have allowed arguing, put-downs, and other forms of blaming in their past sessions. It is my job to be the authority in the room—the person who will contain the process. Therapists need to set boundaries around reactive behavior in order for both individuals in the couple to feel safe. There is security in knowing that the therapist can manage the energy in the office, which then creates permission to discuss the sensitive topics around sexuality.

For example, when John and Julie came to couples therapy, it became clear by the second session that they were there to address their conflict around desire discrepancy. Julie expressed a litany of provoking and blaming comments in a raised voice, "You only think about yourself. This is all your fault. You don't initiate sex ever. It is never the right time for you. You are a narcissist." Upon hearing this, John stood up, kicked the trash can, and left the room. He came back about 10 minutes later. At that time, I made the boundaries clear to both of them: "It is important to slow down and speak for yourself. It is my job to keep the space in the therapy room safe by helping you both to slow yourselves down and begin to listen to each other. When you speak everything that comes to your mind, instead of monitoring your own thoughts, your partner is not able to stay present to you. Additionally, physical reactions, such as kicking the trash can, will frighten your partner and are not okay in the session."

I inform couples that this type of contract is essential to keep the therapy room as a safe container where they can explore the more vulnerable feelings around their sexual relationship. I ask each of them to verbally agree to this contract. In later sessions, if it is needed, I remind them that they have made a contract with me to this effect.

In addition to setting boundaries, the following are some other ways therapists can help clients feel safe discussing sexuality:

- Educate clients about sexuality as it relates to their problem. This gives them confidence and hope that the therapist can help them. For example, when working with a female with hypoactive sexual desire, I inform the client about the difference between spontaneous versus responsive desire. In other words, desire often comes after arousal. Women are relieved and validated by this knowledge. Whether they have a male or female partner, this information is a relief to the partner, as they have often taken their partner's lack of desire to mean that there is something wrong with them.

- Use correct sexuality terms. For example, speak openly and plainly, using the correct words for body parts: penis, vagina, oral sex, and sexual intercourse.

- Normalize clients' anxiety about discussing sex with a therapist who was until now, a stranger, by saying things like, "This must be uncomfortable, talking about the most intimate details of your life. I want you to know there is little I haven't heard in this office."

- Use good listening skills and validate their experiences.

LIMITED INFORMATION

Limited Information is the process of providing basic education regarding the topic at hand. It is synonymous with the process of helping clients change their cognitions in CBT. Cultural, familial, religious, and societal norms usually do not provide clients with education about healthy sexual attitudes and beliefs. It is this history that therapists need to access to make attuned interventions.

Consider the case of Lauren and Ron, who came in for therapy to discuss their sexual issues and who were both quite emotional. Lauren had grown distant from Ron. As a coping mechanism, Ron was viewing pornography more frequently than he was comfortable with. His wife interpreted this behavior to mean that Ron was not attracted to her and wanted women who looked similar to the pornographic actors. She often became angry in this discussion, both at home and in the sessions, and eventually became quite tearful.

An important intervention for the therapist to make in this situation is to teach the couple about the use of pornography by giving limited information on the topic. Some examples of giving important limited information might be:

- Pornography and fantasy can sometimes be a way to create more arousal.

- Pornography can help bring the brain into the sexual experience.

- Most people are not interested in doing what they see in a video.

- Viewing more pornography than a person is comfortable with is often a coping mechanism.

However, some new therapists, in their excitement to help clients achieve results, can give too much information in a way that is not attuned to the couple. It is important to use limited information in session only when the therapist clearly understands the problem and has made space for clients to explore the necessary emotions underlying their beliefs. If a therapist were to offer this information too soon in the course of treatment, the opportunity could be missed to go deeper and explore the client's underlying emotions. For example, Lauren thought she was not enough for her husband both in terms of her body image and as a partner. These were important places to explore in order to help both Lauren and Ron as a couple.

Therefore, therapists should ask themselves a number of questions before offering important limited information, beginning with, "Why am I giving this information, and this amount of information, at this time?" Some other questions for the therapist to ask themselves when considering when to give attuned limited information include:

- Am I anxious about the amount of emotion shown and thus interrupting the flow?

- Have I fully understood the client(s) before I offer information?

- Am I uncomfortable with the subject they are discussing?

There are many examples of how limited information might be helpful in an integrative sex and couples therapy session and facilitate cognitive restructuring. Some examples that are helpful include:

- Most of the time, anxiety and sexuality are incompatible physiological responses. Blood vessels close when people are anxious and open when they are relaxed. Blood flowing into the genitals is the primary mechanism for physiological arousal in the pelvic and genital areas.

- Sexuality is about options. When something is not working, do something else rather than continuing to do the same thing over and over or withdrawing from one's partner. Remember the quote by Albert Einstein, "Insanity is doing the same thing over and over again and expecting different results."

- Sex is a journey. Pay attention to the journey instead of worrying about or focusing on arriving at the destination (the orgasm or intercourse).

- A sexual experience is similar to meditation. When someone gets distracted by their thoughts, they can notice them, let them go, and return to focusing on the sensations in the moment.

- Other than medical problems, the brain is the primary organ in the body that interferes with sexual functioning.

- Different and multiple types of stimulation help enhance arousal.

- The use of fantasy is another form of stimulation that can help a person focus more on sensations, rather than observing or worrying about their own or their partner's arousal. Using fantasy is not necessarily a sign that a person is not attracted to their partner or wants a different partner. Fantasy is a thought, not (necessarily) a desired action.

- The goal of sexual encounters is not performance; rather, it is about pleasure, connection, fun, and stress relief. Focus on the many positive aspects of sex instead of how each person is performing.

- Touch has two points of contact. When a person is touched, their focus is on the specific body part being touched. The other person's focus is on touching and noticing what they experience in touching. Pleasure can be experienced in both ways.

- Accepting differentiation in sexual relationships helps deepen sexual intimacy and connection. Examples of this are:
  - Couples are not always aroused by the same type of sexual activities. This is not a sign of incompatibility. For example, individuals can address different arousal triggers by taking turns.
  - Welcome one's own sexuality, as well as that of one's partner. Shaming a partner for their desires is often based in one's own fear and can be damaging to the relationship.

- Many people have different doors into their sexuality. Despite the differences, pay attention to what stimulates sexual interest in the partner.

SPECIFIC SUGGESTIONS

Specific Suggestions involves giving clients specific suggestions for behavior changes that can help improve sexual satisfaction or functioning. It is similar to treating anxiety within a CBT framework, in which clients work their way up a hierarchy of anxiety-provoking situations. For example, clients with a fear of flying may first begin treatment by looking at pictures of airplanes until they habituate to the anxiety that this stimulus causes. The next step in the hierarchy might be going to the airport, followed by walking into the airport, going to the gate, getting on the plane, and eventually flying. This method of systematic desensitization helps clients gradually overcome their anxiety to become comfortable with flying.

Helping clients change in integrative sex and couples therapy is based on the same principles. Sex therapists offer couples a ladder of activities to help them work through their sexual anxiety to become more comfortable and present in their sexual interactions. Sensate focus, which is an intervention developed by Masters and Johnson, is a prime example of using an anxiety hierarchy. The purpose of sensate focus, which is a form of mindfulness, is to help people create an experience in the present moment wherein they concentrate on the sensations in their body instead of focusing on their thoughts. In doing so, it releases people from the anxiety of performance and pleasing their partner. In the long run, this creates a more satisfying, pleasurable, and sensual experience. The hierarchy of exercises involved in this process could be as follows:

1. The couple is first given directions to explore their partner's body through touch, while not touching the breasts or genitals.

2. After a comfort level has been achieved by both partners with the nonsexual touch, exercises include incorporating gentle touch that adds the breasts and genitals.

3. Positive verbal and nonverbal communication are added in order for individuals to guide their partner's touch.

4. Eventually intercourse is experienced, focusing on mindfulness.

However, the anxiety hierarchy may not always work as planned. Sometimes, difficulties with compliance occur when therapists do not have the client's "buy-in" when it comes to the exercises. Other times, clients may simply be asked to start with activities that are too far up the ladder for them. For example, a couple may not be ready to start with a naked-body touching exercise. To avoid these challenges, it is more useful for the therapist to first define the overall concept of sensate focus, educating the couple on the purposes of sensate focus and then asking them what touching exercise might work for them. In other words, cocreating the exercise together makes it more likely that there will be buy-in from the couple, and it ensures the therapist does not inadvertently assign the couple a starting exercise that elicits too much sexual anxiety.

There are other reasons couples have difficulty with compliance in "doing the exercises" between sessions. The explanation for this noncompliance can be found in the complexities of sex and couples therapy. If CBT is not working, therapists need to turn to other factors affecting sexuality: the relationship and intrapsychic beliefs about one's sexuality. This is when the therapist turns to the final step of the PLISSIT model: intensive therapy.

INTENSIVE THERAPY

The final level of the PLISSIT model is *Intensive Therapy*, in which the therapist works to uncover the underlying issues contributing to the sexual difficulty at hand. To address these issues, the sex therapist needs to explore two important factors: (1) the dynamics of the couple's relationship and (2) the formation of each partner's sexual self-esteem.

Exploring the Relationship Dynamic

Becoming a skilled relationship therapist is an essential component in sex therapy. Addressing a sexual problem, dysfunction, or issue cannot be easily accomplished through individual therapy alone, especially if the client is in a relationship. Often, a partner unknowingly contributes to the sexual difficulty in unconscious, unaware ways. Generally, the sooner the therapist can work with the couple, the more effective the therapy.

In couples therapy, therapists work with the relationship. In fact, the relationship *is* the client rather than the individual. Indeed, there are three entities in every dyadic couple's relationship: Partner A, Partner B, and the relationship itself. It is the therapist's job to help clients see the relationship as an entity unto itself. The relationship is the energy that a therapist observes between the couple. The easiest way to initially understand this concept is to ask a couple what the energy between them feels like when they are in an argument. If partners have an argument and retreat from each other, they will describe a negative, tense energy between them. Partner A could be on the second floor of a house and Partner B in the basement. They will feel tension all the way from the basement to the second floor. Most couples identify with this example.

It is the therapist's job to help the clients understand they are responsible for the energy between them. This energy between couples is described as the "relational space" or "the space in between," both in Imago Relationship Therapy (IRT) and Emotionally Focused Therapy (EFT). Philosophers, such as Martin Buber and Jalāl ad-Din Muhammad Rumi (most often known as Rumi), have described this space as well. Martin Buber says, "When two people relate to each other authentically and humanly, God is the electricity that surges between them." Similarly, Rumi notes, "Beyond our ideas of right-doing and wrong-doing, there is a field. I'll meet you there. When the soul lies down in that grass, the world is too full to talk about. Ideas, language, even the phrase 'each other' doesn't make sense anymore." It is the therapist's job to teach couples about this space and how to take care of it.

In order to take care of this relational space, each partner needs to understand they contribute to creating ruptures within it. When a person feels unsafe in the relationship, they instinctually respond in ways to protect themselves and make themselves feel safe, even though that behavior often causes ruptures in the relational space. For example, they may withdraw, lash out, or leave their partner alone following a conflict. These adaptive coping mechanisms reflect the body's instinctual fight, flight, or freeze response. They mobilize the body for action in response to a threatening situation, regardless of whether the threat is real or imagined.

What shows up in the therapist's office is an interaction between couples—a dance of sorts—that reflects the disconnection between them. The relational conflict observed in the therapist's office is a microcosm of the interaction occurring between them at home. It reflects the couple's pattern of relating that is driven by their adaptive coping mechanisms, which, in turn, creates the disconnection. It is the job of the couples therapist to help couples change this pattern of relating so each partner can relax their protective behaviors and share their underlying feelings, beliefs, fears, and values. This type of sharing reflects an expression of what is often called the individual's "essence," "Self," "true identity," or "centered self."

As individuals express their essence, the relational space becomes more connected, safe, and intimate, and each partner begins to feel calmer and more fully alive. Differentiation in connection, which is the ability for each partner to express their individuality and remain connected, is achieved as well. There is then room for each partner to fully express themselves, no matter their differences, and still feel connected in the relational space.[1] The following diagram reflects the creation of differentiation in connection in the relational space.

Relational Paradigm

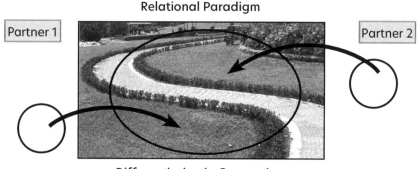

Differentiation in Connection

The goal of couples therapy is to change the process between the partners in the relationship instead of focusing on the details of the conflict (i.e., the content). It is the therapist's job to help the couple see their sexuality dance *and* speak about what is underneath the dance. However, in integrative sex and couples therapy, therapists also offer feedback about the content of the problem (i.e., the sexual issues) to help the

---

[1] The same types of interactions are seen in dyadic partnerships or polyamorous relationships. At times, in polyamorous relationships, the dance may be more complex, as more people are involved, but the dynamics are similar. Therefore, any of the information presented in this chapter can be applicable to polyamorous relationships.

couple change their emotional and sexual interaction. As they change their dance and take care of the relational space, differences in sexuality can then be welcomed, and these differences can enhance their sexual connection.

Ultimately, it is possible to help couples relax their coping mechanisms and share their underlying feelings, beliefs, fears, and needs to restore connection, safety, and aliveness, both emotionally and sexually. In the following section, a discussion of these coping mechanisms and interventions to address them will be explored through the lens of IRT, EFT, and Internal Family Systems (IFS). At the heart of each of these theories is the notion that these coping mechanisms create disconnection in the relational space by "polluting it with trash."

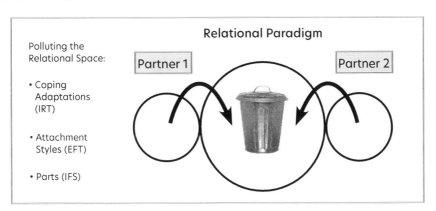

Imago Relationship Therapy

Through the lens of IRT, the protective mechanisms that individuals engage in when they feel unsafe in the relationship are referred to as coping adaptations. These coping adaptations are expressed through behaviors that reflect energy-out adaptations (e.g., fighting, overtalking, verbal shaming) or energy-in adaptations (e.g., withdrawing, stonewalling, fleeing, freezing). Individuals with energy-out coping mechanisms are called maximizers, "tigers," or "hailstorms," and those with energy-in styles are called minimizers or "turtles."

The following example illustrates how the coping adaptations that individuals engage in can create ruptures in the relational space. Mary and Joe were referred to me for help with their sexual dysfunction. Joe was diagnosed with premature ejaculation, as he ejaculated shortly after intercourse began. As a result, he developed secondary erectile dysfunction. In other words, he became anxious about his ability to maintain an erection because of his anxiety about having an orgasm prematurely. He also had low testosterone, which resulted in lower sexual desire, and he was taking testosterone prescribed by his urologist to address this concern. Mary had no functional sexual problems, but she was avoiding sexual encounters with Joe because of his frustration about his own lack of sexual response.

In their fourth therapy session, we explored their sexual interaction in detail, which revealed their sexual pattern (or "dance"). At some point in the beginning of each sexual interaction, Joe would have difficulty with his erection or ejaculate within minutes of insertion into Mary's vagina. Joe would grow frustrated and leave the bedroom in a fit of anger. Mary would be upset but unable to express her feelings. Instead, she would withdraw and begin to avoid sex as often as possible.

The ways Mary and Joe protected themselves and created a rupture in their relationship are clear. Joe protected himself by getting angry. As long as he felt angry, he was unaware of his underlying feelings about his lack of sexual responsivity and functioning. Mary responded by withdrawing and did not express her feelings. Joe was a "maximizer," coping by "blowing up" and leaving the room. Mary was a "minimizer," withdrawing from Joe and withholding sex.

Using the steps involved in the "Imago Dialogue"—which include mirroring, validation, and empathy—Mary and Joe were able to actively listen to each other with understanding and without reactivity. In listening intently and without reactivity, both partners were able to express the deeper roots of their internal struggle, which originated from injuries they experienced in childhood. Joe was not angry with Mary, but it looked and felt that way to her. Joe was, in fact, angry at himself. Joe grew up in a family where he was shamed for his "failures." Joe felt shame and inadequacy when he was not able to respond sexually. In therapy, he was able to share this with Mary because she was truly listening and present to him. I helped Mary set aside her defenses so she could be present to Joe, which allowed her to feel empathy toward him.

With the safety of the Imago Dialogue, Mary shared the root of her coping strategies that were triggered by Joe's anger. In her childhood, Mary's mother would often "blow up" at her in a way that made Mary feel she was responsible for her mother's anger. Mary was angry at her mother for blaming her for things that were not her responsibility. Mary was quite tearful in telling her story, and underneath she also felt responsible and shamed, like Joe. Similarly, she felt blamed in the relationship. She thought Joe was blaming her for his sexual difficulties. She felt she did not deserve his anger and blame, and thus withheld sex from him to punish him. Withholding gave her a sense of control and power, something she did not have as a child.

As Joe listened in the session, he heard the origins of Mary's pain and anger. He was empathetic and moved by her feelings and story, actually leaning toward her and listening deeply. He reached for her physically and hugged her. This loving response healed old wounds inside of Mary, as her mother had never responded to her in an empathic way. This session created a change in their relationship in which the relational space, emotionally and sexually, felt warmer to both of them. They described the energy between them as more loving and said they felt more connected.

Emotionally Focused Therapy

Emotionally Focused Therapy (EFT) is another type of therapy from which the relationship paradigm can be understood. EFT is a form of couples therapy developed by Susan Johnson and her peers based on attachment theory, which helps couples create a secure, safe attachment with one another. It helps couples stop their negative cycle of interacting by teaching them to speak up and express their underlying vulnerabilities, feelings, and needs (Johnson, 2004, 2008). In EFT, coping adaptations are reflected in people's attachment styles.

When a person experiences inconsistent availability and abandonment by a parent or primary caregiver in their early years, they often develop an "anxious preoccupied" attachment style that persists into adulthood. In relationships, they may pursue their partner and perpetually seek attention as a way to get their emotional needs met. In contrast, individuals who grow up with a parent who is detached, unavailable, and cold will often develop a "dismissive avoidant" attachment style, in which they keep an emotional distance between themselves and their partner. Finally, individuals who grew up in an erratic household characterized by oscillating patterns of abuse/distance and warmth may develop a "disorganized" attachment style. They often are in inconsistent connections in adulthood and exhibit the same "come hither, go away" dynamic. All of these attachment styles reflect ways individuals cope with pain and anxiety in an effort to get their needs met. These attachment styles create a dance, which creates ruptures in the adult relationship.

In working with Mary and Joe around their sexual relationship, it became clear that Joe was the pursuer ("anxious preoccupied") and Mary was the distancer ("dismissive avoidant"). These attachment styles created a dance in the relational space because each partner was unable to speak about their needs or their true feelings. The goal of EFT would be to help them recognize this dance and join together to fight it. Through EFT, Mary and Joe would express their underlying feelings—including their fears of being shamed or abandoned—and their needs to be valued and connected. Sex therapy techniques could then be used to help them express their needs sexually, as well as address their specific sexual dysfunctions.

Internal Family Systems Therapy

Internal Family Systems (IFS) theory maintains that everyone has a system of parts inside themselves that relate to each other, similar to those in a family (Schwartz, 2001). Some of these parts are protective, which explains why in IFS therapy, the coping adaptations are described as "protective parts." These protective parts often come into being because they are taking care of younger parts that were hurt as a child. These younger parts are termed "exiles." People have to protect and hide their exiles in order to survive. For instance, Mary's exiled part was her shame for being blamed unjustly for others' problems. Joe's protective part was created as a result of his underlying feelings of inadequacy.

All protective parts serve a purpose, as they help people to function and protect themselves. Sometimes, though, the protective part takes over, causing it to be the only part that others see. In IFS therapy, the goal is for the "Adult Self" (or Self-Energy) to be in charge so it can recognize the protective parts, heal the exiled parts, and speak for these parts as well. In the context of couples therapy, this process occurs through a method of IFS therapy known as Intimacy From the Inside Out (IFIO; Herbine-Blank, 2015). In IFIO, the therapist works to dissect the sequence (or dance) occurring between partners, as this sequence reflects an interaction between the protective parts. When the sequence becomes unraveled, each partner can begin to speak "for" their protective and exiled parts, rather than "from" their parts. As the Adult Self begins to speak for the parts, communication between partners becomes more authentic, open, and vulnerable. It is through this "courageous communication" that the relational space becomes more intimate, safe, and alive.

Though the IFS lens, the dance between Mary and Joe can be seen. Joe had a protective part that was reactive and responded with anger. In IFS, this protective part is called a "firefighter," a part that thinks there is an emergency and needs to react immediately to avoid danger. This protective part existed to protect Joe's exiled part from feeling shame related to his perceived sexual inadequacy.

In the dance, Mary responded by withdrawing and shutting down her unexpressed anger. This protective part is called a "manager," and it tried to prevent Mary from feeling blamed and responsible for another's feelings. She too was protecting a younger part, an exile, that was hurt and shamed unjustly. By unraveling the sequence between them, Mary and Joe could have a courageous conversation, in which they would speak for their protective parts, as well as the younger parts they were protecting. Communication between Mary and Joe might look as follows:

Mary: "I have a part of me that is female, called my 'righteous indignation' part. The righteous indignation part withdraws from you. She feels mad because she believes you blame her for your sexual difficulties when you storm out of the room in anger. She wants you to suffer for hurting me. The righteous indignation part protects me from hurt and shame."

Joe: "Wow! I was not aware that you were experiencing this. I feel so sorry for hurting you. I have a part that feels angry and takes over. When that angry part shows up, I have another part that comes in—the 'runaway' part—that tells me to leave the room. The 'runaway part' of me is protecting my 'inadequacy' part, which feels so much shame about my sexual performance. It is much easier for my anger and 'runaway part' to take over so I don't feel the pain and shame carried by the 'inadequacy' part."

Mary: "I had no idea that was what your anger meant. It sounds so painful. Now that I understand it, let's see if we can work together to help each other feel more relaxed as we try to figure out our sexual relationship."

This conversation helps them take care of the relational space and create connection, warmth, intimacy, and aliveness. Subsequently, sex therapy techniques could be incorporated to help Mary and Joe express their sexual needs, as well as CBT techniques to address any specific sexual dysfunctions.

No matter what type of couples therapy a therapist uses, they are employing methods to help couples change their dance and express what is underneath in terms of beliefs, fears, needs, and emotions. Such communication helps couples find connection and takes care of the relational space. When sex therapists help couples unravel the dance, they are then able to teach them more positive cognitions about sex and help them make the necessary behavioral changes to improve sexual functioning. However, the intrapsychic beliefs people have about themselves regarding their sexuality may still interfere with couples' ability to create a thriving sexual connection, which is when exploration of each partner's sexual self-esteem becomes necessary.

Exploring the Formation of Sexual Self-Esteem

Sexual self-esteem is created by a multitude of factors. Culture, religious upbringing, ethnicity, gender roles, and family influences contribute in intricate ways to the beliefs, feelings, and self-esteem people have related to sexuality. When CBT or relational therapy techniques are not enough, it is time to explore the internal beliefs clients have about themselves as sexual beings and in sexual relationships. Therapists need to delve into historical issues that influence the relationship and sexual dynamics. Through my experience, certain themes consistently show up in the context of this deeper exploration: (1) the three P's (performance, pleasing, and play) and (2) shame, guilt, and trauma.

The first P is related to **performance**. When men are focused on their erection, they might ask themselves: "Am I hard?" or "Can I stay hard?" or "Can I stay hard long enough for my partner to have an orgasm?" As discussed, this focus creates performance anxiety, which interferes with sexual responsivity. When a client finds it difficult to move out of this anxiety, it is helpful to explore how that person experienced performance pressure growing up.

For example, a married couple, Jack and Amy, came to see me because Jack was experiencing difficulty keeping his erection. He was not progressing with the CBT protocols for erectile dysfunction. When asked about his experiences with performance pressure growing up, he told a number of stories about being chastised whenever he didn't make all A's in school. He also experienced shaming when he made mistakes in sports. As his wife, Amy, heard these stories, she felt compassion for his pain and expressed this to him. Amy reached for Jack. Her voice softened and her eyes filled with tears. She said, "I had no idea you experienced so much pressure to perform when you were younger. I feel sad seeing your pain." She also saw that, at times, she triggered this reaction in him when she felt disappointed in his waning erection. Amy apologized and also comforted Jack about his childhood experiences.

She said, "You never deserved to have so much pressure as a child. I would never want you to feel that way with me." In sharing his story and through the healing and owning of his past, Jack received empathy from Amy and accepted the natural waxing and waning of his erections. He was able to try different options when his erection waned, which helped them to reconnect sexually in a more loving, positive way.

The second P is **pleasing**. In sexual encounters, people are often focused more on their partner's pleasure than their own, which represents another form of performance pressure. Sometimes, pleasing the partner is the only way an individual can relax enough to enjoy their own sensations. However, this focus creates pressure for both partners. The person who needs to please the other feels badly about themselves when that does not happen, which can result in low sexual self-esteem. Similarly, the partner being pleased feels pressure to respond in a certain way, which creates anxiety and lack of responsivity, or results in their faking a response to please the other person. In order to address issues related to sexual self-esteem, it is important to discuss the root of this need to please others as well.

I once worked with a lesbian couple, Sue and Betsy, in which I clearly saw this dynamic. Sue had a mother who was volatile on a whim. She learned to watch her mother's moods and tried to please her to protect herself from her mother's explosiveness. Sue did the same with her wife, Betsy. This pressure to please interfered with both Sue and Betsy's ability to enjoy their sexual encounters. Sue was focused on Betsy's pleasure, not on herself or her own experience. Betsy felt anxious to feel pleasure because it was so important for Sue to please her. Betsy would often shut down in response to Sue's desire to please her. This resulted in anxiety for both of them, with little pleasure for either.

When Sue saw she was creating so much pressure for Betsy, she wanted to learn how to let go of this need to please. I asked Sue if that part of her would be willing to stay in a different room of the house when they engaged sexually. She agreed, and she started making that mental separation prior to sex. She also worked on her own self-soothing. She had the adult within her be present and compassionate to this younger part of her that wanted to please when she became fearful of Betsy's lack of arousal. She reminded herself that while Betsy could "blow up" about other things, she did not blow up in the sexual encounter. This helped Sue's younger part to relax a little. Betsy began to understand Sue's fears and was able to become more reassuring and loving, which helped Sue relax during sex. Betsy wanted to provide some healing for Sue around her childhood experiences by staying present in a loving way no matter what happened sexually.

The third P is **play.** Sensuality and sexuality reflect the ways adults engage in play. At its best, sexuality is a fun endeavor that brings pleasure to those involved. Unfortunately, many individuals are taught that play happens only after work is done. For example, children who come home after school are often told by their parents or caregivers that they must complete their homework before they can play. This message is often carried into adulthood, often making sex the last thing on anyone's list.

A couple with whom I worked illustrates the importance of discussing play in treatment. At the time of our discussion, I had been working with George and Lisa for about one year. They had addressed a number of issues that had little to do with sex. However, George was still upset by the infrequency of their sexual interactions. Lisa enjoyed sex when they had sex, but it was the last thing on her list. Lisa had a high-powered job and two children at home. Her tasks felt never-ending. At one session, I asked Lisa about her childhood as it related to her need to work so hard at home and work. She told a powerful story.

From the time Lisa was five years old, her mother woke her up at 5:00 a.m. on Saturdays to clean the house. Cleaning the house was often a process that continued until noon. By noon, the Saturday morning cartoons on television were over. The message Lisa took from this childhood experience into her adulthood was: "There is no play until the work is done." Her demanding job and desire to be a good mother resulted in the experience that her work was never done. Therefore, play was never a possibility. After Lisa understood this and saw the origin of this story, she decided she was no longer willing to put play last on their list. She and George began to find ways to connect sexually *before* all of the work was done.

In addition to the three P's, experiences related to shame, trauma, and cultural, religious, and gender messages can interfere with sexuality. When clients have experienced sexual abuse, sexual assault, rape, or sexual harassment, they may internalize a variety of sexual messages, such as, "Men are only interested in one thing," "It is my fault that I was raped," "I will never be good enough because I am broken," "I wore something that was too provocative," or "I was special because my father/mother/clergy/family friend chose me." These negative messages are endless. It is important to note that any time a therapist sees clients who were shamed or experienced trauma, there may be sexual dysfunction or sexual acting out as a result. One couple with whom I worked, Andy and Susan, provides a good illustration of both.

Andy had a history of paying sex workers for sex, which had begun prior to his marriage to Susan. He had secretly been engaging in this behavior once or twice a week for over 25 years. After 20 years of being with his wife, Andy finally told Susan about his compulsive behavior. In delving deeper into the root of his sexual acting out, it was revealed that there were two traumatic sexual events in Andy's childhood and adolescence. In each, he had been publicly shamed for his natural sexual impulses. At the age of five, his mother discovered him playing naked with and touching other children's genitals (who were of the same age). His mother chastised him in front of the others, leaving him with feelings of shame and an internalized message of, "I am bad." At age 17, he engaged in heavy petting with a girl without intercourse. However, the girl subsequently told their religious community that she was pregnant. Andy was publicly shamed for a behavior of which he was innocent. He was forced to publicly apologize to the religious community and be baptized again for his sins.

In addition, Andy had received religious messages about sexuality that further affected his sexual self-esteem. In particular, he had internalized the message "No sex before marriage." Therefore, the worst thing that Andy could have experienced was being publicly shamed by his religious community for an action he did not do. This public shaming resulted in Andy feeling ashamed of his sexuality and unconsciously acting out through compulsive interactions with sex workers. Whenever his shame and inadequacy would build up inside of him, Andy would contact a sex worker, as being with them made the terrible internal feelings go away temporarily. However, after the sexual encounter was over, his feelings of shame would come back with even more force. Without understanding the experiences of shame and trauma in Andy's life, it would have been impossible to help him heal his own pain and the pain he caused in his marriage.

Another factor to explore in the development of sexual self-esteem is the messages that have been communicated through an individual's ethnicity or culture. Hannah, a client of Hispanic origin, provides a good example. Hannah was big breasted and small in her hips. She told me that wide hips were important and attractive in her culture. She believed her Caucasian husband found her unattractive because of her small hips and feared he would tire of her and leave her. Over time, we explored these messages and her fears of losing someone important to her. By looking underneath her belief, she was able to recognize her fear of abandonment. She was able to provide healing to herself around her self-worth, as well as speak openly to her husband about her fears. He was able to help her heal by proving he loved her as she was. Therapy helped her understand that her hips had little to do with his commitment to her.

In addition, gender roles can affect sexual self-esteem. While there are vast changes in the perception of gender and gender roles over the last 40 years, sexual gender roles continue to be rigid and can create performance issues. Males still have many damaging conceptions that affect sexual relationships, such as, "I should be able to be erect at any time" and "I should know what is necessary to please my partner, whether they are male or female." Females may also carry messages, such as, "I am inadequate because I don't have orgasms with my partner through intercourse" and "I will offend my partner if I ask to have my needs met." Ultimately, it is the therapist's job to uncover these internalized messages and help clients explore their underlying fears. The goal is to help clients feel safe in their present adult sexual encounters by creating new, more positive internal messages.

CONCLUSION

The complexities of sex and couples therapy are obvious. Integrative sex and couples therapists are required to know the mechanisms of healthy sexuality and the methods to communicate this information to clients. Any time sex therapists feel stuck in a CBT-form of sex therapy, it is necessary to unravel the dance between the couple and help them speak their truth; explore their essence, fears, longings, and desires; and take care of the relational space.

It is also imperative to take a deeper dive into clients' history, beliefs, sexual messages, and traumas. The sexual messages and beliefs people carry about themselves are created to protect themselves from underlying hurt, low self-esteem, and fear of being hurt, enmeshed, controlled, or abandoned. When sex and couples therapy stalls, therapists need to explore these protective beliefs to help clients heal some of their past hurts, both for themselves and for their relationships. This healing will help individuals achieve a better sexual self-concept and allow them to develop relationships that are more connected, alive, and differentiated. By working with the past, clients can let old beliefs go and develop a new, positive, and healthy sexual self-concept.

For professionals who are couples therapists or who are just beginning to learn about sex therapy, do not be afraid to ask clients about their sexuality. Most people feel relieved when we create a space to discuss sexuality. If a couple's dance is obvious, ask how this dance shows up in sexuality. If they talk about the influence of their family, ask how their family has influenced their sexuality. If they talk about performance anxieties, ask if this shows up in their sex lives. If they talk about their traumas, ask how these have affected their sex lives.

Most importantly, take the risk to ask this simple question at any time: "How are things going for you sexually?" If clients do not want to talk about sex, they won't. This is not a question based on the agenda of the therapist. This is a question based on the fact that sexuality is a part of living, and it needs to be welcomed into people's lives in order for them to be fully alive and connected.

Chapter 2

Sex Therapy and Sexual Medicine with Couples: The Collaborative Sexual Wellness Model

Daniel Rosen, LCSW-R, CST, and
Pebble Kranz, MD, FECSM

SEX AND MEDICAL ISSUES: BARRIERS IN THE FIELD

The World Health Organization defines sexual health as "a state of physical, emotional, mental and social well-being in relation to sexuality" (WHO, 2006). However, barriers abound when individuals attempt to receive care for sexual concerns that is comprehensive and whole-person-centered. These barriers are a result of the fact that, historically, there has been inadequate cross-pollination between the fields of couples counseling and sex therapy. Likewise, there is poor integration between the medical care of sexual concerns and psychotherapeutic approaches. This disconnect is problematic, given that sexual concerns may have aspects that are related to medical illness or treatments. To offer just a few examples, erectile dysfunction may be caused by vascular disease or diabetes. Anorgasmia may result from treatment with a selective serotonin reuptake inhibitor. Sexual pain may result from radiation for cancer. Furthermore, the physical aspects of sexual problems often have a bidirectional relationship with psychological or relational elements. Erectile dysfunction may be both caused by and a result of mood disorders. Painful intercourse may be exacerbated by anxiety and may result in anxiety.

In the United States, medical training programs that offer multidisciplinary, comprehensive training on sexual function, dysfunction, and psychological aspects of sexuality are rare. While there is a discrete medical specialty called "sexual medicine"—which deals with the medical aspects of sexual problems and the sexual aspects of medical problems (Moser, 1999)—this branch of medicine is not recognized in the United States and has only recently been recognized by the European Union's board of medical specialties.[1] Therefore, many physicians are not aware of sexual medicine as an area of study and receive minimal training on sexual function in medical school. This is true even in postgraduate training for specialties in which most clients *expect* to have sexual concerns addressed, such as gynecology, urology, and primary care. While most physicians are aware of medical interventions for erectile dysfunction, they may be unaware of methods to assess and treat many other sexual concerns.

As a result, clients encounter multiple barriers in addressing sexual concerns in their medical care, and they rarely get a comprehensive assessment and treatment plan that encompasses both the medical and psychosocial aspects of their concern. Sex therapists may not have training in couples counseling, and couples counselors may not have training in sexology. Similarly, medical providers are not typically aware of the methods and approaches used in sex and couples therapy. Yet a significant portion of couples have *both* relational and sexual problems that require *both* medical and psychotherapeutic interventions.

Therefore, successful treatment requires a consideration of medical, psychodynamic, social, and cultural factors that impact each individual partner and the couple as a whole. The biopsychosocial model, which was developed in the late 1970s, is an ideal model to address sexual concerns in the context of couples counseling, as it articulates a holistic approach to medical issues by accounting for physical, mental, and social factors (Engel, 1977). In this chapter, we describe how this holistic approach can be used to develop the foundation for a more contemporary biopsychosocial model that addresses sexual concerns with couples.

COLLABORATIVE SEXUAL WELLNESS

Given the many structural barriers to providing biopsychosocial care for couples with sexual concerns, we developed an integrated resource to bridge these gaps. Coauthor Dr. Kranz provides sexual medicine and behavioral and psychoeducational counseling, while coauthor Mr. Rosen provides sex therapy for individuals, couples, and groups utilizing the Feedback-Informed Treatment (FIT) model (Miller & Donahey, 2012).

We believe that a nonhierarchical, colocated, integrated collaboration between a sex therapist and a sexual medicine specialist facilitates constructive dialogue between the medical and therapy sides of the team to determine clinical decisions and maximize rapid clinical change. We are fortunate that our collaboration is facilitated by our personal relationship. As partners, not only in business but in life, we share a passion for helping people achieve health, pleasure, and satisfaction with themselves as

---

[1] Europe's Multidisciplinary Joint Committee on Sexual Medicine (MJCSM) defines sexual medicine as the branch of medicine concerned with human sexuality and its disorders, addressing: (1) sexual function and dysfunction, (2) sexual and/or partnership experience and behavior, (3) gender identity, (4) sexual trauma and its consequences, (5) both the individual and couple, and (6) a biopsychosocial basis. Sexual medicine clinicians have a deeper than average knowledge of the effects that many medical conditions and/or their treatment have on sexual function. The MJCSM offers a fellowship certification for sexual medicine specialists (FECSM) from a wide variety of specialties, including gynecology, urology, primary care, psychiatry, and endocrinology.

sexual beings. While medical and psychological treatments are our focus, validating, affirming, and supporting growth goes beyond treatment to creating a place where each unique sexuality is celebrated as a core element of the human experience. We are both committed to providing safe and effective treatments. We find it most rewarding to work in a holistic way with individuals, couples, and other family systems. We call our model Collaborative Sexual Wellness.

Triage of New Clients

The Collaborative Sexual Wellness model has several phases: triage, intake, treatment delivery, and follow-up. We collaborate on mutual clients and consult with each other on other cases. Dr. Kranz or Mr. Rosen conducts an initial brief phone consultation and then directs the client to initiate care with either sex therapy or sexual medicine. In some cases, we offer a joint intake, including when clients are traveling long distances, if it seems likely they will need both services, or at their request.

The following case example illustrates how this first phase of the Collaborative Sexual Wellness model looks in practice. Valerie, a woman in her late forties, sought out Dr. Kranz for help with sexual pain. A perimenopausal woman with multiple sclerosis and endometriosis, Valerie had many reasons for sexual pain: (1) the muscular spasticity in multiple sclerosis can have an impact on any area of the body, including the pelvic floor; (2) vaginal dryness and irritation may begin in perimenopause; and (3) endometriosis is known to cause deep dyspareunia (i.e., sexual pain that occurs with penetration).

During the triage phone call with Dr. Kranz, Valerie identified several concerns in her relationship with her husband, Michael. However, her most pressing concern was decreasing the pain that was becoming more severe every year. She had discussed this issue with her gynecologist but didn't feel she was making progress with the current treatment plan, which involved hormonal contraceptives to manage endometriosis and a recommendation for dilators without direction on how to use them.

Sexual Medicine Intake

Dr. Kranz's intake starts with a form that the client completes prior to the appointment. This form covers demographic information, goals for the consultation, information about client-identified gender and sexual orientation, as well as general medical issues, medications, surgical history, urological or gynecological treatment history, and diet, exercise, and recreational substance habits.

We use this written intake form for a couple of reasons. First, it is challenging to cover the full range of issues that can have an impact on sexual function during an initial intake session. Second, there are some issues that clients find easier to reveal on paper and some that are easier to reveal in discussion. Clients complete a treatment consent form and forms authorizing the exchange of information with other medical and mental health providers. The rationale for information exchange is discussed with the client during the initial appointment.

A Model for a Biopsychosocial Diagnosis of Sexual Concerns
(Bitzer, Giraldi, & Pfaus, 2013)

	Biomedical (e.g., chronic diseases, medications, hormonal factors)	**Psychological** (e.g., mental illness, personality, attachment style)	**Social/ Relationship**	**Cultural**
Predisposing Factors				
Precipitating Factors				
Maintaining Factors				

The first intake session is 90 minutes long and is focused primarily on history taking. Depending on the concern, there may be a physical exam. The rationale for performing a physical exam is discussed, and the client's specific, verbalized consent is elicited for each aspect of the exam. For issues of sexual pain, exams occur on the second visit to decrease anxiety and increase comfort with the examiner. Psychosexual function and anatomy education are provided, and books on sexual function are occasionally recommended. Labs and imaging may be ordered. If the client gives permission, Dr. Kranz gathers information from other providers to assure medication and medical problem lists are complete, and to see what has previously been done about the presenting concern. During the intake, Dr. Kranz develops a formulation regarding the client's sexual concerns with attention to predisposing, precipitating, and maintaining factors (see table).

Several weeks later, there is a second treatment planning session, where the information gathered and biopsychosocial diagnosis are reviewed with the client and a proposed treatment plan is discussed. This plan may include medical or behavioral interventions, as well as recommendations for couples or individual therapy, pelvic floor physical therapy, or other interventions. Identifying concerns within the categories of predisposing, precipitating, and maintaining factors helps target suggested interventions. If a medical intervention targets *only* predisposing factors, progress on a sexual issue will be challenging. Factors maintaining a problem must be addressed in the initial stages of treatment.

Returning to Valerie's case example, during her initial sessions with Dr. Kranz, it became clear that Valerie had endured many painful sexual experiences that led to further pelvic floor muscle tension and worsened pain. Additionally, both tolerating pain during sex and avoiding sex were having an impact on her relationship. Valerie and her husband, Michael, attempted consensual non-monogamy (CNM) to meet her husband's sexual needs, but this caused some residual anger, tension, and shame for Valerie.[2]

---

[2] In no way should this couple's experience be interpreted as a refutation of consensual non-monogamy (CNM). While residual feelings emerged, the experiment was helpful to them. At the time of the experiment, it seemed there were no further options to treat Valerie's sexual pain or elicit changes in their sexual relationship. CNM remains a reasonable choice for some couples.

Valerie also revealed a history of childhood messages that caused ongoing shame and fear about sex. In her family of origin, sex was dirty and not appropriate for discussion. She learned that pleasure, specifically, was shameful. Between the two initial visits, Dr. Kranz discussed Valerie's pain with her gynecologist, who felt that Valerie's report of sexual pain was not significant enough to warrant additional treatment because she had been able to tolerate a speculum exam. However, Valerie's physical exam revealed that there were multiple tender points on her vulvar vestibule, in addition to tender and spastic pelvic floor muscles. During the exam, anything that caused a pain level above a threshold of 3 out of 10 was discontinued. Lab evaluation showed significantly reduced estradiol, progesterone, and calculated free testosterone levels, indicating that the pain at her vulvar vestibule could be at least partially due to low hormone levels. A biopsychosocial formulation regarding Valerie's sexual concerns is presented in the following table.

Valerie's Initial Biopsychosocial Assessment
Diagnosis: Sexual Pain Due to Hormonally-Mediated Vestibulodynia and Pelvic Floor Dysfunction

	Biomedical (e.g., chronic diseases, medications, hormonal factors)	**Psychological** (e.g., mental illness, personality, attachment style)	**Social/ Relationship**	**Cultural**
Predisposing Factors	Endometriosis; multiple sclerosis	No concerns identified	No concerns identified	History of shaming sexual messages in childhood
Precipitating Factors	Long-term hormonal contraceptives to manage endometriosis; perimenopausal hormonal changes	No concerns identified	Tolerating repeated painful vaginal penetration experiences, both sexually and in her medical care	
Maintaining Factors	Pelvic floor dysfunction due to multiple sclerosis-related spasticity and as a consequence of tolerating painful penetration; possible adhesions related to endometriosis; low bioavailable sex hormones due to both perimenopause and long-term hormonal contraceptives	Ongoing sexual shame; residual anger, resentment, and anxiety about the monogamy contract	Avoidance of most sexual play; worry about marriage ending as a consequence of her inability to tolerate sex	Sexual pain concerns under-addressed in medical care

Sex and Couples Therapy Intake

Mr. Rosen's couples intake starts with either one individual or the couple together. If only one person wishes to come alone at first, it is made clear that for couples therapy to be effective, the therapist must not be seen as the therapist of just one party. The intake occurs over one to three hour-long sessions, in which a general mental health evaluation, a sexual history, and a history of the relationship are obtained.

During the first therapy session, the rationale for FIT is explained, as well as how to complete the measures. Clients complete scoresheets at the beginning and end of each session. These scoresheets include the Outcome Rating Scale (ORS)—which measures personal, interpersonal, social, and overall well-being at the beginning of each session—and the Session Rating Scale (SRS), which measures the client's assessment of the alliance with the therapist, the degree to which they have common goals and methods, and an overall sense of the session. A rising ORS score (or for high initial ORS scores minimal declining) indicates positive, clinically meaningful change, whereas a low SRS score signifies a potential rupture in the therapeutic alliance that needs attending to. Therefore, both scales provide an opportunity for the therapist and client(s) to discuss how well treatment is progressing.[3]

During intake and early treatment, it may become clear that one or both parties would benefit from a medical assessment. Sometimes, a medical assessment can help develop compassion and understanding for a partner as they both come to recognize the *physiological* components that have led to their distress. Since clients may be misinformed by the Internet or other sources, receiving reliable medical information about sexual function from a knowledgeable physician is healing, even if the diagnosis is "you are perfectly normal."

Sharing one's sexual history is often deeply satisfying for clients. At a minimum, a sexual problem history with psychosocial components is necessary for the Collaborative Sexual Wellness approach. Gaining a fuller understanding of clients' sexuality and history may be required if that is where the therapist is led, if treatment focuses more on the clients' past, or if treatment seems to stall.[4]

Treatment

While an enjoyable sex life has a modest positive effect on a couple's satisfaction, sexual problems have a significant negative impact (McCarthy, 2015). Couples are often wistful and want to return to the "way it was" before the sexual problem manifested. Our clinic takes the stance that changes in sexual functioning inevitably occur in

---

[3] For more information on Feedback-Informed Therapy and scoring, please see https://www.centerforclinical excellence.com. Instructions and interpretation here are in abbreviated form.

[4] In the field of medicine, a "sexual history" is equivalent to what sex therapists call a "sexual problem history." A full sexual history expands on a sexual problem history by including information such as childhood sexual experiences, fantasies, unwanted touch, use of erotica, moral conflicts, and family-of-origin messages. In *The Behavioral Treatment of Sexual Problems*, Jack Annon defines a sexual problem history as including the following: description; onset and course; the client's concept of cause and continuation of the problem; past treatment (both psychological and medical); self-help; and finally, expectations. Annon suggests that a sexual problem history is relevant for shorter-term sex therapy and a full sexual history for longer-term intensive therapy.

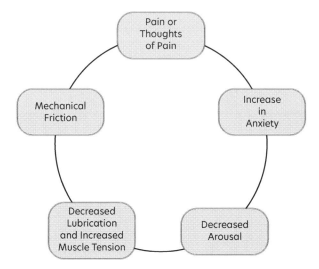

long-term relationships and that rather than striving to return to the "good old days," couples are best served when they aim to deepen and improve their sex lives with a focus on the present moment and current sexual functioning. This involves building new patterns of communication, increasing sexual repertoire, deepening emotional connection, understanding the function of sexual intimacy, and allowing space for couples to explore sexual interests.

When the management of sexual pain is a focus of treatment, the goal is to minimize future painful sexual experiences while maintaining the couple's physical intimacy and building positive sexual expectations. Painful sexual experiences lead to a vicious cycle where pain or thoughts of pain lead to anxiety and bracing, which in turn leads to muscle tension that then cuts off blood supply to tissues. Decreased circulation leads to decreased lubrication and increased muscle tension, which leads to further pain, and so on. The cycle of pain must be interrupted. Often, treatments to decrease the source of pain take time to implement—at least three months and sometimes longer. During this time, it is critical for both the individual and the couple to maintain hope (even in the face of setbacks), expand their sexual repertoire, and work on other ways to maintain intimacy.

Dr. Kranz began treating Valerie to improve her pain by discussing vulvar skin care and prescribing topical hormones to improve the strength and resiliency of her vulvar skin. In addition to other medication adjustments, Valerie received instructions on safe lubrications for penetration and how to work with dilators and vibrators. She was also referred for pelvic floor physical therapy.[5] While Valerie made progress with

---

[5] Pelvic floor physical therapy (PFPT) is a specialized area of physical therapy practice that requires additional training. PFPT can assist in treating urinary and bowel problems, chronic pelvic pain, and painful intercourse. It may also be useful for the treatment of vaginismus (also known as bulbocavernosus muscle spasm), endometriosis, painful ejaculation, and premature ejaculation. PFPT techniques include education on anatomy and function of the pelvic floor; pelvic floor exercises, such as Kegels; and, often more important, pelvic floor relaxation, hands-on massage or stretching, pelvic floor biofeedback (a probe inserted into a woman's vagina or a man's anus with results displayed on a computer screen), electrical stimulation, and vaginal dilators.

being able to tolerate and even enjoy penetration with dilators and vibrators, she was still having difficulty with partnered penetration and worried that her avoidance of penetrative sex was having a negative impact on both her husband's sexual well-being and their relationship. She and her husband agreed to enroll in sex and couples therapy with Mr. Rosen.

Mr. Rosen's Treatment Approach

In our collaborative setting, the sex therapist helps clients integrate the gains made through medical and physical therapy interventions. Unlike general psychotherapy, which may take a neutral stance toward medical treatments for sexual concerns, sex therapy *advocates* for medical treatments that enhance sexual functioning. Therefore, the sex therapist may need to work through a client's resistance to medical interventions or provide accurate information to the client about sexual functioning. Often, the sex therapist will also need to treat the relational and intrapsychic elements of sexual concerns in order to address the problem fully.

With regard to the relational components of treating pelvic pain in particular—which was of relevance to Valerie and Michael—there are three general stances that the partner of a woman with sexual pain can take: negative, accommodating, and facilitative (Goldstein, Clayton, Goldstein, Kim, & Kingsberg, 2018). A **negative**, or hostile, response understandably impairs both relational and individual healing from sexual pain. Michael had previously adopted an **accommodating** stance in which he avoided asking for sex. He had internalized a belief that he was harming his wife with sex, even simply by asking for it. Although one may expect that an accommodating stance would be helpful, this stance impairs both relational and individual healing. While this stance may maintain emotional intimacy, it often does not lead to an improvement in pain. Moreover, it can lead individuals to suppress their own sexual needs. For Michael, his battle to deny his sexual needs created self-loathing and a fear of his sexual thoughts, impulses, and behavior.

A **facilitative** stance is one where the partner remains positive, hopeful, and emotionally *and physically* engaged with a partner suffering from sexual pain. The facilitative partner maintains and strengthens intimacy and closeness while also being helpful in the resolution of pain. Through therapy, both Michael and Valerie assumed a more facilitative, engaged stance as Valerie's pain improved. As Michael moved to a more facilitative style, Valerie could demonstrate her own desire for him, and they initially rekindled a new sexual relationship, although without intercourse.

Checking in regularly on the sexual concern is important, as resolving relational problems without returning to the sexual problem leaves clients unsatisfied. Although therapeutic goals may change during the course of treatment, and clients' sense of well-being may improve, the goals should still include improving both sexual satisfaction and sexual functioning.

Clients are encouraged and coached to discuss their sexual concerns (including what is and is not going well), as doing so builds sexual communication skills. Directly modeling how to listen and share information is often helpful. Creating in-session enactments of difficult discussions blends cognitive and emotional gains with behavioral gains. Throughout these discussions, it is often productive to move deeper to uncover familial patterns, deep personal pain, conflict, and existential components that have contributed to the sexual concern.

As Valerie and Michael worked to improve their communication skills, Valerie clearly stated that she felt increasingly comfortable with Michael expressing his sexual concerns to her. Michael, of course, worried that his negative thoughts about sex (such as addressing his sexual frustration and anger) would stimulate guilty feelings in Valerie. To some extent, this did occur. However, Valerie and Michael were fortunate to possess strong character structure and the capacity to modulate intense affect. Therefore, their problems lay not in *oversharing* but in *undersharing*. Michael's anxieties and sexual urges initially elicited guilty feelings in Valerie, but ongoing dialogue resolved Valerie's guilt and decreased Michael's fear of hurting Valerie.

Although sexual symptoms may sometimes mask deeper issues, this is not always the case, so it is an error to assume that a sexual problem is always an indication of another psychological or relational problem. For example, Michael and Valerie's relationship was strong despite their sexual problem. Similarly, men with lifelong premature ejaculation may harbor feelings of inadequacy that are resolved with medical intervention alone. We have seen cases in which the medical resolution of the sexual symptom has profound impact on an individual's mental health and relational well-being, and we have seen medical resolution leaving relational and psychological problems untouched.

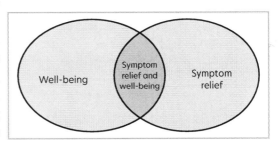

In our Collaborative Sexual Wellness model, the goals of symptom remission and overall well-being often overlap, but not always. For example, people unable to achieve change in sexual function through counseling alone (e.g., those with treatment-resistant depression, painful intercourse, or sexual dysfunctions attributable to medications, medical procedures, vascular, or neurogenic factors) may gain only partial symptom remission from psychotherapeutic work. However, processing their grief, loss, and anxiety may provide significant gains in well-being. Things can go the other way too: People who resolve problems in sexual functioning may find that their well-being has not improved much.

For Valerie and Michael, a graphical representation of their ORS scores showed that each client made sustained and significant growth in their sense of well-being. However, Michael's SRS scores did not peak until mid-treatment, indicating that he initially did not feel entirely connected to the session activities. This allowed Mr. Rosen to adjust the therapeutic space as needed and more fully engage Michael in the process of healing. Michael's continued progress on both scales demonstrated that the feedback provided by the SRS allowed Mr. Rosen to guide him—and the couple overall—to a positive outcome.

Michael and Valerie's trial of opening up their marriage (i.e., through CNM) was mixed for them. Fundamentally, they wanted intercourse together. However, prior

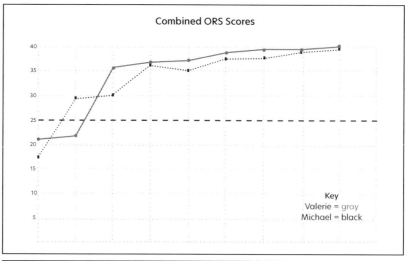

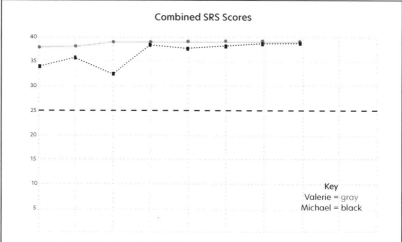

to receiving treatment in our clinic, they both considered a future that included intercourse together unlikely. While the CNM experiment was emotionally difficult for Valerie, Michael had some positive gains from the experience. He realized that he was not hopelessly resigned to a sexless life, and it revived in him a sense that intercourse was permissible and enjoyable and that he could do it successfully without hurting a sexual partner.

Therapy opened a space for Michael to have sexual desire, and it allowed him to trust that he would not be criticized for his desire. Positive and emphatic requests for sexual pleasure were encouraged, centering the responsibility for sexual pleasure away from the couple as a dyad and into each person individually. Valerie's physical therapy involved the use of a vibrator and dilators to relax pelvic floor muscles and improve blood flow for vaginal skin elasticity. During a counseling session, they decided that when Valerie was using the vibrator and dilator they would bring Michael into the room to help with the dilator and vibrator. The goal was for him to be involved in her healing and to ignite desire for both of them. This helped Michael overcome some of the repression of his sexual urges and helped him understand what was comfortable and pleasurable for Valerie. Valerie's physical therapy exercises were also arousing for her. Valerie's desire for Michael to be involved in the exercises helped him feel wanted. This was the rebirth of his sexual engagement with her.

The couple's goal of vaginal intercourse became secondary and almost totally dissolved. It had reformulated itself as the true desire underneath—a longing to be sexually wanted by the other partner. Ironically, as the prospect of intercourse grew closer, the necessity of it diminished. Painless sexual contact (without intercourse) can be a therapeutic success in its own right. As it happens, Valerie and Michael have now successfully reintroduced intercourse into their sexual life together.

Follow-Up

Six months after the initial treatment phase, Valerie and Michael had maintained sexual intimacy and emotional closeness, as well as intercourse. Valerie reported an extended period where the couple had intercourse at least weekly. During this period, Valerie discontinued dilators and topical medications without recurrence of pain. Subsequently, a series of health and travel-related events kept them from having intercourse for several months. Meanwhile, Valerie did not reinitiate the use of dilators, vibration, and topical treatments. When she and Michael tried to have intercourse, the pain was back. While this felt like a setback, Dr. Kranz reminded Valerie that this experience was useful. It made it clear that in Valerie's case (as in many others), sexual pain due to pelvic floor dysfunction needs ongoing attention. Once topical treatments, progressive dilator use, and other physical therapy interventions were re-incorporated, resolution of symptoms was again achievable. Relapse of sexual concerns is common, making follow-up a critical aspect of effective treatment.

TOOLS FOR COLLABORATION WITH MEDICAL PROVIDERS

In our setting, we have frequent opportunities to discuss the pros and cons of our clinical choices: whether and when to engage clients in couples counseling, when to work individually with a client, or when to have a client's romantic partner(s) come in. For therapists who are not colocated with medical providers, it may be useful to work toward developing relationships with a variety of medical providers who are knowledgeable about sexual concerns.

It is our experience that providers who are invested in the comprehensive care of sexual concerns want to know and collaborate with the therapists in their communities. We recommend seeking out medical providers listed as members of the Sexual Medicine Society of North America (SMSNA), International Society for the Study of Women's Sexual Health (ISSWSH), International Society for Sexual Medicine (ISSM), Scientific Network on Cancer and Female Sexual Health, or other societies studying sexology. The North American Menopause Society (NAMS) may also be a useful resource for finding medical professionals with an understanding of menopausal concerns.

Often, therapists have challenges coordinating with medical providers due to communication obstacles that historically exist between medical and mental health professionals. The book *The Collaborative Psychotherapist* identifies some of these systemic and cultural factors that make communication difficult and offer recommendations for overcoming them (Ruddy, Borresen, & Gunn, 2008). Briefly, medical and mental health providers speak different languages, work on different time frames, don't always share methodologies, and have vastly different caseloads. Nothing substitutes for an in-person meeting to understand each other, but a couple of simple written tools may be useful aides to collaboration when this is not possible:

1. **A post-referral and intake letter**: This can be a simple "thank you for the referral" template letter to be sent after the intake is complete. Filling in fields for diagnosis and a few words about treatment plan are helpful. It is important to understand that there is an expectation in medical care that when a client is referred to another provider, there is a "closing of the loop" regarding the assessment and treatment plan. Medical providers often do not need (nor do they want) details of the history. Be aware that any written communication will become a part of the client's official medical record accessible by other providers and possibly insurers. Both Dr. Kranz and Mr. Rosen find it useful to let the client know what this letter will include and to get verbal consent for each communication.

   Include information about how to contact you for collaboration and case discussion. Some medical providers will be eager to discuss cases, while others may simply be reassured to know that their client is in good hands. Don't be offended or concerned if you do not receive a reply to this letter. Medical providers, especially primary care doctors, receive many notes like this each day on thousands of clients. For the most part, when received from other medical providers, there is no expectation of a response. Communication is understood to be informational. It is appreciated if communications are brief. Ideally, all written communication should be a maximum of one page.

   If you need information in return, include a Release of Information form signed by the client that clearly indicates the specific information desired. This request will likely be signed off on by the provider and then processed by a member of the medical provider's staff, so it must be a clear and direct request for specific information. If you do not receive the information requested, then a call to the medical provider's staff may be all that is required.

2. **Termination letter**: This is also a simple template letter with a statement that the treatment relationship has concluded. This letter can be cocreated with the client as part of the termination process. It may be helpful to include any options for future treatment.

CONCLUSION

We are lucky. We appreciate the ease with which we can work in this way; we created our work environment collaboratively and have clearly shared goals. Part of the reason we arrived here is that we both found it challenging to find opportunities for close collaboration. Both medical and mental health providers may feel alone when caring for clients. It is a comfort to know that the weight is borne across multiple shoulders. We believe clients also benefit from this collaborative approach, as sexual concerns exist at the intersection of multiple domains of health—physical, emotional, mental, spiritual, relational, social, and cultural. These concerns deserve a comprehensive and integrated approach. Integration of treatment modalities and approaches can happen within an individual, as well as within a collaborative team. We encourage and applaud efforts to integrate couples counseling skills, sex therapy skills, and sexual medicine however possible.

Treating No-Sex Couples: Integrating Emotionally Focused Therapy with Sexuality Counseling

Wendy E. Miller, PhD

Jane and Al walked into my office, exuding calmness and connectedness. A middle-aged couple, they lived with their three boys, sharing chores and appreciating each other's quirkiness. Jane, a driven, Type A woman, worked long hours, exercised religiously, and kept a spotless and very organized home. She grew up with a disorganized mother who hoarded. Al was a successful surgeon and enjoyed painting in his free time. He grappled with depression that seemed rooted in a lonely childhood growing up with an ill mother. He remembered spending days on end sitting by his mother's bedside.

When they first met, there was an initial sexual spark, partly ignited by the excitement of a new relationship. Al was head over heels for Jane and wanted to be with her so much that he ignored that the sex felt perfunctory, even in the beginning. Jane had moments of sexual interest, but she had put her sexuality in a box after many years of being alone, following several exciting but difficult relationships. Neither had ever imagined that they would find a partner or start a family. They had children very quickly, but the sex died almost immediately after the children were born. Nonetheless, there was a deep love, appreciation, caring, and warmth between them.

Throughout the years, the couple had created a home, a comfortable retreat for themselves and their three children. They spent entire weekends together with their children, doing the myriad of activities that one does when raising a family. Jane and Al's relationship could be considered a "peer marriage" (Schwartz, 1994) in that they experienced a satisfying, collaborative relationship and considered each other their best friend. Indeed, Jane and Al felt incredibly compatible and couldn't imagine life without each other. There was a solidness to them as a couple, but this seemed in place of any spontaneity or risk taking.

Peer marriage relationships seem to work well except when there are difficulties in the area of sexuality, such as when one or both partners reports low or no desire

(Iasenza, 2006). This was the case for Jane and Al, as they felt extremely close but had no sexual energy between them. Being sexually intimate seemed like visiting a foreign land with no map or directions; they had no idea how to get there, and the years of sexual distance made it seem out of reach. They both lamented the lack of physical intimacy and connection, though it was far more painful for Al. During our sessions together, Al's hopelessness and frustration sometimes erupted in angry outbursts, which only served to make Jane withdraw further and feel like she had to walk on eggshells. Despite these occasional eruptions, they reported that their marriage was satisfying to both of them.

Like Jane and Al, many couples enter my office after being together for years with a happy or "good enough" life—but not having been physically intimate for a long time, even decades. Sometimes, both partners feel the absence of sex equally. Other times, one partner in particular finds the lack of physical intimacy unbearable.

Regardless, the lack of a sex life is always painful for both. For the partner who yearns for sexual connection, feeling attached to their partner while missing this vital piece means living with deprivation. The challenge of feeling good about oneself and one's sexuality can be daunting when a partner is uninterested. Similarly, the partner who has lost interest in sex or cannot find a way to engage sexually is acutely aware of the distress this causes their partner, but they feel helpless to do anything about it. Both feel stuck—held together by a feeling of attachment but haunted by the absence of sexual connection.

For a long time, the fields of couples therapy and sex therapy have had opposing viewpoints regarding how to best address these issues of sexual disconnection. In the couples therapy world, the narrative has been that if you fix the couple's relationship, then the sex will follow. In the sex therapy world, the opposite view has dominated: Fix the sex, and the couple's relationship will improve. While each perspective is true for some couples, integrating both narratives is necessary to address the specific needs of different couples. Therefore, my aim in this chapter is to weave together the unique contributions of sex and couples therapy to create a rich framework from which to approach couples who appear deeply committed and solidly attached to each other, but who are profoundly distressed or confused by their lack of interest or motivation to engage sexually. Jane and Al are one such couple.

I will begin by discussing the complexities of sexuality, as well as by presenting some of the basics of Emotionally Focused Therapy (EFT), which is an enormously popular and useful system for working with distressed couples (Greenberg & Johnson, 1988; Johnson, 2004). My goal is to highlight what EFT brings to the discussion of couples' sexuality, expand its reach when working with couples with resistant sexual issues, and discuss the complex relationship between attachment and sexuality.

THE COMPLEXITY OF SEXUALITY

Sexuality is extraordinarily complex. It encompasses biology, culture, religion, and family issues, and it involves a myriad of factors—past and present, intrapsychic and interpersonal, cognitive, emotional, and symbolic. All these factors shape an individual's sexual identity and contribute to their sexuality in the context of a relationship.

As Weiner and Avery-Clark put it, "sexual functioning and its meaningfulness are so multi-dimensional that understanding just the physiology or just the psychology or just the cultural factors is not enough to explain many sexual problems and dissatisfactions" (2017, p. 1). Rather, there are multiple meanings that impact both the individual personally and the couple interactively.

As a result, the absence of sexual connection can occur for any number of reasons. Sometimes, it has to do with unconscious dynamics and early object relations that interfere with an individual's ability to access desire in the present. Or it can be a consequence of not knowing how to navigate a sexual dysfunction. It can also be due to internalized models of parental intimacy, which can interfere with the expression of sexuality in some peer marriages (Iasenza, 2006).

For Jane and Al, the latter was a significant aspect of their sexual disconnection, as both had experienced developmental trauma and parental rage, and neither had grown up observing parents that were affectionate or in a happy marriage. As a result, they both felt a degree of guilt around their own sexuality and capacity to experience pleasure. Indeed, it is not uncommon for individuals who grew up with unhappy parents to experience guilt about surpassing their parent's capacity for happiness.

How are sex and couples therapists to organize the complex and extensive information presented by the couple into a coherent and useful map so their interventions have purpose, direction, and impact? It is essential that in organizing the material, especially around sex, one does not collapse something that is very complex and multifaceted into a single, descriptive narrative that is overly simplistic. As with individuals, one size does *not* fit all, despite the singular media images and predominant cultural narratives that abound, which suggest a quick medical fix for a much deeper set of issues.

One useful and coherent therapeutic model that can be used to navigate these complexities is EFT. Developed by Sue Johnson, EFT is an elegant system for helping couples who are affectively dysregulated, disconnected, and experiencing conflict. By integrating attachment theory with systemic couples therapy and sex therapy, EFT can help therapists organize what is happening in the room when they sit with a distressed couple to work on issues related to sexuality.

EMOTIONALLY FOCUSED THERAPY

There is a growing trend in some parts of the sex therapy field that prioritizes the biological components of sexual functioning and seeks medical answers to sexual problems. EFT offers an important corrective sway to the overemphasis on biology by stating that sex is essentially about relational and attachment meaning. Although a sexual problem may have initially begun in response to a physiological situation, meaning becomes intertwined with biology even when there are physical components. The meaning that an individual or couple attributes to the sexual problem is often the primary contributor to the development of a chronic and ongoing sexual impasse.

EFT is grounded in attachment theory, which maintains that an individual's ability to form an emotional and physical attachment to another person is critical for creating a sense of emotional stability and security. According to EFT, when individuals have an insecure attachment with their partner, this can lead to fears of abandonment or rejection that underlie most conflicts in the relationship. Due to this attachment insecurity, when one partner attempts to get their emotional needs met, this triggers the other partner's underlying fears (e.g., regarding rejection, isolation, inadequacy), which only serves to worsen the disconnection and ultimately creates a negative cycle. These repetitive self-defeating cycles become overlearned and automatic and leave the couple feeling angry, despairing, and stuck.

One negative pattern frequently identified in EFT includes the pursue-withdraw cycle, which can also be seen as a criticize-defend or a blame-placate cycle. In this negative loop, the insecure or anxious partner tries to make contact or gain reassurance from their partner by reaching out but in a blaming, hostile, or critical manner. Rather than encouraging the type of reassurance and connection the individual is seeking, the behavior only serves to push their partner farther away into a withdrawn, shut-down, or retaliatory response, thus intensifying the pursuer's upset and anxiety. This loop then becomes repeated, often with increasing intensity, leaving both partners alienated and hopeless. Two other common cycles are the withdraw-withdraw cycle and the pursue-pursue (or attack-attack cycle).

The goal of EFT is to create a "new" emotional experience that becomes the basis of a secure attachment. Rather than focusing on the *content* of the problem or the history behind it, the focus of EFT is on the *process* that is happening in the here and now. In particular, the EFT therapist helps the couple observe their interactional patterns as they are unfolding in present time during the therapy session. The focus of sessions is to help each partner become emotionally accessible, expressive, and empathically resonant, thus creating a solid and dependable bond. The stages and steps involved in this process, as outlined by Sue Johnson, are as follows.

Stage One: Assessment, Negative Cycle De-escalation, and Stabilization

1. Create a therapeutic alliance with each partner through the assessment.
2. Begin to identify the negative interactional cycle that expresses the core attachment issues and conflicts.
3. Access and articulate the unacknowledged emotions and attachment yearnings underlying the interactional positions.
4. Reframe the problem in terms of the negative cycle and the deeper attachment needs and fears; the problem is the cycle, not either member of the couple.

In the first stage, EFT therapists work experientially to help partners go beneath the surface problems and complaints and to move toward identifying the destructive patterns between them that cause them to feel so alone and unhappy. By helping the partners go below the surface anger and frustration that fuels their arguments—instead of focusing on the underlying vulnerable emotions of hurt and yearning—their behavior begins to make sense to themselves and the partner in a new way. Arguments should decrease, and the couple should begin to feel like a team with a common enemy: the negative cycle that has them in its grip.

Stage Two: Restructuring Interaction Patterns

1. Help each partner access their implicit needs, fears, and aspects of self that have been unknown or denied and risk expressing these to their partner.
2. Promote the acceptance of each partner's vulnerable underlying feelings and develop new interactional behaviors.
3. Facilitate the expression of each partner's attachment needs through directed bonding events in session, which create new interactions and interactional positions.

In the second stage, partners are encouraged to explore, understand, and share their own attachment needs and fears. By tracking and reflecting emotional moments and interactions in the session, the therapist facilitates bonding experiences that lead to a new here-and-now experience for the couple. The new experiences serve as an antidote to years of marital distress and deprivation. The therapist helps each individual articulate their underlying feelings rather than resort to blaming or avoiding their partner. Re-engaging the withdrawer and softening the pursuer are the two main focuses of this stage.

Stage Three: Consolidation and Integration

1. Facilitate the development of new positions and new cycles of couple interaction.
2. Consolidate new solutions to old relationship problems.

Once the couple completes the deeper experiential work of stage two, they begin to consolidate their gains in stage three. Consolidation consists of the couple creating a narrative of their relationship that supports attachment security and expresses the value they place on the attachment to each other.

Throughout all these stages, the therapist is always working experientially through an attachment lens—whether it is working on de-escalation in stage one or on deeper experiential work in stage two. In doing so, the therapist helps the couple change their ways of interacting so they can have a new experience of vulnerability and receptiveness with each other that they can replicate at home.

EFT purposely does not focus on the specific content that a couple brings up in a session, as the model assumes that couples will successfully navigate these content areas once the interactional process between them operates with vulnerability and responsiveness. However, sex should not be treated the same as other content areas, such as who does the dishes and who walks the dog. Rather, sexual material should be considered a sharing of a very vulnerable part of the self, which should be invited into the therapy session and treated with the utmost importance. Sharing the content of an individual's sexual yearnings and turn-ons is enormously personal and vulnerable. Couples often do not know how to respond to sexual material from each other, and it can cause them to become threatened and easily triggered, which often shuts down the conversation. The therapist's inviting response to sexual material can model for the couple how to respond to each other in a sensitive and accepting manner that makes room for all parts of the person, including their sexual self.

Ultimately, the goal of EFT is to create a secure emotional bond between partners. In Johnson's view, creating this bond optimizes healthy sexuality because it "fosters the ability to play, to put aside defenses and trust bodily responses, to tune in to another person, to express sexual desires and needs, and to deal with sexual differences and problems" (2017, p. 251). This then creates a positively reinforcing feedback loop wherein good feelings support sexual behavior, and sexual behavior contributes to increased good feelings and connection. It is the secure attachment system that is crucial for the sense of security that enables optimal sexuality.

Therefore, through the lens of EFT, solidifying the couple's attachment must be addressed prior to addressing their sexuality. Only after de-escalating the couple's conflict and deepening their emotional bond does the therapist more directly address the couple's sexual issues. In helping the couple learn how to ask for and receive emotional connection with each other, the expectation is that this will transfer into initiating and receiving sexually as well. In turn, sex can become a safe adventure wherein affection and intimacy nurture lust and passion, and feeling secure with one's partner can help individuals navigate and withstand those inevitable moments of mis-attunement and shifts in focus without triggering negative feelings of anxiety and rejection (Johnson, Simakodskya, & Moran, 2018).

For many couples, deepening their emotional bond forms the bedrock from which playful, exploratory sexuality emerges. When these couples feel more deeply connected and are no longer mired in friction and resentment, they can finally begin to experience satisfying sex. However, this is not always the case. For many other couples, looking through the attachment lens of EFT is not enough, and strengthening the couple's attachment bond does not always facilitate positive sexual involvement. For these couples, it can sometimes seem that attachment and sexuality belong to different, and possibly opposing, relational dimensions.

Indeed, in his conceptualization of attachment, Bowlby viewed attachment and sexuality as distinct but overlapping behavioral systems that mutually influence each other. In particular, he considered the attachment system to provide a scaffold for the developmental emergence of sexuality in all of its forms (Bowlby, 1966, 1988). According to this view, though, attachment and sexuality are still conceptually distinct because the two systems are activated differently, at different points in development, and they are directed toward different objects.

Is it possible to integrate attachment and sexuality without subsuming one to the other? Is it possible to instead focus on how the two interact, consolidate, and diverge over a life cycle to elucidate their development? In the section that follows, I'll discuss some theoretical and clinical issues to consider when working to integrate attachment and sexuality in the context of sex and couples therapy, as well as what therapists can do to attend to the sexual and emotional needs of couples.

INTEGRATING LOVE WITH SEX

My position is that attachment and sexuality can be conceptualized as two separate and continuously entwined developmental strands that are wrapped around each other but that maintain their distinctness, like the human gene helix. This places sexuality not simply as a behavioral expression of attachment but as a distinct thread with a unique developmental trajectory.

How attachment and sexuality are conceptualized is not just a theoretical question, though. The manner in which these constructs are conceptualized is also of clinical significance. If sexuality is viewed as its own primary and unique developmental pathway, then therapists will give sexuality more credence in the context of therapy. In contrast, if sexuality is conceptualized as an outgrowth of attachment or as its behavioral expression, then therapists will primarily attend to a couple's attachment and security needs instead, believing sexuality will inevitably follow. However, for many couples, it doesn't happen this way. For couples like Jane and Al, their relationship may be deeply satisfying in many ways while the sexual connection remains frozen or absent.

Therefore, it is important to view sexuality as its own developmental thread, for often what ignites sexuality may not be the same as what nurtures attachment. Many clients report that what makes for good attachment may not make for good sex. Some describe the best sex they have ever had with the worst and most inappropriate of partners, people with whom they would never want to construct a life. *Partners can be intensely attached to each other with little sexual interest, and people can be intensely sexually involved with an absence of emotional attachment.*

When individuals exhibit difficulty in bringing love and desire together, it may be reflective of a "love/lust" split (Morin, 1995; Perel, 2006). The integration of love and attachment with sex and desire proves particularly challenging to some people and creates an internal rift that can seem impossible to knit together. For these individuals, sex and love are connected to different self-states, and while love might be accessed with the primary partner, sex is not.

Sam and Naomi illustrate the power of a love/lust split. Naomi, Sam's wife of 25 years, dragged him into my office in a last-ditch effort to see if they could initiate any kind of sexual relationship. Their oldest child had left for college the previous fall, and it was unclear whether the marriage would survive. What had started wildly, with sex in restaurants and airplanes, died down before they were even married. The excitement and daringness of their early trysts turned into rote sexual repetition. Although this loss of sexual interest had ended all of Sam's previous relationships, when Sam and Naomi got married, they each thought this time would be different.

Predictably, though, the sex stopped altogether soon after marriage and kids. One decade became two decades, and then almost three with no sex. They had grown older together and traversed many extremely challenging life experiences having each other's back but never entering a sexual realm together. It wasn't that Sam had no sexual interest, as evidenced by his solo masturbating while watching porn. Rather, he couldn't understand why anyone would want to have sex with someone they saw every day, claiming, "What's interesting about that?" As an introvert, much of his social interactions felt like obligations. Sex was one place where he had drawn a line in the sand, and he was not willing to cross it, not even for Naomi.

Meanwhile, Naomi yearned to be desired. She saw herself as a sexual adventurer and was open to most kinds of sexual exploration, even coming to his office one day in only a trench coat. He greeted her with annoyance. She seemed to experience little sexual conflict or anxiety, and yet she had allowed herself to be in a sexless marriage for 25 years. She did not want to have an affair or find a lover, as she feared this would be the end of her marriage. She wanted to have sex with Sam, but he could not imagine experiencing sexual desire in a relationship with someone he cared about and felt connected to. While he had a gruffness about him, he had a soft underbelly as well, and he cared deeply about Naomi. He was generous in many ways, but not sexually. What are we to do in cases like this where attachment and sexuality seem to exist in profoundly disconnected universes?

Turning more deeply to what has been said in the psychoanalytic literature offers some help with understanding the complex relationship between attachment needs and sexuality. According to Stephen Mitchell (2002), a psychoanalyst and author, we flatten out passion in long-term relationships in order to feel safe and secure, opting instead for a kind of sexual inertia in an attempt to avoid the anxiety and risk inherent in an exciting and vibrant intimacy. In this view, the sexual boredom and ennui of long-term relationships is actually rooted in resistance to engaging in a vitally alive intimate sexual relationship with the person on whom we depend the most. The idea that this person with whom our life is so entwined might actually not be so familiar, predictable, and known by us is a terrifying thought, so we opt instead to deaden romance and passion with our long-term partners. We unconsciously trade the excitement that may come from approaching a mystery for the safety and familiarity of the known.

Other psychanalytic theories offer additional explanations for the love/lust split. For example, Morris Eagle maintains that sexual excitement is fueled by newness, novelty, and the forbidden, whereas what we look for in a solid attachment figure is characterized by familiarity, predictability, and availability—which are not necessarily the ingredients of sexual energy. Therefore, being in a long-term monogamous relationship results in contradictory "pulls" between the interconnected, yet functionally separate, attachment and sexual systems (Eagle, 2007). Integrating these two systems is a developmental challenge that is more easily accomplished by those who have smoothly resolved their relationships with early attachment objects and, in turn, have attained a secure attachment organization. However, if an individual is unable to achieve psychological integration, both in resolving their own early attachment relationships and in integrating their caretaking part with their sexual self, this may contribute to a love/lust split.

Returning to the case of Naomi and Sam, therapy revealed that Sam had suffered early attachment trauma at the hands of his parents, which interfered with the development of secure attachment. Sam was an only child, and when he was five years old, he reported feeling that his parents never should have had him. He would frequently get painfully smacked in the face by his mother for minor infractions. He also remembered the confusion he felt as a child when a strange man would visit his mother shortly after his father had died in an accident. Sam came to understand why he did not allow himself to feel vulnerable and desiring with Naomi, a woman on whom he was also dependent. However, this realization did not initially free Sam to be more affectionate or sexually available, as he was unable to reconcile his attachment relationship with Naomi versus his mother.

When an individual is unable to shift their primary attachment from an early parental figure to their current partner, they may unconsciously equate the current partner with their original caretaker, which intensifies the incest taboo and causes them to suppress their sexual feelings. When children are added to the current family matrix (resulting in one's partner becoming a parent in actuality), these feelings can grow and potentially interfere with the ability to experience one's partner as a sexual being. When this occurs, accessing sexual desire can feel easier and less complicated with an extraneous and less intimate person who does not play the role of a caretaker in one's life. This was the case for Sam. After all, how can one reveal and share a primitive, uncensored, and base part of yourself with the person you also depend on to do the laundry, pay the bills, and plan the playdates? It can feel like there is far less at risk in revealing a lustful loosening of control with someone other than the person you turn to in times of need. It can feel easier to be sexually free and experimental with someone who is not tied to a particular definition of the self as developed and constrained by a shared history.

However, others argue that attachment and excitement can coexist. For example, Virginia Goldner argues that attachment is not a steady state but, rather, that there are inevitable undulations of connection and disconnection throughout all long-term relationships. It is in these unavoidable fluctuations of feeling both more and less connected that there is the possibility for newness and excitement as individuals re-find their partner, again and again (Goldner, 2004). Similarly, Peggy Kleinplatz maintains that emotional risk is an essential ingredient for erotic energy but so is deep attunement and connection. Her work has found that being embodied, fully present in the moment, and deeply "in sync," connected, and aligned with one's partner—along with extraordinary communication—form the conditions for optimal sex (Kleinplatz, 2003, 2012; Kleinplatz et al., 2009).

How do we reconcile these theories under the lens of EFT? Is a secure attachment bond necessary to jump into the adventure of sex? Is feeling safe a necessary prerequisite to allow lust, passion, and playfulness to emerge? The crucial question may be how safe is just safe enough and when does the comforting ease of safety risk becoming a sense of complacency that deadens the daring ruthlessness of intense erotic yearning? As Virginia Goldner suggests, safety and dependency may well create erotic energy, but this is "not the flaccid safety of permanent coziness, but a dynamic safety whose robustness is established via the couple's lived history of risk taking and its resolution" (2004, p. 388).

Therefore, I suggest that we need to make room for *multiple* pathways to a rich erotic life that may look and operate differently for different couples and operate differently for each member of the same couple. If therapists have ideas about the "right" or best kind of sex (e.g., deeply loving connected sex), then they are likely to foreclose or shut down what could be a rich exploration of and path toward integration, both for the individual and the couple.

I also suggest that we make room to allow for the creative use of aggression in creating sexual excitement instead of packaging sexual desire solely into a loving attachment box. Doing so can foster disassociation by splitting off one's aggressive lust, and it increases the risk of its finding expression in clandestine affairs or secret activities. Good sex is often selfish, devouring, demanding, ravenous, and uncensored. Ideally, these feelings can be located within a loving, attached relationship, but there is a risk that they can feel incongruent with caring attachment and therefore be suppressed and denied.

In order to integrate attachment and sexuality, it is necessary for sex and couples therapists to act like tightrope walkers, leaning a little this way and a little that way to hold both the emotional and sexual life of the couple in a delicate balancing act. If the therapist puts a couple's sexuality on the back burner until they are securely attached, then the message to the couple may be that sex is of secondary importance. This may also serve to deprive the couple of a powerful means to promote connectedness. Some couples may even unconsciously sustain ongoing conflict so as not to have to deal with the anxiety stirred up by the prospect of making sexual contact.

For some couples coming into therapy, elevating their sexual relationship as the initial and primary focus of therapy can help them revitalize and reactivate their sexual connection in a way that leads to de-escalation of conflict and creates a secure bond. For these couples, sexuality does not flow from attachment; rather, it creates a stronger attachment. For other couples, there needs to be initial work done in therapy to develop a reliable connection between the partners before sex can be usefully addressed. For some couples, both issues need to be held in mind. In any event, it is important that sex and couples therapists not neglect the developmental history and emotional world of the individuals they are working with to resolve sexual issues. This is never truer than when dealing with couples who have difficulties integrating love with sex.

THE IMPORTANCE OF TAKING A SEX HISTORY

Taking a thorough, in-depth sexual history is essential at the beginning of any work with couples that involves their sexuality (Iasenza, 2010). Sexuality is not only about the couple and what happens between them, but it also involves the individual and that person's sense of self, particularly how they experience themselves as a sexual being and all that has influenced this.

The sexual history provides information that allows the therapist to make potentially useful connections between the individual's background, defenses, fantasies, and behavior that inform the treatment intervention. It also provides an opportunity for the therapist to conduct an in-depth inquiry about sexual trauma. Often, therapists are the first people to learn about a traumatic experience that is deeply buried in layers of shame and self-blame. Trauma, shame, sexual conflict, and cultural values all contribute to the molding of one's unique sexuality.

When taking a sex history, each person is met with individually, and the development of their sexuality is reviewed, from childhood to the present, giving particular attention to the impact and meaning attributed to these experiences by the individual. It is also important to assess for the presence of any medical and physiological conditions that may be contributing to the couple's sexual life. This includes all medications, erectile issues, dyspareunia, and any other pain issues. In addition to reviewing the individual's developmental experiences around sexuality and medical conditions, some of the questions to ask include:

- What did you learn about sex and love from growing up in your family?

- What did you learn by observing your parents as a couple?

- How do you think this might be influencing you today?

- How did your family respond to your sexuality, and what kind of physical contact was there?

- How do you feel about, and in, your body? Does your body image or body discomfort obfuscate being present and experiencing pleasure?

- How do you feel about pleasure? What kinds of pleasure do you experience physically?

- Are you able to surrender to how it feels when your partner touches you, or are you in your head grading yourself rather than being fully present in your experience?

- What have you learned from your peer group about sex? From the media and culture? What are your ideas about how sex happens? What makes for good sex?

These questions can be used to unpack the narratives that may be interfering with a couple's sex life, such as the preconceived notion that all good sex is spontaneous, easy, lustful, and always ends in orgasm. What is the couple's working model of how sex operates? Is their understanding linear, like Masters and Johnson's model (1996), wherein desire leads to arousal, which leads to orgasm? Or does it allow for complexity, like Rosemary Basson's nonlinear model (2001), wherein many points of engagement and exit create multiple possible positive pathways, which can (but don't have to) include arousal and orgasm? Most couples find it helpful to shift toward this more expansive understanding of sex that moves away from a singular focus on intercourse and orgasm.

For Sam, as well as for many couples with whom I have worked who have not been sexually intimate with their partners for a very long time, the idea of how sex operates is that it just happens spontaneously and that one shouldn't have to do anything to make it happen or put effort into it. Sam had never considered that willingness without desire was one way to engage in a sexual interaction with Naomi or that he could do anything to enhance the conditions that might lead to desire. Sam's narrative was that he used to have desire, and now he didn't. End of story.

Because sex is so rarely talked about in an open and honest way, even in therapy, it can easily become disassociated, and early experiences that have impacted one's sexual development can remain unrecognized and unintegrated, giving these experiences unseen power to inform one's narratives. Individuals learn about love and intimacy from how they were held and loved, and what they observed in their parents. Trust and comfort in one's desires and bodily experiences, especially sex, is influenced by early caregivers who may have passed on their own anxious or distorted views regarding their relationship to their body.

Inviting clients to talk about all aspects of their physical and sexual experiences, particularly when taking an in-depth sexual history, opens a pathway to integration and healing. By integrating the information garnered from the sexual history, therapists can identify where movement is possible, address individual vulnerabilities, and help the couple construct a narrative that includes and honors each person's unique history. It is important to help clients define erotic intimacy expansively, decenter orgasm, and put effort into creating the conditions that facilitate a regenerative erotic space together.

Using Sensate Focus

In addition to taking a sexual history, the use of sensate focus exercises can help couples who struggle with sexuality to connect on a sexual and emotional level. Sensate focus is a series of touch exercises that begin with instructions for each person to touch and explore the other with a sense of interest and curiosity (Weiner & Avery-Clark, 2017). Arousal and pleasure are specifically not the focus of the exercise because even that degree of intentionality can lead to pressure, as pleasure is not something one can "make" happen. Sexual responsivity is paradoxical in that the more one tries to achieve desire, arousal, or orgasm, the less likely it is to occur. This idea may seem counterintuitive, but the assumption underlying the use of sensate focus is that sexuality is a natural bodily response that occurs as a result of being present and tuning in to one's own felt sensations in the moment. Not focusing on a partner's experience greatly reduces expectation, worry, and performance anxiety.

Engaging in non-demand touching exercises and having space to not attend to or worry about one's partner's experience or feelings is often a novel experience. Some couples find this exercise profoundly intimate. During this process, couples can also observe any feelings or thoughts that may interfere with being present, and these observations can provide important information about unresolved conflicts and underlying anxieties.

For example, after conducting individual sex histories with Jane and Al, they were directed to begin sensate focus exercises. Initially, they were excited at the new intimacy they felt from doing the non-demand touching exercises. However, this excitement was very quickly followed by Al's anger at all the deprivation he had suffered in this area for the previous many years. "What am I supposed to do with all those feelings just because we are now doing something positive?" he would angrily ask.

Through the lens of EFT, Al's pain and longstanding frustration were validated in the moment as important feelings for him to be able to share with Jane, and she was helped to respond from a place of deep understanding. However, over time, these feelings were also seen as a form of resistance that prevented anything new from happening between them. On the surface, Al was talking about the many years he had gone without sex from Jane, but he was also harboring the experience of deprivation and loneliness that characterized his childhood, and these feelings were not going to be erased with a few sessions of touching. Given his history, it made sense that he was going to struggle with letting his guard down and trusting that Jane could be there for him in this way.

Therefore, after the initial positive response to the use of sensate focus, Jane and Al stopped completing the exercises altogether and reported they could not find time to do the exercises. Avoidance of homework is a common issue for couples in this situation, and it allows for a deeper exploration and understanding of the anxieties, fears, and discomfort that can be provoked in attempting to change sexual behavior after many years. These moments are clinically useful, as they bring to the surface the unacknowledged ambivalence to change that may be operating. Individuals may deeply desire change but, at the same time, feel scared and conflicted for a variety of reasons that contribute to their avoidance. For Jane and Al, it wasn't that the touching exercises didn't work. They just got anxious and couldn't do them.

To address this issue, it was necessary to work on several levels congruently. First, it was necessary to help Al become vulnerable and to be able to express his deep longing to be sexual, and for Jane to become emotionally responsive to this. Doing so involved increasing their physical intimacy behavior and working to resolve the interpersonal impact of their trauma histories. Second, Jane needed to look at her reliance on overfunctioning at the expense of pleasure or fun as a response to a dysfunctional and chaotic childhood characterized by little emotional connection. She also needed to reconsider her sense of self as "just not a very sexual person." Challenging this self-concept was enormously freeing and left her feeling hopeful. In addition, Al needed to feel entitled to ask for what he needed without fear of rejection.

Therapy also helped them find other ways to insert physical intimacy into their routines. For example, they started walking their dog together regularly, which gave them some time alone not in front of the television. Often, these walks included holding hands, which they found to be a very positive change.

Finally, the idea of taking a bath together emerged as something they could do since they could make sensual contact while washing each other, effectively multitasking, which Jane liked. This shared activity helped Al feel more normal and hopeful, and his frustration receded some. As the small changes they made began to have a positive impact, they began to feel less distress and confusion over their sexual disconnection and instead felt confident that they could build a positive and satisfying sexual life together.

CONCLUSION

The effectiveness of EFT in addressing the sexual dimension of a relationship is enhanced by an understanding of sexuality that encompasses more variety, more complexity, and many paths to optimal sexuality. It should be clear by now that sex can serve many purposes and is never about one thing, not even attachment. Attachment is often the bedrock of sexuality, but sex can also function to soothe, distract, procrastinate, reassure, entertain, connect, reward, and even to punish. Just as there is no one "right" way to be sexual, there is no right way to address sexual issues in sex and couples therapy.

For some couples, increasing security, emotional accessibility, and responsiveness opens the door to a rich erotic life together. However, for others, this is not sufficient. With these couples, the therapist must hold a myriad of possibilities and avenues of exploration in mind. A multidimensional model that invites a deep exploration of both the sexual and emotional life of the individual, as well as the couple—and that locates these in an ongoing state of interaction and tension—is the most effective approach when working with the complex and diverse couples that sex and couples therapists see every day.

Chapter 4

Sex and Imago Relationship Therapy

Tammy Nelson, PhD

with contributions by Orli Wahrman, MSW,
Sylvia Rosenfeld, LCSW, and Sophie Slade, PhD

Imago is Latin for "image" and also reflects "the mature stage of a butterfly." Imago Relationship Therapy (IRT) is based on the theory that the frustrations, conflicts, or feelings experienced during childhood often manifest themselves in our adult relationships when we seek a partner who is the image of a childhood caretaker. This partner choice reflects a longing to integrate a part of ourselves wounded in childhood. We imagine we can be healed by a partner who reflects what we have denied in our psyche and need to heal. There is no coincidence that we choose the partners we do, as we do so based on their similarities or differences to our parents.

Even in the best of childhoods, people don't always get all their needs met. Although this enables individuals to grow up and take care of themselves as independent functioning adults, it can also mean they may seek another person who will fulfill those unmet needs when they grow up. In the initial romantic stage of a relationship, those unmet needs are met as each partner feels safe, connected, and relaxed.

However, when the romantic phase ends, or they no longer fulfill each other's needs, emotionally or sexually, one or both partners may become critical or shaming. They can withdraw or attack. Neither partner is sure how to get their emotional or attachment needs met. They then enter into the power struggle or conflict stage of the relationship. They may split off their sexual needs or compartmentalize them, hoping that at some point they will work things out.

In IRT, therapists help couples work with this dynamic in order to heal each other from their childhood wounds and create a healthy relationship they desire by facilitating a dialogue characterized by active listening, mirroring, empathy, validation, and behavior/change requests. The couple learns how to be both connected and differentiated. From one session to the next, a new positive imprint is created, and gradually the couple can move from the power struggle to a joined journey of understanding and connection.

For example, George and Helen came into my office to talk about their issues around sexuality. For many years, they had been in a sexless marriage. They had each experienced difficult childhoods and had felt a kinship and deep emotional connection when they first met. Since their children had grown up and moved out, there had been a split between them. George had turned to pornography, and Helen was depressed and withdrawn. In relating their problems, they told me the following:

> **Helen:** "Sometimes, if I give into George when he wants sex, we seem to be happier. When I do, all is well for a while. However, slowly we slide back into conflict and start fighting, and out come the sweatpants, and we find ourselves back in that same struggle. Our sex becomes maintenance sex, and I feel alone."

> **George:** "I guess I use sex as scorekeeping. If she is mad at me, then she doesn't want sex. If she's mad, then how can I have sex with her? I can't do it if we're fighting."

George and Helen explained that they wanted to learn to talk about sex and share their erotic needs. They hoped to create safety and to trust each other again. I told them that learning to talk with each other in a way that focuses on validation and empathy could help. Most of the time, I said, when we are having a conversation with our partner, especially if it is about something conflictual, we are not really listening. We have a tendency to prepare our rebuttal before they even finish their sentence. We respond and cut them off before they finish their thought. We make assumptions about what they are thinking and cut them off without giving them space to share.

Helen acknowledged that having conversations about sex was very difficult with her and George. The topic brought up emotional conflict and pain, and they avoided it as a result. She also noted they had trouble listening to each other, so having a conversation about their lack of sex was particularly hard. George also related that he wanted to be able to communicate with Helen and restore their sex life, but he was at a loss regarding what to do. In response, I introduced them to the Imago Dialogue.

THE IMAGO DIALOGUE PROCESS

The Imago Dialogue is a structured technique that therapists can use to help couples communicate around sexual frustration and difficulties. This dialogue process starts with one person (the sender) sharing their thoughts and feelings while the other partner (the receiver) listens, validates, and emphathizes, and then the partners switch roles.

Through mirroring, validating, and empathizing, this structured active listening process is a way to deal with conflict in a relationship while letting both partners feel heard. To practice the technique, a therapist can have each partner share their thoughts and feelings on an agreed-upon topic. It is best to start with something easy and not too triggering. Although this structured dialogue is led by the therapist, the couple participates fully in the process.

The couple chooses who will be the sender and who will be the receiver. The sender begins by saying one thing they feel about the chosen topic, and then the receiver mirrors back what they hear. Mirroring is simply listening, but in an active way, without inserting one's opinion. It involves responding by repeating what one has heard and "sending" the information back.

The therapist leads the couple through the process, keeping the container of the dialogue safe and allowing the couple enough structure so they can relax into the back-and-forth conversation, encouraging them to go deeper into their feelings if needed. Whenever the sender shares their feelings and the receiver mirrors back what was said, the therapist encourages the receiver to ask, "Is there more?" This is a way to let the sender know that whatever they say is welcome, and it gives the receiver a chance to listen as closely as possible. The receiver continues to mirror and ask, "Is there more?" until the sender says, "That's enough for now."

The receiver is then encouraged to validate what the sender has said (e.g., "It makes sense, knowing you the way I know you, that you feel this way"). Next, the receiver exhibits empathy by sharing some feeling words to see if they understand what the sender is feeling about what they are expressing (e.g., "And I imagine you feel . . ."). In doing so, the receiver tries to express their understanding of what their partner might be going through, even if they don't agree with it or aren't having the same experience. This process allows each partner to share their experiences while feeling heard and understood. The goal is not to agree, but simply to be heard and to find empathy. Next, the partners switch roles, and the receiver shares their thoughts about the topic.

The following conversation template summarizes what this Imago Dialogue process could look like.

Sender: "One thing I would like to say about this topic is _____."

Receiver: "So one thing you would like to say about this topic is [*simply repeat what they say*]. Is there more?" [*Mirroring*]

Sender: "Yes, I _____."

Receiver: "Is there more?" [*Mirroring*]

Sender: "No, that's good for now."

Receiver: "Knowing you the way I know you, it makes sense you would feel that because _____. Did I get that?" [*Validate*]
[*Or, if it does not make sense,* "Tell me more about that."]

Sender: "Yes, you got it."

Receiver: "I imagine you must feel _____. Are there other things you feel?" [*Empathy*]

Sender: "You got it. I also feel _____."

Receiver: "Thank you for sharing this with me."

Ultimately, the Imago Dialogue helps each partner feel seen and heard, and it gives a space to the conversation so the therapist does not have to be in control of the conversation; the dialogue is turned over to the couple. It also allows time for the couple and the therapist to listen and hear what is being said without having to reply or jump into any action.

The therapist's role throughout this process is to facilitate mirroring, keep the sender and receiver in the process, and help them contain anything that triggers so much emotion that it may prevent them from staying in the process. The goal is not to become so rigid that fluid conversation is banned from the treatment room. Mirroring does not need to be so perfect that the couple feels ashamed or embarrassed when they don't get it right. At the same time, there should be enough structure to allow the couple to take a break from their regular routine and decrease the power struggle that may follow them into treatment from their normal lives.

Once the dialogue process feels comfortable, the therapist can guide the couple into more difficult and deeper conversations. It is a particularly good container for conversations about sex and intimacy—including issues surrounding affairs, desire issues, and sexual dysfunctions—which have been traditionally more triggering or emotionally loaded for many couples (Nelson, 2008).

SEX AND COUPLES THERAPY

Couples have a greater likelihood of staying together for longer periods of time when they improve their communication skills around sexuality (Nelson, 2008). Indeed, the process of facilitating erotic recovery and restoring long-term passion begins with teaching good communication skills in the context of couples therapy. As couples begin to communicate their sexual needs together in couples therapy, the Imago Dialogue techniques specific to IRT can provide a unique structure from which they can explore their fantasies and desires.

Using the Imago Dialogue technique, couples can practice being totally present for the other, creating a safe place, and allowing their thoughts and feelings to be truly heard and valued in the session (Masters, Johnson, & Kolodny, 1982; Nelson, 2008). Paradoxically, experiencing the safety to talk to each other in couples therapy begins to loosen the tension that has been held with the secrets that often come with sexual dysfunctions and problems in sexual relationships. Sometimes, though, the secrets themselves are what has kept the erotic energy in the relationship, and this possibility must be explored as well (Bader, 2002).

Imago Dialogue techniques can be introduced in the initial phases of sex and couples therapy, though it may continue into the secondary stages of treatment and most certainly into the final stages where the vision of the couple's relationship can be established (Hendrix, 1998; Nelson, 2008). Couples can also take the skills of the Imago Dialogue home with them to practice after the session.

APPRECIATION DIALOGUE

Couples are much more open to hearing what their partner has to say when the conversation in a session begins with an "appreciation." An appreciation can be a compliment or something positive that one partner notices about the other but may fail to mention normally. Many times, in the later stages of a relationship (after the first three months), partners fail to mention the positives and start focusing instead on what makes them unhappy. They begin to criticize each other and are open about what makes them unhappy in the relationship, or they are vocal about how they are not getting what they want.

Behaviorists tell us that to extinguish a negative behavior, we should ignore it as opposed to exerting pressure on someone to change it. Similarly, to enhance a positive behavior, we should appreciate it. Remind your partner what you appreciate about them and you will get more of that behavior. This works particularly well when talking to a partner about their sex life.

To have a conversation about erotic needs, it is important *not* to mention the things that don't seem to be working, as doing so can wound or shame a partner in ways that are hurtful and embarrassing. In order to avoid inflicting harm, couples can start off the conversation with an appreciation dialogue that uses the three aspects of the Imago technique. Returning to the example of Helen and George, on their sixth session, we expanded on what was working. Their appreciation dialogue looked as follows:

Therapist: "Let's use this exercise to practice appreciation. Talk about something you appreciate about sex with your partner. Be specific. I'd like you each to think about what you appreciate and say it to your partner in the following way, 'One thing I appreciate about you is . . .'"

George: "Helen, I really appreciate you taking the time to massage my back this morning when we were lying in bed together."

Therapist: "So, Helen, can you please mirror back what George said to you?"

Helen: "So what I hear you saying, George, is you really appreciate me taking the time to massage your back this morning when we made love." [*Mirroring*]

Therapist: "In order to let George know that you understand his point of view, can you validate his experience? You don't necessarily have to agree. It might sound like, 'George, this makes sense to me; I know you really love it when I massage you.'"

George: "Yes, and it really helped me to relax and want to have sex today."

Helen: "It makes sense, George, that you like it when I massage you because it relaxes you." [*Validation*]

After helping Helen and George through the first two components of the Imago Dialogue, I explained the third part of the technique (empathy) and encouraged Helen to incorporate this into the conversation as the receiver.

Therapist: "The receiver imagines what the sender might be feeling and tries to step into their shoes, checking out if they have an idea what the sender is experiencing. It might sound like, 'So I imagine you feel happy and turned on when I massage you.'"

Helen: "So, George, you really appreciate it when I massage you [*Empathy*], and I am so happy that you are turned on."

George: "Yes, I really like it, and it makes me excited to make love to you."

Therapist: "To take this to the next level, you can use this dialogue process to talk about your sexual desires or even fantasies. There is nothing you or your partner need to do except listen and just mirror. The only response needed is empathy and validation. You don't need to react to hearing your partner's desires or fantasies by promising to take them into action, nor do you need to refuse to act them out. All you need to do for each other is hold the space by having the dialogue."

When we concluded our conversation practice, I reminded Helen and George about three important things pertaining to the Imago Dialogue. First, when you want to have a conversation about your needs, remember to always ask your partner if now is a good time to talk. Sometimes, we set ourselves up for disappointment if our timing is off. Second, when you want to have a conversation *about sex*, also always ask if now is a good time. Setting up an appointment to talk about sex is a great idea since a longer lead time leads to a great erotic charge. In addition, your partner might need a safer time or space to talk about erotic needs. Make sure your partner can commit to a later date or time. And third, always start your dialogue with an appreciation.

SEXUAL FANTASY DIALOGUE

Helen and George had gotten to the point in therapy where Helen was open and willing to hear George's fantasies. She had not felt ready to talk about his needs up until now, as she had been harboring anger and resentment toward him based on things that had happened in their past. He had been using pornography, and she was upset that he had been hiding it from her. As a result of using the Imago Dialogue process, she now felt comfortable enough to have these difficult conversations about the pornography and could talk about what she wanted in her sex life going forward.

George had never shared his fantasies with her before, and she was somewhat anxious but also excited to hear what he had to say. George's fears about telling Helen his true fantasies were deeply rooted in his past. He had some homoerotic fantasies and feelings that had been part of his erotic template for many years. However, he had been afraid to talk about his fantasies of sex with men because of his childhood. When he was growing up, his church members and his family had been clear with him that being gay was a sin.

In the session, I told both George and Helen that talking about sex didn't mean agreeing to act out fantasies. It simply meant they were appreciating each other. By talking and empathizing with each other about their desires, they were showing real respect and care for each other. Appreciation was a sign of integrity in a relationship. I reminded them that all they needed to do was to listen, empathize, and validate.

Still, Helen was nervous about George asking her to do something that she did not want to consent to. Throughout her childhood, Helen's mother had taught her that "good girls" did what they were told, and when men asked her to do something, she was to listen and never argue. I assured her that listening did not mean saying yes. It simply meant that she could empathize with his experience and that empathy did not mean acquiescence.

After several sessions of using the appreciation dialogue and practicing empathy and validation, they were both more confident and ready to share their true desires with each other.

George: "I feel more confident and trusting."

Therapist: "Can you tell Helen your thoughts? Do you feel like you can share with her without worrying that she will judge you?"

George: "Yes, I can use the Imago Dialogue."

Therapist: "Can you ask Helen if she is ready to hear your fantasies?"

George: "Helen, is now a good time to tell you about one of my fantasies?"

Helen: "Yes, now is fine."

George: "I am nervous, but I want to share this fantasy with you."

Helen: "So you are nervous, but you want to share this fantasy with me. Is that right?" [*Mirroring*]

George: "Yes. Please don't judge me, but . . ."

Helen: "Oh, so you are asking if I would please not judge you." [*Mirroring*]

George: "Yes. One of my secret erotic fantasies is to be with a man."

Helen did not respond. I asked if she could just mirror what George had said instead of reacting in any way. I encouraged her to hold the space for now and just mirror. Helen blanched, but instead of shaming George, she just mirrored his words.

Helen: "So one of your secret fantasies is to be with a man. Did I get that?"

George: "Yes, I guess I have wanted that for a long time."

Helen: "So, what I hear you saying is that you have wanted this for a long time. Is there more?"

George went on to describe a little bit more of his thoughts about being with a man. Helen was able to hear what he described, and more about why he felt the way he did, and I encouraged her to stop him when she felt like she had enough. Instead, she allowed him to talk more about his fears.

George: "I don't think I'm gay, I am just curious."

Helen: "So you don't think you're gay, just curious." [*Mirroring*]

George then talked about his pornography use, and how he used porn to explore some of his sexual fantasies. When I asked Helen if she could empathize and validate George's response, she initially struggled to express understanding about his feelings.

Helen: "I know you have a lot of interest in sex. I get that you have fantasies about . . . things."

Therapist: "Well, you are two different people. Does it make sense George has different thoughts, just like you have different appetites for different foods? And you might sometimes have different sexual fantasies?"

George: "I do feel like I can tell you anything."

In response, Helen began to cry in the session. I reiterated to George that I could imagine how telling this fantasy was hard for him, but that I imagined it also made him feel relieved. I then asked both of them if they could share an appreciation for each other for this dialogue. It is important in IRT and sex therapy to close the session with appreciations, as it leaves the couple with a positive sense of what was experienced in the session and acts as a review of the progress made.

George: "Helen, I appreciate that you listened to me without judging me."

Helen: "George, I appreciate and love that you were so honest with me. Thank you."

FINDING THE SEX THAT HAS BEEN LOST

Though it is not evident when we first meet our partners, when the infatuation or romantic stage is over, how our differences manifest becomes quite clear. Couples come to therapy saying they are sexually incompatible because they have different sexual templates, are interested in different sexual behaviors or ways of being sexual, or have discrepant desire levels.

However, this perceived incompatibility can serve as an opportunity to explore the messages individuals have received surrounding sexuality, and promote growth and healing. Often, individuals attempt to find a balance between keeping their sexual essence and fitting into what culture or society has deemed acceptable sexual behavior. As a result, aspects of their sexual self either become overdeveloped or underdeveloped. For example, individuals who received appropriate messages about sex were taught to embrace their sexuality. Some of these appropriate sexual messages include:

- It's okay to think about sex and to fantasize.

- It's okay to be you sexually.

- It's okay to experience all your bodily senses, including sexual ones.

- It's okay to move your body.

- It's okay to talk about sex and your sexual problems.

- It's okay to be sexually alive.

- It's okay to feel and express your sexual feelings.

- It's okay to initiate sexual contact.

However, other people grew up with repressive or negative messages around sex that influence their present relationships. These messages can negatively impact their sexuality in the domains of thinking, sensing, feeling, and acting.

For example, individuals who received negative messages related to thinking may have a restricted or absent fantasy life. They may not know what they like sexually, or they can't tell their partner what they like. They may also be obsessive, anxious, and in their head during a sexual experience.

Individuals who received negative messages regarding sensing may rush through sexual experiences and be goal- and performance-oriented when it comes to sex. Similarly, those who received negative messages regarding feeling may inhibit pleasure or find it easier to be sexual when not intimate.

Thinking	Sensing	Feeling	Acting
• Don't think about sex. • Don't think certain sexual thoughts. • Don't talk about sex. • Don't express certain thoughts. • Don't be curious or know about sex.	• Don't experience your body. • Don't touch yourself. • Don't smell bad. • Don't experience all your senses.	• Don't feel aroused or excited. • Don't enjoy your sexual feelings. • Don't show your sexual feelings or sexual pleasure. • You should feel ashamed of yourself.	• Don't move your body. • Don't move your hips, thighs, or pelvis. • Don't initiate physical or sexual contact. • Don't be spontaneous.

Finally, those who received negative messages regarding acting may have difficulty initiating a sexual experience. They may restrict themselves with regard to positions, only moving a little and being rigid during sex rather than loose and relaxed (Rosenfeld & Slade, 2019). The previous table summarizes some of the negative messages that individuals may have received across these domains.

In order to help couples form a secure and functioning relationship, understand each other sexually, and collaborate in having a more positive sexual relationship, it is important to assist each partner in exploring the messages they received growing up around sexuality. The Lost Sexual Self Dialogue (Rosenfeld & Slade, 2019) is a structured technique that couples can use to explore how these messages affect the current sexual partnership and move the couple into a healthier, more rewarding relationship.[1] Using the following sentence stems, both individuals and couples can talk about how their childhood influences led to their current relationship decisions.

A positive message I received in childhood about sex was . . .

A negative message I received about sex in childhood was . . .

A decision I made as a result of these messages was . . .

The way that this impacted my past sexual experiences was . . .

The way that this impacts my current sexual experience (with you) is . . .

A new message I can give myself is . . .

An action I can practice reflecting that new message is . . .

As I complete this process, what I experience is . . .

This dialogue can be used in a session or at home. Each partner can complete the sentence stem and share the dialogue with their partner, either privately or with a therapist in session. The partner can mirror back each statement, reflecting, validating, and empathizing what they hear. These sentence stems can be the beginning of a longer conversation or a deeper session.

SEX THERAPY AND IMAGO THERAPY IN AN ISRAELI CLINIC

Orli Wahrman is a sex therapist in Israel who combines IRT with sex therapy in the context of couples work. She works collaboratively with a physiotherapist, or a pelvic floor therapist as it is known in the United States, to treat sexual pain and penetration disorders. This collaborative approach allows the physical therapy portion of treatment to focus on mechanical interventions, whereas sex and couples therapy focuses on increasing insight, improving communication, and creating an atmosphere that helps the couple enhance their sexual relationship. The following vignette illustrates how this team approach was used to address a sex therapy case that involved issues related to culture, religion, and sexual pain.

---

[1] Sylvia Rosenfeld, LCSW, and Sophie Slade, PhD, are both certified Imago therapists who created a clinical training for therapists on the application of Imago theory to sexuality issues called "Finding the Sex You Lost." The Lost Sexual Self Dialogue, which is an adaption of the Imago Lost Self Dialogue, is part of this training.

Shoshana and her husband, Eliezer, were referred for treatment due to Shoshana's experience with vaginismus and pain upon penetration. As it is currently defined in the *Diagnostic and Statistical Manual of Mental Disorders* (*DSM-5*), vaginismus is a genito-pelvic pain/penetration disorder (American Psychiatric Association, 2013). It is the inability to achieve vaginal penetration despite a desire to do so, which results in sexual and non-sexual (e.g., gynecological examination, tampon, dilators) aversion to vaginal penetration owing to actual or anticipated pain. Shoshana's sexual pain was negatively affecting their relationship, and they needed a therapist to help with communication, as well as to heal the sexual dysfunction.

Shoshana and Eliezer, who were both in their twenties, were from closed, conservative families where girls marry early and where there is pressure to have children and maintain a large family. Shoshana didn't cover her hair as many married traditional or religious women do. They were well educated and had a loving relationship.

Shoshana and Eliezer decided to get help after a year of marriage and daily attempts to have sex. They were starting to feel the pressure in their marriage and from Shoshana's mother. Apart from the sexual penetration problems, they said that they had become extremely worried about being able to "succeed" and that even hugging and kissing was not "as sweet" as it had been in the beginning of their relationship.

They were referred for pelvic floor therapy far enough away from their home village to maintain their privacy. Their work with the physiotherapist continued for eight months, and the couple came to sex therapy once a week during this time. Each sex therapy session lasted an hour and a half. The first half was spent discussing their sex life and learning how to enjoy their sexuality and bodies without penetration, and the second half was devoted to the Imago Dialogue. In the office, they sat in separate chairs, facing each other, looking into each other's eyes and talking in turns, one at a time. This structured framework invited a way for each partner to be present, understand, validate, and empathize with the other, without the need to agree.

The first task in sex therapy involved helping Shoshana ease her anxiety and gain trust in the physiotherapist. She felt inadequate, full of shame and guilt. What developed was a parallel process: The safer she felt with both the sex therapist and the physiotherapist, the more her body relaxed, and the more confident and satisfied she felt with herself and therapy. At times, Eliezer came alone to therapy to help him understand the problem, learn to be empathic, and manage his overwhelming feelings. He worked on his feelings of perceived inadequacy as a man, his perception that he was not desired by his wife, and his feelings of blame (e.g., "If she only wanted me enough, there wouldn't be any problem" and "If I'd be more of a man, she would . . .").

Early in therapy, it became clear that Shoshana was the highly competitive partner in the couple. As a little girl, she grew up in a family that didn't allow for any mistakes. She was also an independent woman in a society led by men, making her own decisions, including what to study and where, choosing to live in a dorm during college, and moving away from home. She was close to her mother, but she guarded her boundaries and her independence. She was petrified of telling her mother about her "failure" (i.e., her vaginismus "problem").

Eliezer came from a family of girls, and his older sister was always like a mother to him. He wanted to be the "man of the house" but presented as quite diffuse in what he was asking for, and he had a hard time with Shoshana's strong will. Other times, Eliezer could be quite manipulative in getting what he desired, instead of being honest and direct. Whenever Shoshana would discover this scheme, she would become quite upset and angry, which resulted in Eliezer pulling away. In turn, the couple might not talk or connect for days.

At each therapy session, Shoshana and Eliezer discussed this long-lived dynamic between them. They also processed their family histories, childhood wounds, and defenses, including how these things influenced the relationship and their sex life. Using the Imago Dialogue, Shoshana talked about how difficult it was to enjoy their lovemaking, as she kept thinking about her vaginismus and her difficulties with penetration. Eliezer was able to mirror, validate, and empathize with her concerns. When it came Eliezer's turn to use the dialogue, he complained about Shoshana not appreciating his efforts to be patient and empathic, and about her not making the efforts to find out what gave him pleasure.

At the end of each session, Shoshana and Eliezer worked on each partner needing to be appreciated by the other. They came to appreciate that even though their situation was not perfect, they could enjoy each other and be emotionally and sexually satisfied. Eliezer was able to see that Shoshana could be more attentive to him and less preoccupied with the vaginismus if he expressed his desires in a specific way. He was encouraged to say more, initiate more, and ask for what he liked—both in life and in sex.

Similarly, competitive Shoshana was encouraged to not work so hard and to appreciate Eliezer's efforts in stating what gave him pleasure. Eventually, sensate focus exercises were used to help the couple learn how to give and receive pleasure as they gradually moved from learning to touch, explore, and enjoy different body parts, to eventually the sexual organs.

Sex therapy was a parallel process to Shoshana's work with her physiotherapist, where she learned to loosen up and open her body first, and then her vagina. In doing so, she was able to work on issues of control and achievement. After five months, the couple both reported that they had a more satisfying sex life without penetration. They both reached an orgasm and enjoyed touching and exploring each other's bodies.

After eight months, Shoshana had a positive response to the vaginismus treatment, which can be persistent and difficult to treat. She had learned to use the vaginal extender to widen her vagina and to allow her fingers and tampons to penetrate. She felt that she had the knowledge and ability to loosen up and open herself, and she saw the problem as solved.

CONCLUSION

Sex therapy is more than just a mechanical or physical intervention. It also involves talking about sexuality so couples can ignite more passion in their relationship. Therefore, couples must engage in dialogues about how sexual issues have affected their adult selves, explore sex and its physical effects on their erotic lives, and talk about how messages about sex have been brought into their relationship. Doing so can help them heal childhood wounds that arise in the context of their adult relationships, thus allowing them to achieve emotional and sexual satisfaction. Using the Imago Dialogue and the techniques in *Getting the Sex You Want* (Nelson, 2008) therapists can enhance communication between couples and help them create an atmosphere for erotic connection. Desire starts in the mind, and encouraging couples to communicate about their sexual fantasies can lead to erotic recovery.

Chapter 5

Internal Family Systems and Sex Therapy

Gail Guttman, LCSW

Internal Family Systems (IFS) therapy is a type of therapy originally created by Richard Schwartz (1997, 2001), which was later adapted by Toni Herbine-Blank into a theory and method of couples therapy called Intimacy From the Inside Out (IFIO; Herbine-Blank, 2015). Given that both IFS and IFIO provide a framework for integrating sex and couples therapy, this chapter explores each model in greater detail. IFIO can be used as a springboard for integrating IFS in the context of couples work that addresses relational and sexual concerns.

INTERNAL FAMILY SYSTEMS

Internal Family Systems (IFS) therapy was first developed by Richard Schwartz after he began to notice that all of his clients had a system of "parts," or subpersonalities, within themselves. He found that each of these parts served a purpose, as they helped people deal with difficult situations or feelings. While other theorists had previously described these parts or subpersonalities (e.g., Berne, 1964; Jung, 1970; Rowan, 1990), Schwartz noticed that these parts were related to each other, similar to the relationships family members have with one another. This was a revolutionary concept at the time. Schwartz began to work with these parts in a similar way that he worked with families. Through this revelation and his resultant process with clients, Schwartz developed the theory and method behind IFS therapy.

One concept central to IFS therapy is the notion that all people have protective parts. These protective parts often reflect a person's strengths, and they are intended to help people navigate life by protecting them from real or perceived danger. In particular, these protective parts often come into being to protect people from painful feelings, memories, or experiences that occurred in childhood. They protect younger parts, known as "exiles," who were often not allowed to express their thoughts or feelings regarding their hurtful or traumatic experiences. They protect the exiles from reexperiencing the hurt, fear, and uncomfortable feelings of being alone. According to IFS, these protective parts reveal themselves as managers or firefighters.

Managers

Managers are the protective parts that try to guard the individual from real or perceived danger that could happen in the future. One example is a controlling manager, which tries to keep the individual from harm by being in charge of everything that could go wrong. For example, one client, Paula, had a strong need for structure and organization to feel safe and calm. Paula had a demanding job and two small children. She tried to manage her family's activities with a strict calendar in order to handle their busy lives. This helped Paula to feel calmer and kept the whole family on a tight schedule.

However, when managers are too controlling, they may not be useful in other ways. For example, the manager part can cause problems in sexual relationships. When Paula's controlling manager was in charge, she often demanded that her wife, Jane, only touch her in certain ways, with little variety. Paula also needed Jane to like the stimulation she was giving her, even if it did not fit for Jane. In this circumstance, the manager's need to be in control harmed Paula, Jane, and their relational, sexual connection.

However, at other times, a controlling manager can be used as a tool to enhance sexual play. When agreed upon, the manager can control the sexual situation in a way that both partners find arousing. For example, Paula asked her wife if it was okay to tie her up with silk scarves. Her wife agreed, they found a safe word, and they were able to act out Paula's control in a satisfying sexual way that brought pleasure to both of them.

Managers can also help when a client has been sexually abused in childhood. These managers protect the exiles from emotional pain, hide abusive memories, and control sexuality and sexual situations. One client, Diane, had been sexually molested by a babysitter when she was a child. She had a protective manager that numbed the sexual sensations in her vulva, resulting in little or no sensation. Whenever others touched her genitals, the manager protected her younger exile by shutting down arousal in her vulva.

However, in an attempt to protect Diane from the traumatic memory of her sexual abuse, this manager also kept Diane from masturbating. She would not touch her genitals, and even in the shower, she would only touch herself with a washcloth. Diane discussed how this "numbing" protector prevented her exile from feeling anything sexual by physically numbing that part of her body.

In therapy, Diane began to share more detail about the younger part who was molested, including the story of what happened to this exile. As she began to open up, it appeared there were two different parts of her that were present during the molestation, one which experienced some pleasure in her body and another that experienced pain, violation, and fear. As a five-year-old child, this experience was confusing. As an adult, Diane's manager protected her from reliving this experience. It functioned to keep her exiled part from suffering through the memory of the trauma, as well as the associated feelings of shame and terror.

Firefighters

In addition to managers, IFS theory also identifies another type of protective part known as the firefighter. In contrast to managers, which preemptively attempt to protect the individual from harm, firefighters perceive real or immediate danger that requires immediate attention and, at times, impulsive action to protect the more vulnerable, exiled parts of the self. Examples of a firefighter can be reflected in substance abuse, overeating, gambling, sexual acting out, or compulsivity.

For example, Mark came to my office seeking treatment for problems with his sex life and stress in his marriage. He considered himself a "compulsive masturbator." Any time he felt something unpleasant, such as an argument with his wife or a conflict at work, a part of him responded by masturbating as soon as he could get to a private place to do so. Mark's firefighter (his compulsive masturbation) numbed him and kept him from experiencing any uncomfortable, painful feelings in his current life, as well as the feelings of shame, anger, or fear carried by other protective parts and exiles. At the time, he did not think about what he was doing or the frequency with which his firefighter was constantly pulling at him. Afterward, though, his exile was often left feeling ashamed.

During therapy, we began to explore Mark's firefighter and its function, including how this compulsive masturbator part was helping him. As Mark's firefighter relaxed some, he slowly began to recall detailed memories of emotional abuse from his childhood. He remembered seeing his mother have sex with what appeared to be a stranger when he was five years old. When a child sees sexual behavior at too young of an age, without explanation, they are often unable to process their sexuality developmentally. In turn, they can develop protective parts that act similarly to the events witnessed through sexual actions. For Mark, he began to use masturbation as a self-soothing mechanism as a child. At a young age, he started to touch and play with his penis whenever he felt scared, lonely, or sad. Through this discussion, Mark began to see that his firefighting behavior numbed him to protect this exile from the traumatic memories of his childhood.

Unblending and Unburdening

The question in therapy is, how does the therapist help individuals with their protective parts and exiled parts? Although protective parts serve a useful purpose, they can take over at times, with little sense of any of the other parts and their needs. This can create difficulties and real-life problems. For example, Diane's manager had been protecting her from releasing her trauma and feeling any genital pleasure. Similarly, Mark's firefighter had prevented him from releasing his shame and the feelings of responsibility that he did something wrong. In order to help these managers and firefighters, clients need to learn how to be in relationship to these parts.

In particular, therapy requires focusing on the system as an internal family system to access a more centered energy. According to IFS, everyone has a core "Self" (also known as "Adult Self" or "Self-Energy") that embodies a variety of qualities, known as the eight C's: calmness, curiosity, compassion, confidence, courage, clarity, creativity, and connectedness.[1,2] In IFS therapy, the goal is to help the Self or Self-Energy be in charge of the system and in a relationship with the protectors and exiles. To do so, therapists must help clients "unblend" from the manager or firefighter parts to prevent them from taking over. Unblending is a way to help clients get space from the protective parts and let those parts know that the Self is present. When clients are able to unblend from the protective parts, the Self is in charge. The Self recognizes the ways the protectors are helpful or harmful and sees that the protectors are trying to keep the younger, hurt parts safe.

The first step in the process of unblending involves asking the protective part, "Do you know that the Self is here?" Once a protective part can understand the concept of the Self and feel its presence, the Self begins to interview the protective part to find out more about its role. The therapist can accomplish this task by asking clients to take a deep breath, relax, and continue viewing the protective part outside themselves or with some distance. Then the therapist asks the following questions, waiting for an answer before moving on to the next question:

- Where is this part in your body?

- What are the feelings of this part?

- How do you ("Self") feel toward it? (This question lets you know if there is Self-Energy on board. If the client answers with any of the adjectives (eight C's) to describe the Self, then the therapist knows some Self-Energy is on board. For example, the client might say, "I feel with the part," "I feel compassionate toward it," or "I feel curious about that part.")

- What are the beliefs that this part carries?

- What is it protecting? Or how has this part helped you?

- What has been its job?

- What is its hope?

- Is there a story it carries?

- Would this part be willing to step aside for a few moments to allow you to get present to the part that is underneath, either the exile or another protector? This part can come back anytime it is needed.

- Is the protective part willing to do that? If so, thank it and let it know that it can return at any moment.

---

[1] I like to add these traits as well: warmth, acceptance, presence, and consistency. A supervisor of mine, John Palmer, also describes the Self as being "free from anxiety."

[2] I often refer to the Self as the "Adult Self" in order to help clients understand the concept of a complete, aware self-concept. The terms Self, Self-Energy, and Adult Self will be used interchangeably throughout the rest of this chapter.

When the protective parts have stepped back and the Self is present, the therapist can help "unburden" or release the pain of the exiles. When the exiles release their burden, the protectors begin to relax. The Self can then unburden the pain, negative messages, and beliefs that the exiles carry. This unburdening can free up the exiles and protectors to bring in the useful traits they do have. If the exiles feel unburdened and healed, then the protectors can relax and be freed to help the system without taking over when one is in fear.

The following is an illustration of the internal system that is within every individual. The Self is in charge of the system and is located in the middle of the circle. The protectors (i.e., the managers and firefighters) and exiles are all in a relationship with the Self. The firefighters and managers are next to the exiles, as they serve to protect the exiles. Additionally, the firefighters and managers touch as they relate to each other and often help and protect each other. This illustration shows the importance of all parts being in relationship with each other, helping each other, and working toward the internal system that is led by the Self.

In individual therapy, both Diane and Mark were able to experience some unblending from their protectors and unburdening of their exiles. However, the processes of unblending and unburdening are rarely linear processes and are often complicated. Unblending and unburdening happen repeatedly and often over many sessions, particularly with trauma. When a person is in Self-Energy and starts to unblend from an exile, other protectors usually reveal themselves to protect the exile. An example of this process is illustrated through Diane's case. In therapy, we worked

to help Diane unblend from the protective part that did not want her or anyone else to touch her genitals by asking some of the questions identified earlier. For example, when Diane was asked how she felt about the protective part that surrounded her entire genital area, she said she was grateful it was there. This expression of gratitude gave the signal that Diane had some Self-Energy present and that her Self was in a relationship with this protective part. This protective part believed that people would hurt her badly if it was not there. Its job was to keep her safe from men, as she believed that men were not to be trusted.

When asked about the story that this part carried, the protective part revealed the story of her sexual molestation by a babysitter at five years old. At that point, Diane began to cry. She noticed that the protective part faded further into the background, and when it did, she saw the little girl, a younger version of herself, who was terrified, alone, and abandoned. This was the exile she was protecting. Many times in therapy sessions, the protective part would return to protect this younger girl (who she came to refer to as "Little Diane") from feelings of fear, shame, and anger over her childhood abandonment.

When Little Diane was present, I asked Diane's Adult Self how she felt toward Little Diane. Over time, Little Diane began to see that Diane's Adult Self was present for this little girl. Little Diane began to share more of her story to Diane's Adult Self, and in doing so, more details of the abuse were revealed. I asked Little Diane if she could begin to create a new story, an internal image, of Diane telling her family that they should have protected her. In turn, Little Diane began to imagine Diane's Adult Self telling her family that they should have protected her, listened to her, and seen how scared she was when the abusive babysitter came to take care of her. I also asked Diane's Adult Self to help Little Diane speak up about her anger toward her family.

Little Diane asked Diane's Adult Self, "Is it my fault that this happened?" and Diane's Adult Self let her know that "no child deserved this." As therapy continued, Diane began to imagine holding the young girl in her lap, comforting her, and letting her know she was not alone. I asked Diane to ask Little Diane, "Would you like to be taken away to a safe place?" Even though this work was primarily internal, Little Diane was able to say that she wanted to go to Diane's adult home, as that was a place where she always felt safe.

We then worked to uncover the beliefs held by Diane's younger, exiled part. When I asked Diane's Adult Self to ask this exile about its beliefs, Little Diane said, "No matter what you say, I know I am responsible for this abuse" and "I am damaged goods." She also felt that "No one will really be there for me." We began an unburdening process of helping Little Diane release these beliefs with the presence and help of Diane's Adult Self. This process was done in a number of ways. With Diane's Adult Self, Little Diane started to see that it could never be true that she was responsible for the babysitter having molested her. With the presence of Diane's Adult Self, Little Diane was able to challenge the belief that she was "damaged goods" by imagining a ritual in which she frees herself from this message. The door then opened for her to develop new beliefs about her sexuality.

Her inexperience with self-touch and genital touching was now the biggest hurdle in her sexual life. She accessed her Adult Self and began to explore touch on her own, exploring her own body in a slow and gentle way. Little Diane began to learn that her Adult Self was safe, would not judge her, and would always be there for her.

As Diane released her burdens and practiced gentle self-touch, Diane's Self-Energy began to grow more curious about her genitals. At this time, I began to use some cognitive behvior techniques and sex therapy. To help Diane get to know her own genitals and experience pleasure, I encouraged her to look at her genitals using a hand mirror. For the first time, she bought a vibrator and, with education and patience, was able to reach orgasm. Eventually, she was able to tell her partner how she like to be touched. Slowly, her Adult Self became present in order for her to get to know her body and experience pleasure.

Mark was taken through a similar process to that of Diane, which involved a slow unblending and unburdening process and the use of related questions. In individual therapy, Mark often talked of a vague memory of seeing his mother have sex with someone. By asking questions of his firefighter (i.e., his compulsive masturbator part), the firefighter was able to step back and become more unblended. In turn,

Mark's Self-Energy became more present. In his Adult Self, he was able to see that his firefighter was protecting an exile that felt shame about seeing his mother having sex with another man and the pressure of keeping this information a secret. This exile, a child part, believed that by witnessing this secretive incident, he was "bad."

The exile began to see that the firefighter part masturbated compulsively as a way to protect it from the shame that it felt in carrying a secret. With Self-Energy on board, the exile was able to unburden and release the negative belief "I am bad." Many of the associated feelings of shame were released as well. Through these unblending and unburdening processes, the firefighter began to masturbate less compulsively. Using CBT practices in the context of sex therapy, Mark's Adult Self began to ask for what he wanted from his wife, explaining to her that their sexual connection was a way that he could feel close to her.

INTIMACY FROM THE INSIDE OUT

Intimacy From the Inside Out (IFIO) is a theory and method of IFS couples therapy created by Toni Herbine-Blank (2015). IFIO maintains there is a sequence that happens between partners, and this sequence represents an interaction between the protective parts that can be dissected in the context of couples therapy.[3] In unraveling the sequence, the Adult Self speaks "for" their protective parts, rather than "from" their parts. This means that individuals begin to describe how the protective parts are trying to help the other more vulnerable parts. When protective parts are validated for the ways they are trying to help, the parts often relax, and there is room for the Adult Self to speak about the underlying exiles' feelings, beliefs, emotions, and needs. Self-healing the exiles and speaking "for" the parts are necessary prerequisites to healing. If people are speaking for their parts, then it is possible to restore, heal, deepen connection, and promote differentiation.

In couples therapy using IFIO, the Adult Self is present for the individual and is responsible for healing them internally, which means the partner is not responsible for saving the other. This transfer of ownership regarding the Self's responsibility is often a slow, difficult process, as most couples come to therapy in an attempt to get their partner to change. Looking inside themselves instead of focusing on their partner is often a learning curve. The goal is for therapists to ultimately teach inner differentiation in order to promote "outer" differentiation (i.e., differentiation with their partner). This process involves four steps: (1) making a therapeutic relationship, (2) tracking a sequence, (3) unblending from the parts, and (4) courageously communicating or doing individual work. The following sections describes each of these phases.

Making a Therapeutic Relationship

Building and maintaining a therapeutic relationship is an essential component of all forms of therapy. Therapists try to create a safe place wherein people can share

---

[3] In IFIO, the dance between partners is described as a sequence. The terms "dance" and "sequence" will be used interchangeably throughout this chapter.

and explore themselves in order to work toward change. In couples therapy, it is important for therapists to make it safe and stay out of the middle of the couple's relationship. To create this safe space, the therapist needs to be in charge and have the authority in the session. Slowing down and mirroring each person in the session, as well as teaching them to mirror their partner, helps couples develop trust that the therapist will not let things get out of control or allow blaming of the other.

Therapists can also develop a strong therapeutic relationship by reassuring couples that therapy can help them. Indeed, Schwartz often says that therapists are "hope merchants" in that they give clients hope for their future. Asking couples to create a contract with the therapist to jointly create a safe space for each of them is a way to get their buy-in to work with the therapist. The contract is created, stressing the importance of safety and helping individuals understand "parts" work.

In the first session in IFIO, the therapist teaches the couple about parts and describes the basic theory of IFS. Clients are helped to see that we all have a multiplicity of parts. They are taught that they each have parts that protect them and that these parts are there for good reason. The therapist's job is to help each partner recognize the parts that show up in their relationship—that is, to be a "parts detector"— and to help them to see that these parts can cause ruptures in the relationship. The therapist lets the clients know that instead of looking at their partner as the problem, the focus will be "taking a U-turn" to encourage them to look back at themselves to understand what is going on inside. One of the most essential aspects of IFS is helping clients to look at themselves versus blaming or focusing on their partner.

Therapists need to be their own "parts detectors" as well, as couples therapy can stimulate the therapist's protective parts and exiles. For example, if a therapist grew up with conservative religious sexual values, a discussion of polyamorous relationships could stimulate a judgmental part inside the therapist. This judgmental part may be protecting a part that carries fear about open relationships. Therefore, therapists must go slow in the treatment process and pay particular attention to parts that might get stimulated within themselves, as doing so will keep both the therapist and clients directed toward healing and connection. Maintaining an awareness of their own parts helps therapists stay out of the middle of the couple's relationship. While any subject can trigger a therapist's protective parts, sexuality is often a vulnerable place for therapists.

Tracking a Sequence

As in any type of couples therapy, IFIO focuses on the dance between the couple. Therefore, after initially creating safety for the couple, therapists will begin to notice the couple interacting in a predictable pattern. The sequence often represents an interaction between the protective parts, which are attempting to protect the exiles from feelings of fear, hurt, abandonment, or anger. While these protective parts have good intentions, this dance actually ends up creating disconnection between the couple. It is the therapist's job to help the couple recognize the sequence, stop the dysfunctional pattern, and relate in a more differentiated and connected way.

The therapist takes charge of the session by slowing down the interaction (the "sequence") between the couple and helping each partner look at the part that is showing up in the relationship. The therapist speaks to one partner about the part they see and might say, "I notice you have a part of you that [*insert part's behavior*]. I would like to know more about this part. Would that be okay with you?" The therapist then begins a process of helping the client know and understand this part by asking the following questions:

- What are the sensations in your body?

- What do you say to yourself?

- What is its first impulse?

- What does it actually do in your relationship?

The therapist then turns toward the other partner and asks, "How did you react to your partner?" The therapist would begin a process of asking the same questions to the other partner to help them understand their protective parts and which parts show up in the sequence. By asking this series of questions, the therapist begins to see a pattern. This process is called "tracking a sequence."

There are many goals behind tracking the sequence. Tracking the sequence slows down the interaction between the couple and allows each partner to begin the "U-turn" process of looking inside themselves versus focusing on their partner. The partners begin to recognize that their protective parts are trying to help them get their own needs met—the needs for love, safety, warmth, connection, and closeness. However, they also begin to see that these parts may not be helping them get their needs met and, instead, are creating a rupture in their relationship. By recognizing this, the couple can begin to see change is up to them. As therapists help clients recognize their contributions, hope is instilled by asking the couple if they would like to work together to do this dance differently and, in turn, create more self-esteem, connection, and room for accepting of differences.

The following example illustrates the process of tracking the sequence. Larry and Louise, who had been together for four years, came to therapy to address sexual issues. Specifically, Larry experienced premature ejaculation. Louise felt very dissatisfied with their sexual relationship and thought Larry was not present sexually. He did not take time to stimulate her, and she often felt pain in the lower third of her vagina when intercourse began due to lack of arousal. Because there was so little stimulation of any kind, Louise did not have orgasms through intercourse or manual stimulation of her vulva area by herself or her partner.

In the second session, Louise shared that she had never been with a man who ejaculated so quickly. She thought there was something wrong with Larry. She experienced him as only thinking about himself during sex. She did not experience him as present or connected during lovemaking. Larry responded by saying that he too had never experienced this before, as other women he had been with had never complained about the timing of his ejaculation. As these responses began and they acted out their sequence, I started to slow them down and asked the questions mentioned previously. I asked Louise to describe the sensations she was experiencing at the moment. She said she felt tightness in her chest and stomach. Her first impulse was to criticize him, and she said she told herself that Larry only thought about himself and didn't care about her pleasure.

I then turned to Larry and asked him what happened inside when Louise criticized him. He felt tension in his chest. "I cannot ever get it right with Louise," he said. Larry's first impulse was to defend himself, and he then told Louise, "No one else has ever complained before."

As we began to unravel this sequence, I asked Louise and Larry if they would like to do this interaction differently to feel more connected with each other. They agreed that if this was possible, they would feel hopeful that they could improve their sexual relationship. They agreed to this process.

The course of couples therapy is never linear. Clients often say they want to change the sequence. However, changing the dance is not easy to do. Most of the time, couples therapy requires unraveling sequences throughout every phase of therapy.

Unblending from the Parts

As discussed earlier, unblending is a process of getting Self-Energy on board wherein the Adult Self can establish a relationship with the protectors and the exiles. In this third step of IFIO, the couples therapist begins to help each partner look closer at the parts that show up in their dance or sequence.

Unblending, or speaking "for" the parts, is a process in which an individual turns inward to explore the stories, emotions, fears, roles, and hopes of the part. Larry and Louise's example demonstrates this unblending process in the context of couples therapy. Louise had a part that criticized Larry. Helping her to get Self-Energy on board was not easy. However, in exploring this critical protective part further, she eventually got in touch with more Self-Energy. The beliefs of Louise's critical part were that Larry only thought about himself and did not really care about her. This part's job was to blame Larry rather than feel her own vulnerability and insecurity. Underneath, Louise's critical part was protecting an exile, a part of her that feared she would not be good enough and that all men, any man, would only want her for sex. This part also protected her from depending on any another person, in this case, her husband.

As Louise's story began to unravel, she revealed that her mother had gotten pregnant with her before marriage. When Louise was a child, her mother had told her that getting pregnant had ruined her life. Her mother warned Louise to be careful about men and not to depend on them. Additionally, Louise's mother was constantly critical of her. As we explored the criticism, Louise was able to see that she had a part that her mother had taught her: to be critical when she felt scared. Underneath the criticism, Louise had an exile that feared she would never be enough. Her exile carried the legacy burden that men only wanted her for sex and not for who she was. This vulnerable exile had several fears. If her husband could not "perform," then it was her fault because she must not be good enough. The other fear was that she would be abandoned because she was not good enough. Louise had developed another protective part that told her she could only count on herself.

As we began to explore these parts, Louise was able to get some space from the part that criticized Larry. Slowly, the Adult Self became compassionate to the exile who felt she was never enough and could never count on anyone. She realized that the critical part was a survival mechanism she had learned from childhood through internalizing the voice of her mother.

As with Louise, it took some exploring before Larry could acquire more Self-Energy. Larry held a protective part that believed "the best defense is a good offense." As we discussed this part, we discovered that a part of him had always felt sexually inadequate. From the time Larry was a teenager, he had a part that compared his penis size to that of the other boys in the locker room. Additionally, when he masturbated, he came quickly. This part feared that his penis was too small and that he would, literally and figuratively, never be enough. Larry's blaming part was protecting Larry from his feelings of inadequacy about the size of his penis and his premature ejaculation. This part's hope was that Larry could disguise himself to prevent Louise from seeing how inadequate he was; she would only see him as a fully adequate sexual male.

Underneath this protective part was an exile that never felt good enough sexually. When I asked about this part's story, Larry said that his family often told him how great he was. The exile that carried beliefs of sexual inadequacy underneath was his only part that felt so inadequate. His protective part—"the best defense is a good offense"— kept the exile from feeling bad about itself. As we began to explore these protectors and the exiles underneath, both Louise and Larry became more compassionate to each other, and they both reported a growing closeness between them.

Courageously Communicating

In the fourth stage of IFIO, partners learn courageous communication and engage in their own individual work to unburden their exiles. Courageous communication involves speaking for the protective parts and the exiles underneath that are vulnerable and fearful. In courageous communication, the sequence is disrupted and each partner takes more responsibility for their parts. The vulnerable parts (the exiles) can relax as they begin to trust the Self to speak for them. Speaking for the exiles and protectors is both healing for the individual and the couple. When couples begin to speak for these parts, intimacy and connection are restored, and it becomes more likely that the individual will get their needs met. It is also healing emotionally and psychologically, especially if in the family of origin there were few experiences in which the caregivers' parts took responsibility for the ways they hurt others.

When speaking for the protectors, the Adult Self no longer blames the other and, instead, takes responsibility for the protective parts that created the relational rupture. The space between the couple is often experienced now as deep, safe, and warm. Differentiation is created, and closeness ensues.

During the process of courageous communication with Louise and Larry, both of them began to speak for their exiles. Louise spoke of the exiles that feared she would not be wanted for who she is. She also spoke of the exile that feared no one would ever be there for her. Similarly, Larry talked of his exile that had an insecurity about whether he would be enough if he had a flaw (i.e., premature ejaculation) and, in his opinion, a small penis. Both Larry and Louise were in their Adult Selves and were compassionate to each other's young parts. This was courageous communication. They also found compassion for these young parts within themselves.

As Larry and Louise learned to unblend from the protectors, their sequence was no longer the same. We then began to use CBT techniques within the context of sex therapy. Larry worked on the "stop, start" sex therapy exercises prescribed for premature ejaculation (McCarthy & Metz, 2004). At times, he still continued to ejaculate quickly after starting intercourse, and we thus agreed that it was best to temporarily take intercourse off the table for the time being. Instead, I instructed Larry and Louise to begin to touch each other in different ways. Larry worked on being present to their shared sexual experience instead of focusing on his own sexual performance. Louise worked on noticing Larry's emotional presence during sex.

In doing so, with the presence of Louise's Adult Self, she began to notice Larry's presence and how much he tried to be with her. Louise's blaming protector relaxed, and her exile began to heal. Louise became more present in the sexual relationship. Larry worked hard to let Louise's young part know she could count on him. Louise reinforced Larry's exile that he was enough, even if he was not perfect.

CONCLUSION

At the time of this writing, Larry and Louise have developed a more fulfilling sexual relationship. Larry has worked to be more present. While he still ejaculates early at times, Louise knows now that his premature ejaculation is not her fault. Larry has learned to stimulate her and bring her to orgasm after he ejaculates. Their sexual relationship has become more open, allowing for more options between them, without their old messages and young parts controlling the communication and their sexual relationship.

Any time a sex therapist gets stuck in couples therapy, using IFIO to unravel the sequence between the couple and create courageous communication can be of tremendous benefit. Helping individuals to speak for their underlying protective and vulnerable parts creates closeness, deeper connection, and empathy. It is then possible for couples to change the sequence that shows up sexually and to make use of valuable CBT techniques that sex and couples therapy has to offer.

Chapter 6

Healing Sexual Trauma with Couples Therapy in Groups

Pamela Finnerty, PhD

THEORETICAL UNDERPINNINGS: GROUP THERAPY AND SEXUAL TRAUMA

There is a rich history and practice regarding the use of groups as a powerful healing mechanism for a variety of psychological issues. Group therapy can foster a culture of cohesion, support, and integration that provides the necessary vehicle from which to facilitate change (Yalom, 1995).

The use of group psychotherapy is particularly valuable for the healing of sexual trauma, as it provides an atmosphere that is simultaneously intimate and public. By listening to other group member's experiences and sharing their own, individuals are able to release themselves from the burden of shame they have been carrying as a result of their trauma. Isolation is gradually replaced by a feeling of community and being understood and accepted, which helps free individuals from the self-blame often associated with sexual trauma (Buchele, 2000).

When conducted with couples, group therapy can heal and transform relationships that have been complicated and limited by the effects of sexual trauma. It allows couples to work through the complicated territory of trauma repair by bringing buried memories and feelings to the surface. Often, couples have never directly discussed the trauma history with each other, and this history only emerges as the couple gradually works on the relationship issues that brought them to therapy. For example, they enter into therapy with their narrative of what has gone wrong in the relationship, such as "his porn use," "she never wants to have sex," or "we just don't communicate." Sometimes, this surface narrative may be unexpectedly masking a trauma that has not been addressed.

Couples group therapy addresses this complicated territory in a variety of manners. For example, the presence of the group in the consulting room, and internally in the bedroom, can help soothe the person so they can stay in the here and now and attune to their partner in the present moment. Often, individuals who have experienced sexual trauma have difficulty experiencing arousal in the context of consensual sexual encounters because of their underlying anxiety related to the trauma. The experience of having the "company" and soothing of the group members can help the individual remember how to "ride out" the anxiety, mindfully remain in the present, and attune to their body's sexual responses (Brotto, 2018).

In addition, the group format can be particularly useful in healing relationship ruptures by helping group members increase their ability to connect with others. Frequently, individuals with a history of sexual or attachment trauma overreact to differences, have difficulties accepting others' views, and struggle to engage with their partner after conflict (Solomon, 2003). The group structure provides opportunities to witness more adaptive behavior from group members and from the therapist, and it provides the assistance, support, and encouragement needed to modify the rupturing behavior. The larger container of the group process can help hold the couple, where one member of the couple turns to another relationship in the group, and to the therapist, while they calm themselves and reduce the adrenaline rush triggered by the old trauma. They can then reengage their partner in an appropriate and modulated interaction.

Finally, the security provided in the context of the group environment can help reconfigure associative networks connected with trauma by providing a new relational framework characterized by trust and safety (Buchele, 2000). Just as each couple, and each individual, forms a relationship with the therapist, group members form alliances with other couples as they work on their relationship issues, including their sexual issues. The relationships that form become deep and multifaceted, and individuals find a sense of healing as they identify with other couples and find a sense of community. Many members report a sense of "we are not the only ones who are struggling." As in all group therapy, the relationships between the members of the group are powerful elements of healing. Increased freedom, ease, and comfort with sexuality is often a result from this powerful type of therapy. The process of creating this group crucible for change has several steps.

STEP ONE: ASSESSING EACH COUPLE FOR COUPLES GROUP THERAPY

Sexual trauma often disrupts individuals' capacity to sustain engagement and reconnect in the context of relationships. Often, a series of small "t" traumas have negatively affected the relationship across time, which are not big traumas per se but smaller betrayals and resentments that have happened over the years (Shapiro, 2001). These small "t" traumas, which often intertwine with past histories of sexual and attachment traumas, may manifest in a variety of responses in the relationship, such as vague uneasiness around heavy drinking or unexpectedly intense emotional reactions that observers would characterize as a relatively minor slight or misstep on the part of a partner. For individuals who have experienced sexual trauma, these responses often reflect preverbal memories of the trauma—memories that the individual has repressed or dissociated from—that manifest in emotional reactions in the context of the relationship (Solomon, 2003).

During the initial consultative process, the therapist ascertains the level of trauma and attendant dysfunction for each of the partners relative to the appropriate level of functioning for group therapy. Every exchange within the couple and with each client and the therapist is diagnostic. Are they both open to the possibility that the issues that bring them to therapy may be shared problems? It frequently occurs that one member of the couple feels the need for therapy more urgently than the other. Exploring the roles of each member, the couple's narrative about the relationship, and the history of each partner in the couple can lead to the realization that the relationship issues are shared and that each member is responsible for their half of the troublesome dynamics.

One particularly critical dynamic is how each member of the couple responds to conflict, both in the relationship and with the therapist. When conflict comes to the surface with the therapist—for example, as a result of a disagreement over the cancellation policy—this is an opportunity for the therapist to experience the client's capacity to dislike something and still be committed to it. The therapist can then strengthen the alliance with the couple when there has been a conflict and find an appropriate level of resolution prior to beginning the work in the challenging and supportive environment of a group.

For example, if a woman is angry because she believes the cancellation policy is unfair, then the therapist can let her know that she hears her feelings, that she understands how this might be difficult, and that agreeing to abide by the policy does not mean she has to like it. Of course, the client has the option to not agree to the therapy contract, and in some instances a referral is made at this point. The therapist helps process the dynamics of agreeing to some things that the client does not like in the interest of staying committed in a valuable relationship. As in all strong relationships, compromises are made and feelings are heard.

After working with several couples for a period of time, the therapist begins to determine which couples might work well in a group. In making this determination, the therapist must ascertain each partner's ability to tolerate conflict, exhibit forgiveness, and accept compromises. They must be willing to push themselves beyond their present level of functioning by tolerating and speaking about their discomforts.

In addition, they must have sufficient ego strength, self-awareness, and openness to hearing difficult feedback. Even if a couple exhibits signs that they would be a good fit for group therapy, the actual process of making the change from couples therapy to group therapy can only be fully known by actually making the transition. In those instances, where the couple's capacities decline or it becomes evident that they are not sufficiently strong for the group therapy process, the therapist implements modifications in the therapeutic strategy. There might be less confrontation, more identification of emotional triggers, or more processing of trauma for this group member's needs.

STEP TWO: DETERMINING GROUP COMPOSITION AND BEGINNING THE GROUP THERAPY PROCESS

The group begins with three to four couples, and other couples may be added as there are openings. In order to benefit from the group format, it is critical that every client has already shown the ability to navigate through their emotions. It is possible that dynamics will appear in the group that were not present in the initial consultative period. Therefore, it is important to balance group members' differing personalities, interactional styles, family of origin issues, tolerance for conflict and intimacy, and other relational factors when considering whether to add members. Normally, no more than two couples with evidence of clearly traumatic histories can be added to a group, considering the amount of work that needs to be processed.

Sexual trauma can be present in people of all ages, ethnic groups, and sexual orientations and identities. Therefore, it is important to develop an understanding of each person's experiences and history, including how that might affect the couples work and, when relevant, the trauma work. In addition, the mix of couples in the group should be balanced as much as possible. Although therapists should proactively attempt to balance the composition of group members to the extent they can, only when the group actually starts does the therapist find out the true makeup of the group.

While it is best to have at least two group members from a diverse group, a group can function if the relative lack of diversity is acknowledged and sufficient alliances are formed. For example, if there is one lesbian couple, or one couple in which one of the partners is transgender, the group process needs to include an exploration of the feelings and possible issues that affect group members. This can be a delicate process that evolves over time, and group selection includes an assessment as to whether all of the group members have the potential to be able to engage in such a process. When accomplished successfully, it can certainly be transformative. The nature and strength of the alliances that do form can sometimes be surprising and are part of the magic of group psychotherapy.

When couples group work begins, the group members meet once a week for 75 minutes. The groups are open-ended in that they are not time limited regarding the number of weeks that couples may attend. When they contract with the therapist, they are told that the group process is ongoing and that they can continue as long as the process is determined to be beneficial. The efficacy of the group process is discussed with the couple and with the therapist on a regular basis. When the group appears to be of benefit and couples are making good use of the group therapy, they can opt to stay for prolonged periods of time, from months to years, to continue to grow in their evolving relationship. Each couple is seen in relationship therapy for varying lengths of time prior to introducing them into a couples group, although the preferred method of couples group therapy is mentioned early in the consultative process.

In couples group therapy, each individual—as well as the couple's relationship itself—are considered "clients," though the relationship of each couple is considered the primary client. Each of these clients are held within the community, or the "group." The group develops its own culture, and alliances within the community are formed. There are many relationships in the room where these connections can be fostered: in the partnerships within the couple, between the couples, between each individual and all of the other members of the group, and between each person and each couple with the therapist.

STEP THREE: STARTING A GROUP

The birth of a new group is creative, exciting, and sometimes unnerving. When a group is first starting out, it is important to establish group norms and ground rules, which include rules around keeping all identities private and making an agreement that group members are not to speak outside of the group about the work done in the group. There is also a discussion about refraining from speaking to or identifying anyone seen in the waiting room, including any of the therapists. The therapist establishes clear guidelines about time, fee payment, lateness, and absentee policies.

Whenever a new couple joins the group, it is important to reiterate these ground rules and boundary expectations, and group members' reactions are openly invited. Often, the process takes place over a period of time as group members process and gradually become aware of the effects of the change of having a new couple in the group. It can be helpful to identify that adding new members is a form of a new beginning—a type of "new group"—as it can cause the group culture to change in unexpected and often challenging ways.

In the early stages of the group, the therapist may open a session with an invitation to the group members by asking a question, such as, "What are you hoping to achieve?" or "How is it to be here with other couples?" Therapists may comment on some element of the process, such as noting that the amount of laughter may be an indication of nervousness or excitement, and they invite the group members to use some self-awareness to know more about what they are experiencing as well.

At this point, the group may be asked a question to follow up on previous work. This can be a way to open a discussion and process anything left over from the previous sessions. Usually the group members will begin to comment, share feelings, and ask such questions of one another. With any group, the normal process may be to watch and wait for the group to begin itself as members ask for time, "line up," and agree to take turns. Couples may also go home and continue a process triggered in the group, subsequently returning with insights and behavioral change that occurred over the week. While they are not required to report their process with the group, it often is beneficial to do so.

Observing the dynamics between members of a couple is part of the process, similar to individual group therapy. At times, the therapist facilitates a substantial piece of work in one or both members of the couple, and other times group members step in to provide support. While the therapist is involved in and responsible for all of the work in the room, some of that work is allowing the couples to help one another. The therapist's decision to move in or stand back is governed by an assessment of what would be most beneficial for the couple or group dynamic at the time. Is it best to let the open argument proceed? Or would it be more helpful to slow things down and encourage active listening? How are the other group members responding? Do they need tending to as well? What is this like for every member of the group at all times? Are there any silent problems?

The power of the group is something to be both managed and allowed to take its course. The balance of overmanaging and letting the members run the group for its own best interest evolves with time. With the therapist's own continued growth, supervision, consultation, and experience, group leaders can continue to grow, change, and improve as facilitators. It is important to face, and hopefully accept, their own imperfections along the way.

TWO CASES: TRAUMA, LOW DESIRE, COMPULSIVE BEHAVIOR, AND SUBSTANCE ABUSE[1]

Case Example #1

Sarah and Joseph came to therapy a few months after the birth of their second child. Joseph was a handsome and gregarious 52-year-old man who was previously married and had a teenage daughter. Sarah, 40 years old, was vibrant and attractive, though she complained of the weight she had gained since her two pregnancies. The two met working on Capitol Hill in Washington, DC. He was a former staff director who currently worked at a successful lobbying firm. Sarah was a lawyer who represented various environmental advocacy organizations. She worked three days a week and said she was always exhausted and wondered how she could continue. She was anxious and exacting, and she was having a great deal of trouble balancing her career, her two children, and her relationship with her husband. She said she felt like she was "a failure" as a wife. Their once intense and passionate sex life with all of its experimentation and openness had become boring and burdensome.

In discussing her childhood, Sarah related a family history of substantial alcohol and addiction issues. Her father was an alcoholic who was very "sweet" and overly physical, or as Sarah had described it, was "all over" his two young daughters. Her mother was "always angry," and there was "a lot of screaming" when her father would stay out later than he had "promised." This happened often, sometimes several nights a week.

She married Joseph when she was 36 years old because he seemed "safe" to her. She stated she did not feel threatened by him, unlike her previous partners whom she described as "exciting bad boys." She never found Joseph to be especially "hot," but she was comfortable with him and found the sex with him to be exciting, and she had orgasms regularly through his manual stimulation. In her younger years, she and her boyfriends drank heavily, and she had what she called "hot sex," although she reported that she normally did not have an orgasm.

Sarah gained a great deal of weight with her first pregnancy, as her longstanding pattern of fasting, intense exercise, and tightly controlled eating ceased. Although her mood remained stable during the pregnancy, she reported a "collapse" after the birth of her first child, which involved feeling anxious, sad, and out of control. The strain of having a baby who was difficult to soothe and her husband's frequent absence for long workdays and business travel left her feeling depressed and "incompetent as a mother."

Joseph came from a working-class Irish Catholic family and had a family history of alcoholism. He reported not having any current issues with alcohol, but he did enjoy two glasses of wine nightly. Sarah used to join him in drinking, but since her first pregnancy, she had either abstained or restricted her use. She complained about Joseph's drinking, and he complained about her lack of interest in sex and how edgy and harsh she had become with him. Joseph's career took off around the same time that his second

---

[1] All of the "clients" described in this chapter are composites of couples I have worked with over the course of my career. The therapy interventions described are depictions of typical interactions in relational couples therapy groups.

child was born. Sarah began to complain bitterly about his late evenings, frequent trips, and excessive drinking. Their once adventurous sex life became an infrequent and rudimentary chore. From the outset, I noticed elements of undiagnosed postpartum depression, disordered eating, and addiction. I also surmised that Sarah's conflictual family history may have been contributing to her low desire.

Case Example #2

Melody, 52, a client for just over two years, was a successful architect with her own business. Although she was sexually adventurous throughout college and her twenties, she currently worked long hours and had little time for her vibrant but limited social life. She first came to therapy after the end of a relationship with a man who also had a demanding career and little availability. He was also distant and emotionally detached. Through the help of therapy, Melody had begun asking him for more emotional connection, more time together, and more sexual connection and closeness. In turn, he became more distant, abruptly ended their eight-year relationship, and started dating another woman.

Melody was well dressed and businesslike. Professionally, she was a combination of aggression and sometimes surprising passivity. Her father was emotionally unavailable, distant, and self-involved. When Melody was a child, he also made inappropriate comments about women in front of his daughters. Melody's mother was a powerful government official who worked long hours, so her parents spent little time together when she was growing up. In turn, Melody saw her parents had little emotional or physical connection between them. Melody later found out her father had been involved in a string of affairs during her childhood, and the couple divorced when Melody was 20. Her father remarried soon after, evidently to a woman with whom he had been having an affair for a number of years.

Melody's new partner, Jake, was an outgoing, warm, and vibrant man. They met on a dating site and hit it off right away. Jake was very engaged with Melody, and it mainly felt like he was a wonderful change from the distant and emotionally unavailable partner of her past. However, at times, Melody felt like Jake's sexual hunger and eagerness were compulsive, causing her to feel "invisible." His porn use, which she knew about and supported, had increasingly grown more intense and consuming. While she enjoyed the sex they had, she also worried about how long she would be able to "keep up with him." She was afraid of hurting his feelings by telling him that she needed more space. She wondered if there was "something wrong with him" and had difficulty bringing anything up with him. With coaching, she was eventually able to ask him if he would join her for a consultation for couples therapy.

Jake reported a childhood of emotional distance from a harsh and intensely focused father whose career as a doctor kept him away from the family and at the hospital. He described his mother, who was French, as beautiful and very warm, but she drank a lot and could be quite seductive with Jake's friends as they grew into young men. The boys were permitted to smoke pot in the basement, and his mother would sometimes join them. Jake reported that her overwhelming closeness could feel claustrophobic, yet he also felt proud to have such a "cool mom."

Melody and Jake came to couples counseling once a week for a period of eight or nine months before the idea of group was proposed. I mentioned that I often worked with couples in groups, and while Jake was reluctant to "tell a bunch of strangers his problems," he agreed to go to couples group therapy "for Melody" if she really wanted it. Neither of them had been in a group before.

The issues that they intended to address included Melody's difficulty opening up and asking for what she wanted from Jake, as well as Jake's difficulty hearing that she wanted more from him. He felt engulfed, overwhelmed, and suffocated by her emotional needs. His marijuana and porn use had increased as her "demands" increased. She reported feeling "unseen" and invisible (e.g., "It's not me he wants; I'm not really here"). As the work in couples therapy progressed, her anxiety and intense demands became evident, as did his anger and withdrawal. Both had difficulty advocating for themselves with the other without blaming or feeling small and helpless, and I indicated that these kinds of issues could be addressed quite powerfully with the increased support and learning opportunities of a couples group.

SEX THERAPY IN COUPLES GROUP THERAPY

Not all couples who enter couples group therapy do so with their sexual relationship being the primary focus. Rather, the group focuses on complex relationship issues, which include (but are not limited to) sexual issues. Elements of sex therapy are integrated into the group as a part of the couples' work.

For example, Sarah began the group wanting to address her relationship with Joseph. "I know you want to have sex, but I just don't feel like it. I'm tired after breastfeeding and keeping up with a three-year-old after working all day. I feel terrible that I can't be there for you, and the last thing I want to do is put on a negligee and have my drippy, heavy breasts touched." Joseph replied, impatiently, "I know you're tired, but I just feel so distant from you, and I am tired of spending night after night with you falling asleep on the couch at 9:30 p.m. or falling asleep when you're putting Adam to bed. We haven't had sex for months."

This is a familiar scenario, with low desire being one of the more daunting and intractable issues presented in sex therapy. The group members talked to Sarah and Joseph, asking about how each of them felt about their lack of sex, and group members shared their own experiences, talking about how they too had worked out similar issues in their own relationships.

Some suggested getting a babysitter once a week, having sex while the children napped on the weekend, and other tactics that couples typically deploy in the early stages of parenting when trying to resurrect their sex life. While the group members discussed practical solutions and offered heartfelt support and encouragement, I noticed that Sarah was becoming increasingly withdrawn and did not seem to be taking in what was being said.

I asked, "Sarah, can you tell me what's happening with you? You don't seem to really be present."

In response, she said, "You don't care. You're not listening to me. No one listens to me."

The group grew quiet. I waited for a moment, sensing Sarah's anger and despair. "Do you know what's going on, Sarah? What are you feeling?"

"I don't want to talk to you," she said. "I don't want to talk to anyone. No one understands me. No one really cares."

"What do you want me to understand?" I asked. "It seems to me you are really up against something and you're having trouble feeling like you are with people who genuinely care about you and want to help you."

Sarah looked at Karen, the group member with whom she had the most connection and seemed to feel the closest. Karen smiled. "I'm here, Sarah. I know all about feeling like no one cares, but I believe Joseph cares, and we, all of us in the group, we all care."

Sarah looked at me, and I asked, "How are you feeling now? How is it going?"

"Better." Sarah looked down and gradually quieted herself by working on her breathing. She shyly smiled, looked at me out of the corner of her eye, and said, "I still don't trust you."

"I don't need you to trust me all the time," I replied. "We both know that sometimes you just don't like what I have to say." I waited a moment and then asked, "Are you feeling like you can trust what Karen is saying to you?"

Sarah looked at Karen. "Yes, it feels like I can hear it from her."

Joseph had been quiet throughout this exchange, so I turned to him and asked, "How are you doing?"

"I hate it when this happens. I'm angry, but I can't tell her. I want to give up."

Sarah turned to Joseph. "I'm sorry I don't want you like I did before. I'm sad we don't have more sex, more everything. I miss you."

Joseph replied, "I miss you too. I get really scared when you do this stuff. I'm afraid I'm going to lose you."

I registered that both partners were angry and scared about what was happening. With the help and support of the group therapy process, Joseph began to let Sarah know more about how their lack of sex, her absence, and her need for control affected him.

A number of features of couples group therapy are evidenced in this example. Whether or not group members are actively participating, they are present and providing the safety of the container. By witnessing and identifying with one another, the group members are doing their own internal work, particularly on issues with which they resonate. The changes in each group member's relationship with their vulnerabilities and relationship patterns develop over time through the following intervention protocol, which works gradually after multiple repetitions as the relationship patterns are inevitably repeated:

1. One or both members of the couple brings up an issue, sometimes in the form of a complaint.

2. The therapist and group members help the couple describe and discuss the issue addressed.

3. Group members weigh in about what they see and feel, with the therapist and fellow group members providing guidance and clarification as needed.

4. Group members learn to identify one another's pitfalls, often from their own work with their partner.

5. Group members recognize themselves in one or both members of the couple doing the work.

6. Group members reflect and gradually learn to take responsibility for their own missteps in the relationship and to catch themselves and hold themselves accountable.

The section that follows discusses some of the change mechanisms that underlie this intervention protocol in greater detail.

Mechanisms for Change in Group Therapy

1. Couples see themselves in others by observing and identifying with the behavioral patterns of other members, and they learn to provide directive feedback.

Being present while other couples are interacting can be a safe way to observe and take ownership of one's own difficult relationship issues. It makes it easier for individuals to absorb difficult feedback and acknowledge that they can sometimes be overly harsh, critical, distant, or unavailable. In the company of other group members, individuals can practice listening to others' experience of being hurt, frightened, or angry in response to yelling or derision. In turn, members think, "I don't want to sound like that. I can see that he is being too harsh with her" or "She's really laying into him. He was out of line, but this feels disproportionate."

For example, in one particular group session, Melody got angry at Jake for wanting too much sex and lashed out at him. In response, one of the group members turned to Melody and said, "When I am in your position, I feel like I'm right and he's wrong. But when you were talking to Jake, I thought it was a bit overblown, and I wouldn't have wanted you to be talking that way to me. At the same time, I also understood your unhappiness and impatience. It's not easy to say no all the time when he asks for sex, and you end up feeling worn out. Although I didn't feel particularly afraid of you when you lashed out, I did feel protective of Jake. Actually, you both had good points. I feel like I want to help both of you." Through the process of being confronted by another group member, Melody was able to see herself and her own reactivity more clearly, while also being able to better see Jake's position.

As group members participate in helping other couples through their interactions, they learn to provide direct and difficult feedback to others in compassionate and measured ways without blame, which helps them develop skills in confronting others and being assertive. In addition, by having the emotional space to observe behavioral patterns in others, they can identify similar patterns in their own relationship. It provides them with their own internal space to see their own reactivity and whether they are, for instance, withholding or controlling.

2. Couples learn to hold themselves and their partner with firmness and compassion.

The community of the group provides a space from which group members can listen to the feelings of others, which provides a felt experience and enables them to change how they relate to themselves and their partner. In particular, it provides a container from which individuals can develop the ability to forgive themselves for any transgressive behaviors they have exhibited in the context of their relationship. One of the keys to changing this behavior is compassionate accountability (e.g., "I can see that I am being overly aggressive and not hate myself for it"), and the group process allows the compassion a group member feels toward others to be transferred to the self.

It is important to remember that these transgressive behaviors once served a critical purpose, as they protected the psyche at a time when there were no other options. Therefore, these behaviors should not be viewed as pathological but, rather, as the "least bad" option during a time when attachment or sexual trauma left them no other choice. While these behaviors may have served them in the past, they are currently interfering with their relationships (Solomon, 2003). Therefore, an important aspect of facilitating behavioral and emotional change is to encourage group members to promote self-compassion for their younger selves who figured out the "least bad" way to survive in an unsafe environment. Clients in the group are encouraged to applaud the ingenuity of their younger selves and to honor their protective defenses even as they are helped to relax these defenses in their current relationships.

The therapist's words can often help in this process. For instance, after Melody lashed out at Jake, I asked her, "Melody, are you able to see what you have done? Can you forgive yourself for having been a bit harsh?" A large part of the journey of couples therapy is for individuals to learn to recognize their untoward behavior without the defensiveness that often arises from deeply held shame.

In developing compassionate accountability, one of the most powerful elements of group therapy is the potential for the ongoing mitigation of self-hatred. For example, Melody was feeling embarrassed about her blowup with Jake. One of the other group members reached out and said, "Melody, we all do that. You've seen me do something very similar. It happens when you are too pressed, we all know that. The yelling is not all of you. Yes, you lost control. You've seen me lose control. Do you hate me for it?"

Melody responded quickly by saying, "Of course not. We all get crazy sometimes."

I asked, "Melody, can that openheartedness apply to you too?"

Melody looked at me and said, "Well, maybe."

Holding oneself firmly accountable is part of an ongoing journey toward self-acceptance without self-hatred. It involves the recognition that "There is something wrong with what I did" as opposed to "There is something wrong with me." Developing this mindset is challenging for individuals who have grown up in abusive families and with sexual abuse, in particular. For the frightened child, the feeling that they are to blame gives them a feeling of agency. The illusion that they were in control, and therefore to blame, protected them from facing the potential annihilation of being overpowered by a much stronger and beloved family member.

3. Groups members are encouraged to hold themselves accountable in working on their issues.

In couples group therapy, the couple is not alone and, in some sense, is more accountable to themselves in having others know about their dilemmas. By having more support, they can be more objective and see their partner through others' eyes. In turn, they may have more compassion for their partner and may find the energy to make an extra effort to connect with them and work through their respective issues. Individual members learn to hold themselves accountable for their own behavior, which is mirrored in front of the other group members.

For example, Melody started the group by saying she wanted to get some help with her relationship with Jake. He became nervous and stiffened, as he generally shut down when discussing her emotional needs. She started to talk about how it sometimes felt when they were having sex. "I start to feel like I'm an object, like you don't really see me. It's okay to be that way some of the time, we all go off into the intensity. But this feels different. You're so determined and intense. Like it's an emergency."

She went on without leaving space for him to respond. "And you never want me to initiate. You're all over me before I have a chance. When I even try, it's almost like you're scared of me."

Jake looked at her, then at me. I asked, "What's happening, Jake?"

He swallowed. "I don't know. I guess I'm getting upset. I just want to shut this down."

He looked away as I said, "Can you tell me where you are, Jake?"

Looking down, he replied, "I don't know. I'm scared. And sad." He then looked up at me. "This is so embarrassing. I don't want anyone to see me this way."

"What way, Jake?"

"Sad, I guess. Upset."

He looked at Melody and said, "I can't believe this is happening. I never get upset, and I certainly never cry, and I feel like crying. I guess I feel hurt."

She looked at him. "I am so sorry. What did I do? I'm so sorry I hurt you."

He shook his head. "No, you didn't do that much. Hell, you should be able to talk about that. There's something wrong with me."

Jake looked at me again. "This is so weird. I feel so uncomfortable. Everyone's looking at me."

I responded, "It's great that you can look at me. Are you okay?"

He nodded.

"Do you think you could look at someone else?"

Jake took a breath and looked at one of the other women in the group, who smiled at him. "It's not a big deal, Jake. We all do this."

He looked at her. "It's just so surprising to have it happen, here, in front of everyone."

His breathing eased, and he looked around the room and then at Melody. He smiled at her. "Wow. What a ride." She reached across the sofa and grabbed his hand.

"We're in this together."

This interaction was part of the beginning of a piece of work for Jake about his family history and his mother's sexual aggression with his father in particular. He had a memory of the nights when he could hear her raised voice as they were having sex on the other side of the thin walls of their apartment. As the memory surfaced, so did the feelings of helplessness, fear, and, as his work progressed, anger.

"I hated what she sounded like. And I hated hearing them."

4. The group format allows couples to participate in healing as they learn how to hold difficult and traumatic content.

The unfolding of early traumatic experiences that have never been identified as abuse occurs slowly, over time. The strong defensive mechanisms that individuals have used to navigate many of life's challenges can only be relaxed gradually. For example, when talking about her sexual issues, Sarah felt shame and initially covered it with belligerence and blame. When anger and contempt have been used to defend against intense shame and vulnerability, the company of the group helps provide a safe container from which individuals can explore their internal reactions to themselves and others. During this time, the therapist stays alert to all of the group members who might get triggered by frequently checking in and making sure everyone is breathing and able to hold themselves and each other through the process.

For example, I helped Sarah explore her tendency to project blame onto her husband by noting, "I can see that when you start out by blaming him, you are pushing him away instead of inviting him into a healing dialogue. It's hard for you to see this in yourself, and you are being very brave in remembering that you were hurt in the past and that he is not hurting you now, in the present."

In turn, Sarah started to wonder about "her half" of the problem. She turned to Joseph and said, "I want to blame you for how our vacation plans are not going well. You promised to make the reservations at the resort and get the flights, and you haven't done it."

He said, "I know."

She continued by saying, "Yes, that's true, but if I turn this into a big fight, then neither one of us is going to feel like doing what it takes to get to Bermuda for that three-day weekend in a hotel room where we always have really fun sex away from the kids and the craziness of our work-home life."

I then asked Sarah, "What's your half? Do you want to blow things up and push him away, or do you want to come closer to him so you can have the 'us' in your relationship that you love?"

As group members participate in these healing dialogues, triggered responses of rage or despondency are recognized as "old feelings," and group members develop the capacity to hold these feelings and share them with their partner. For example, as Sarah and Joseph's work on sexual issues progressed, Joseph noted that she seemed to freeze whenever he engaged with her in oral sex. Instead of blaming him, she acknowledged that she was often not really "there," that she would look up at the ceiling, and that she sometimes dreaded sex and would just "wait for it to be over." While talking about issues related to sex was once very evocative for Sarah, it was now becoming bearable. She noted, "I feel lighter about all of it. I'm able to say that was then, this is now."

Eventually, Sarah was able to develop a new partnership with herself about how her low desire for sex was affecting her husband. She developed more compassion for him, and while she was still angry with him at times, she was increasingly coming to the recognition that she was depriving him, and herself, of the benefits and joy of a vibrant sexual connection. She became more curious about what might be happening for her and how it might be related to how walled off and unresponsive she could be. She became increasingly aware of her own issues and of the particular sexual issues that predated their marriage and the birth of their children.

After several groups, Sarah said, "Maybe this is not just about being tired. Maybe I'm mad, or hurt, or scared of the closeness."

I asked her, "What do you think might be frightening for you?"

"Giving up control. There's so much to lose at this point. I feel more walled off, or maybe more unable to split off. My body is not my own, I'm nursing our baby. And I'm very, very tired. All the time."

I tracked the possibility of unremembered sexual trauma, given the violent atmosphere in which Sarah grew up. I noted, "That must not feel very good, that your body does not belong to you."

"No, it drives me crazy. And it feels like it did when I was a teenager and my body began to change. I felt like I was on another planet, and I didn't like it at all."

I offered, "You don't get to decide when your baby has your body, and you've been having trouble being in your body for yourself and your sexual connection with Joseph."

Joseph said, "I've really been trying to have room for you to have all of these feelings, but it's really hard for me that you're not 'there' when we're together. I get angry about it, but right now I'm just feeling really sad."

Sarah looked at him and said, "I miss you. I miss all the fun and heat we can have. I miss you. And I miss me."

The couple grew increasingly able to remain physically present and able to talk to each other about what they were feeling.

CONCLUSION

As a result of the couples group experience, couples learn new patterns of interaction and new definitions of relatedness. They develop an awareness of their imperfections, and they learn to trust themselves and their partners. They also learn to identify their own sensitive and vulnerable places, where their feelings can be particularly intense and sometimes out of control. Seeing the interactions of other couples helps group members see elements of their own maladaptive approaches with less criticality and harshness. Through modeling, clients learn new behaviors and develop relationship skills they have never seen in their families or prior relationships. Couples are able to change behavioral patterns together and learn a different relationship dance that is more in keeping with the mature and continuously evolving self they have become.

All of the group members bring their unique vulnerabilities, childhood wounds, and patterns of self-preservation that have become obstacles in the intimate, and particularly the sexual, relationship. One of the most powerful tools of couples groups is the ability to watch someone else who is having a struggle and, from a place of inner calm, watch the dynamics unfold without judgment and with the detached observation of a witness. The power of being a witness without judgment enables group members to be compassionate and firm in their own relationship, with themselves, and in relationships with other people. As couples develop the ability to hold themselves and their partner accountable with firmness and compassion, they develop a healthy mutual interdependence and the ability to sustain emotional engagement and reconnect when there has been a rupture.

This process is gradual and ongoing. With the support and encouragement of the group members who believe in them, couples are able to create thriving and vibrant relationships. The group's support, encouragement, good humor, confrontation, acceptance, and affection essentially create a new family: the family of the ongoing therapy group.

Chapter 7

Intersectionality 101 for Sex and Couples Therapists

James C. Wadley, PhD, CST, CST-S,
and Malika O'Neill, MS

In the field of sex and couples therapy, there is a lack of understanding regarding intersectionality and how it affects minority groups, which poses a challenge when it comes to effective treatment. Some therapists may reject the concept of intersectionality altogether because they refuse to acknowledge the complicated and nuanced needs of clients who are not characterized by racial, socioeconomic, and heteronormative privilege. Other therapists may question or resist learning about intersectionality because it is not included in clinical and sexuality training programs. Indeed, the field of sexology has been slow to evolve when it comes to inclusivity of those who are not a part of the dominant culture—that is, those who are not White, able-bodied, middle class, male, heterosexual, cisgender, and so forth. While some sexology programs may offer courses that present a case study or short discussion about intersectionality, few—if any—seek to untangle the complexities of managing multiple identities at the same time.

In addition, most sexuality textbooks are limited in their ability to effectively capture and address issues of diversity and inclusion, and they do not present strategies for addressing the sexual concerns of those who have been traditionally marginalized and oppressed. As a result, few formal conversations occur in this field regarding the influence of colorism, texturism, and even sexual politics (e.g., intercultural intimacy negotiation or severance) on courtship, intimacy, and relational loss (Adams & Lott, 2019; Mbilishaka, 2018; Ryabov, 2019; Williams & Ware, 2019). Without this understanding, treatment for individuals and couples is limited, narrow in scope, sometimes haphazard, and possibly injurious. Therefore, this chapter is devoted to creating a fundamental understanding of the concept of intersectionality by unpacking oppression, highlighting the necessity of self-awareness and therapeutic vulnerability, and discussing the impact of privilege in integrative sex and couples therapy.

WHAT IS INTERSECTIONALITY?

The concept of intersectionality has its foundations within the political evolution of Black, Latina, and other women of color (Carastathis, 2014). Following the feminist movement of the 1960s and 1970s, there emerged a need for public and scholarly discourse to recognize the systemic barriers and invisibility experienced by marginalized groups, including the challenges experienced by women who struggled to navigate their gender and racial identities at the same time.

This discourse came to the forefront again in the 1980s when critical race theory emerged as a movement among a variety of legal scholars. It was in this context that Kimberlé Crenshaw first used the term *intersectionality* to describe how feminist and antiracist politics in the United States served to marginalize issues facing women of color. In her discussion, she noted that "both feminist and antiracist politics have, paradoxically, often helped to marginalize the issue of violence against women of color" (Crenshaw, 1991, p. 1245). The two groups to which she refers are, first, the identity of being a woman in a male-dominated and patriarchal society and, second, the identity of being Black in predominantly White settings. These two groups are often in opposition with each other because of the complexities involved in navigating gender and race. In particular, feminist strategies often perpetuate the marginalization and discrimination of people of color, whereas antiracist policies have the effect of enabling systemic patriarchy. It is here—at the intersection of racial and sexual discrimination—that political intersectionality lives (Crenshaw, 1991).

Similar to Crenshaw, other scholars have recognized the social position of Black women and their experience in navigating racism and sexism. As Collins and Bilge note:

> Intersectionality is a way of understanding and analyzing the complexity in the world, in people, and in human experiences. The events and conditions of the social and political life and the self can seldom be understood as shaped by one factor. They are generally shaped by many factors in diverse and mutually influencing ways. When it comes to social inequality, people's lives and the organization of power in a given society are better understood as being shaped not by a single axis of social division, be it race or gender or class, but by many axes that work together and influence each other. (2016, p. 2)

Moreover, even though some Black women are able to advance professionally and acquire a degree of economic self-sufficiency, racist and gendered stereotypes are still used as a way to define their social identity and behavior (Hooks, 1989).

While the concept of intersectionality was originally intended to describe the experiences of Black, Latina, and other women of color, in order to adequately capture and assess the effects of multiple oppressed identities, there needs to be a "multidimensional conceptualization" of how race, class, gender, religion, ability, and socioeconomic status are woven together and navigated on a daily basis (Roberson, 2013). That is, it is necessary to consider how these categories may form a structure of oppression. This oppressive structure is evident in the United States, where Blacks, Latinos, and immigrants experience exploitation, marginalization, systemic powerlessness, violence, and cultural imperialism (Young, 2013). This experience becomes even more complicated when people experience multiple forms of oppression—such as that involving gender, race, class, ability, and sexual identity—at the same time. The intersection of all these experiences represents intersectionality, and its prevalence explains the need for its clinical recognition in the context of sex and couples therapy.

For example, consider the case of a Black, low-income, chronically ill transwoman who seeks out sex and couples therapy with a therapist who maintains an alternative identity (e.g., a White, middle-class, able-bodied, cisgender man). If the therapist lacks an understanding regarding intersectionality and how it affects his client, then it will be difficult for him to empathize with her experience or to help her discuss the challenges of managing multiple oppressed identities. Similarly, a White therapist trying to understand aesthetic values in communities where lighter complexions are held in higher regard than those of darker complexions needs to be open about their knowledge and skill set when it comes to intersectionality in order to conduct effective therapy.

UNPACKING OPPRESSION AS A SEX AND COUPLES THERAPIST

As the field of sexology continues to move forward in its inescapable migration from singular, hegemonic perspectives to increased ideological pluralism, the evolving social and clinical landscape needs to change. However, unpacking and unraveling oppression as a sex and couples therapist can be a complicated process. What's unfortunate about traditional forms of clinical intervention is that some therapists are not taught about oppression and how it is experienced in relationships. Within the context of sexological discourse, there has been inadequate discussion regarding the need to manage multiple identities (simultaneously or independently), to attend to verbal and nonverbal intercultural communication, and to understand processes of assimilation and oppression.

Moreover, some sex therapists may not have had an opportunity to deconstruct their own feelings and experiences with systemic oppression and its impact on the clinical process. These unprocessed feelings may leave clients feeling unheard, invisible, and misunderstood, and it can possibly lead them to develop the same negative feelings about the therapist as they have for their partner(s).

To avoid perpetuating oppressive conditions in the context of sex and couples therapy, it is vital to ask questions that help clients think about their intersectional identities. The following are some questions that can invite clients to share their stories and experiences about how race, gender, socioeconomic status, sexual identity, and so on impact how they feel about themselves, as well as their relational and sexual decision-making:

1. How do you identify along racial, gender, and socioeconomic lines?

2. How do those identities impact to whom you are attracted romantically?

3. What messages did you learn growing up about race as it may relate to sexuality?

4. What messages did you learn growing up about gender as it may relate to sexuality?

5. What messages did you learn growing up about socioeconomic status (e.g., money and education)?

6. How have your identities impacted courtship and intimacy?

7. How have your identities influenced sexual functioning or dysfunction?

8. How have your identities impacted your history of relationship breakup or divorce?

9. Please share a story about how easy or difficult it's been for you to navigate your identities in spaces where others may appear to have a different experiential narrative.

10. How do your identities influence your sexual fantasies?

11. Do you fantasize about people similar to you or who reflect your experiences?

12. How is power exercised in your relationship?

13. How do you express a sense of feeling validated or affirmed?

14. If someone else were in your shoes and experienced similar challenges related to your racial, gender, socioeconomic, or other identity, what you would suggest to them?

Clinicians need to be intentional and clear about their queries and to let clients know it is okay to refrain if they do not feel comfortable sharing. Therapists must have a grasp of the continuum of gender and be knowledgeable about multicultural counseling techniques to be effective in addressing intersectionality. Therapists should have an understanding of their own feelings and how these feelings may perpetuate oppression in therapy. To be unaware of one's own feelings is potentially detrimental and harmful to the client.

In addition, therapists must recognize how sociopolitical undercurrents may impact how meaningful dialogue occurs in therapy (Sue, Ivey, & Pedersen, 1996). Failing to acknowledge the intersecting constructs of gender, race, sexual identity, and class may prevent or distract the therapist from addressing the couple's core issues. For example, the therapist may inadvertently assume these issues have a personality or characterological basis, when it actually reflects a manifestation of oppressive societal conditions. Or the therapist may attempt to address interpersonal or family factors without a consideration of how these factors are impacted by the larger cultural context (Aldorando, 2007).

Therefore, while traditional sex therapy interventions may be beneficial to some clients or communities, it may be harmful to other clients. For these clients, the use of medical or behavioral models may prevent the therapist from understanding the client's experiences from a larger systemic and societal perspective. This is because, like traditional psychotherapy, sex and couples therapy emerged from Western European culture, so it is grounded within a framework that considers "normative" behavior in the context of those who created it: White males. Any clients who don't fit neatly within this framework are assumed to have a deficit (Arrendondo, 1994). Therefore, it is clinically haphazard to assume that traditional interventions don't need to be contextualized within broader systemic values and assumptions. And it is culturally oppressive for therapists, who are in a dominant position, to impose theories and interventions on those who hold less power: the client (Sue & Sue, 2013).

To be sensitive to issues of intersectionality, practitioners should have an array of culturally sensitive tools and strategies—particularly if the client identifies as a minority (Cayleff, 1986)—making sure to take into account the client's experience with oppression. Although the term *oppression* traditionally refers to the experience of tyranny by a dominant group, not all oppressed groups experience oppression in the same manner, and the interpretations of those experiences vary according to time, context, circumstance, and agenda. Therefore, psychotherapeutic approaches should be tailored in accordance with the client's social identity, including the oppressive experiences that this identity group tends to encounter (Wohl, 1995). At a minimum, this means therapists must have knowledge about a variety of clinical orientations and demonstrate the capability to strategically use them at appropriate times.

When it comes to sex and couples therapy, the therapist must be willing to consider and discuss some of the sociopolitical challenges that may be impacting relational intimacy, negotiation, and maintenance in the relationship. For example, a Black woman in a relationship with a White man may prefer initiating sex because of her perceived lack of power and control in the workplace. The therapist needs to understand how these power dynamics may cause her to be less comfortable allowing her White lover to take control of their sexual interlude. As another example, consider a Latino, Christian, gay male who wants to have a conversation about masturbation with his religiously devout Asian-American partner but is unsure how to do so. Navigating this issue requires an understanding of the religious and cultural values at play between the couple.

Unpacking oppression is often a tedious and complex process as clients are asked to consider how their identities have evolved over their life span and how these identities have impacted their relationship. Ultimately, the therapist must have a sense of themselves to engage clients in this process. Self-awareness is needed in order to be an effective practitioner.

Self-Awareness Cultivates Multicultural Counseling Competence

In sex and couples therapy, three change processes occur at the same time: the one experienced by the therapist and the one experienced by each partner (Helmeke & Sprenkle, 2000). However, therapists are sometimes unable to capture that process within themselves, as well as between themselves and their clients, because of the unique experiences held by each person in the therapeutic relationship. Each person processes past and present events through their own worldview, values, ideas, culture, perceptions, and motivation, which can cause therapy to be disjointed, amorphous, and chaotic. Moreover, if a therapist's worldview and experiences do not allow them to skillfully manage the experience of oppressive identities—and if therapists have difficulty deconstructing intersectionality as well—then therapy may become a space that is emotionally injurious.

In order to address intersectionality, sex and couples therapists must be knowledgeable about their values and biases and be able to skillfully use themselves as a tool to understand, join, empower, and clinically support couples during difficult times. This does not mean therapists must be perfect in their delivery of culturally competent treatment with couples. It merely means therapists must be aware of their own cultural perspective and experiences so they are grounded enough to invite couples to share their experiences. For example, a White, female, middle-class, heterosexual therapist who meets with a Black, male, gay client would need to reflect upon how her relational experiences may be significantly different. She could invite the client to offer his experiences and be willing to query further when the conversation moves into territory that she is unfamiliar with. This self-awareness may have the most impact in cultivating multicultural counseling competence (Torres-Rivera et al., 2001).

When clients and couples experience sexual dysfunction, therapists should be mindful of the variety of sociocultural factors that can influence sexuality and identity management. These include parents, peer relationships, standards of beauty, education, interpretations of language, law and policy, spirituality and religion, social organizations, technology, media and material culture, and values and attitudes. For example, a religiously devout couple, each of whom still resides in their parents' home, may be unwilling to communicate their sexual wants and needs, resulting in dissatisfaction over the frequency of their sexual interactions. Or a Black Caribbean lesbian woman—who experiences vaginismus due to the negative messages she received from her parents regarding the darkness of her skin color—may feel anxious about sexual intimacy with her White partner. Therapists have to take into account individual and systemic challenges such as these that may impede intimacy.

During sex and couples therapy, clinicians have to assess the role these factors play for each individual and be able to help clients empathize with the other's experience. For some clinicians, this is a difficult undertaking because they may be unaware of the impact that each of these factors can have. Clients may also have their individual and relational histories that need to be considered, and sometimes those histories are woven with experiences of trauma or ignorance. For example, for a client who identifies as Afro-Latino, transgendered, and low-income—and who has a history of being in relationships where there is intimate partner violence—it would be the therapist's job to help unpack how the identities and trauma may impact intimacy.

The need to consider sociocultural factors would also be important for a Black gay man who experienced sexual abuse as a child and now struggles with alcoholism. The therapist may help the client explore the extent to which the client's family accepted or rejected his sexual identity and the meanings derived from coming out or not. In addition, the therapist could help deconstruct his childhood abuse, neglect, or abandonment that may have become re-enactments in the form of intimate partner violence experiences. The therapist could then assess the client's history of using coping mechanisms (e.g., withdrawal, aggression, isolation) as a response to traumatic incidents over his lifetime and how they influenced decisions about friendships, romantic relationships, and intimacy. Socioeconomic status would have to be discussed, as it would be helpful to know what resources were available to the client and his family and whether or not they were accessed.

Therapists need to try to help clients navigate these complex histories because of their potential impact on a client's ability to maintain a healthy sexual relationship.

THERAPEUTIC VULNERABILITY

In order for clinicians to connect with a client's experience of intersectionality, as well as how it is managed in intimate relationships, it is also helpful for them to have a sense of their own experience with "brokenness or woundedness." This therapeutic vulnerability may involve the therapist briefly disclosing a similar challenging encounter as that experienced by the client, empathetically acknowledging the difficult experiences the client has managed, or sharing their own affective experience during the session.

Therapeutic vulnerability is important because, as "wounded healers," clinicians may be able to empathize with the woundedness of others (Nouwen, 1972). This means therapists must be able to identity, and possibly articulate, their own feelings so they can connect with clients in a meaningful way. If disclosure and vulnerability are done at the right time during the session, it may be easier for clients to think critically about their experiences with oppression and their multiple identities. When clients are able to sense that the therapist understands the challenges of negotiating their identity over a myriad of settings, including a relationship, then clients may feel more comfortable disclosing their own sense of woundedness and even relational trauma that may be impacting their sexual functioning.

Obviously, therapists should be mindful about the timeliness and the amount of self-disclosure so the focus of the session doesn't become about them instead of the client. But there can still be a moment or two when a therapist shares how they understand the client's experience due to their own personal circumstances. For example, after learning that a client may have experienced the tragic loss of a loved one, therapeutic disclosure may come in the form of the therapist empathizing with the client's experience and briefly sharing a similar story about grief and loss. Or if a client discloses a recent relationship split or divorce—and the therapist has experienced the same challenge—then the therapist may share their own personal understanding of how challenging it is to manage separation and reveal what kind of support they sought out. Skilled therapists are able to use themselves as a tool to join with the client and possibly normalize emergent challenges. The following is an example of therapeutic vulnerability:

Mary: "I never really had a chance to be successful at my company, and I cannot believe that I got fired after only working there for three months. I knew my gender-affirming transition would be a problem when I first interviewed. I could just feel that something was different in the way my boss stared at me."

Therapist: "I'm sorry about what happened at your job and can totally understand how frustrated you are. When I lost my job at the agency years ago, I was really angry at the time, and it took me a while to move past my hurt and resentment."

Mary: "Yes, I am so hurt and angry right now. I don't know what I'm going to do because I need to be able to pay my rent."

Therapist: "If you are open to it, we should consider spending some time talking more about your hurt and anger and how that will impact your job search."

In this case, the therapist vulnerably shares his previous experience of losing his job to empathize with his client's loss. The therapist takes a chance in sharing his own woundedness, and the client is able to feel validated and affirmed. Integrative sex and couples therapists have the privilege of sharing their woundedness or not during therapy. The clinical privilege of disclosure as it relates to intersectionality is not always processed in a meaningful way. The next section addresses the role of privilege in therapy.

THE ROLE OF PRIVILEGE

Recognizing privilege in relationships can be tough if sex and couples therapists have never questioned their own privilege or those unearned rights of their clients. Power is rarely distributed equally in relationships because of its fluid nature. Even in romantic relationships, the partnership is never equal because one partner may systemically enjoy "unearned advantage" or "conferred dominance" (McIntosh, 1990). For example, if a person is able-bodied and their partner struggles with chronic illness, then the able-bodied person may not consider the physical challenges their partner must endure during intimate activities. Or in the case of an interracial couple, it may be that the partner of color is troubled about workplace microaggressions, while the White partner has never been concerned about professional bullying. In both cases, one goal for sex and couples therapy is to give both partners an opportunity to acknowledge how privilege shapes their lives and impacts intimacy.

When privilege and power differentials aren't recognized by both the therapist and the clients, it may never be addressed in a way that helps clients understand the etiology of their sexual or relationship dysfunction. This is especially true when the therapist is trying to address a couple's issues and one partner is more privileged than the other, which can interfere with sex and relationship experiences. This may commonly occur in relationships where one person uses their socioeconomic status to make relational and sexual decisions because of the amount of money they make compared to their partner. Another misuse of privilege may be when one person comes from a racial or ethnic background that is different than their partner, and their partner has not had to consider the challenges of navigating systemic oppression. These challenges may impact the person's ability to be present during sexual encounters, and it would be the responsibility of the therapist to identify, assess, and untangle this complex interaction.

In order for therapists to recognize privilege in relationships, a social justice perspective matters (Parker, 2009), as sexual decision-making and functioning are products of one's history, culture, and family of origin. Taking a look at intersectional identities and their management across time, settings, and circumstances may help couples have an alternative framework for their capacity to form strong attachment bonds. Therapists must be mindful of their own privilege (e.g., race, socioeconomic status, gender, ability) and how it affects their clients. When therapists have this awareness and skill set for addressing privilege, they are better able to join with clients, increasing the likelihood that clients will be authentic. A skilled therapist can help clients develop deeper insight into how their relational and sexual challenges may have their origin in systemic challenges that existed well before the relationship was formed. This form of deeper insight may enable clients to feel affirmed in their unique experiences and make necessary personal and relational shifts. The following are some questions related to privilege to help therapists reflect upon their clinical decision-making:

1. How do your race, gender, socioeconomic status, ability, sexual identity, and family of origin impact the clinical decisions you make during therapy?

2. How do your familial and romantic attachment bonds impact your clinical decision making and relationships you have with your clients?

3. In what manner does privilege influence your ability to help clients address their issues?

Integrative sex and couples therapists should remain aware of their own histories, identities, and roles so they are better positioned to support clients. The next section is a case study that illustrates an example of therapeutic awareness and the clinical use of intersectionality as a framework for addressing the client's concerns.

CASE STUDY

Monique was a 29-year-old, African-American, cisgender, lesbian woman who sought treatment for symptoms related to depression around managing her many different roles and her health. She was the oldest of three siblings and had taken on the guardian role of her brother, who was now 18 years old. Monique came from a low-income background and received housing assistance to help her navigate schooling. She had a master's degree and was currently in graduate school continuing her education. She worked two part-time jobs and described her work as likeable, but she struggled with managing her time and juggling responsibilities, and she described herself as being "burned out." Approximately six years ago, she started a development business that began as a hobby and eventually become one of her part-time jobs. Monique had been in several long-term relationships with men and women, but over the past eight years, she had chosen to date women exclusively. Currently, she was in a same-sex relationship with a woman whom she had dated for over a year and whom she was now living with. When she presented to therapy, Monique and her partner had not engaged in an intimate exchange for over seven months.

Over the past two years, Monique was diagnosed with generalized anxiety disorder, sciatica, and polycystic ovary syndrome, which had caused her several physical challenges. She now had to take several medications to help regulate her hormones, was put on birth control (although she specifically asked not to be), and was informed that she needed to attend physical therapy and adapt to a plant-based diet. These disparities in her everyday way of functioning caused rapid weight gain and triggered an increase in anxiety. She was now experiencing stress on a daily basis and suffering from extreme levels of fatigue. She described "feeling lost in life" and "not knowing where to begin." In response, she began isolating from her family, friends, and partner as a primary coping mechanism. Since Monique was working two part-time jobs, she did not qualify for insurance and had to pay for health insurance as a student for an additional $2,200 annually.

The problems Monique was facing were not just about her multiple identities. They also stemmed from the multiple forms of oppression that accompanied her specific combination of identities. Her situation reflects the experiences of many African-American, low-income women. Specifically, she had to juggle multiple jobs, navigate through several physical challenges in order to function, and fulfill the cultural, gender, and familial expectation that she serve as the caretaker for her siblings. These inequities have a complex genesis that may emerge from a variety of factors, including (1) systemic oppression; (2) lack of accessibility to health resources (e.g., health insurance) to manage chronic illness; (3) sexism, racism, and ableist attitudes; and (4) pervasive heterosexist sentiments.

These overlapping forms of oppression impacted Monique, as well as her relationship, in that it had become difficult for her to experience intimacy and pleasure with her partner. At this point in her relationship, managing her anxiety and chronic illness seemed to be her primary focus. To fully and adequately support Monique, the clinician utilized an intersectional lens, recognizing and conceptualizing the relationship between systems of oppression and the various undercurrents that impacted Monique's multiple marginalized identities. The clinician invited Monique to share her thoughts, feelings, and interpretations of juggling professional responsibilities to make ends meet and her inability to find a balance between work, school, and her relationship. The therapist also allowed Monique an opportunity to deconstruct past intimate and sexual experiences with her partner and the role of chronic illness. In addition to the clinician focusing on internal, subjective, and emotional experiences, he also addressed how the role of multiple socio-structural dimensions (e.g., weight gain, low socioeconomic status, identifying as African American) contributed to her presenting problem.

The use of feminist therapy was beneficial to Monique's case, as it allowed the clinician to use an integrative approach and to focus on the systemic overlapping forms of oppression she identified. The therapist was able to help Monique reframe her experience by focusing on her ability to be resilient throughout her life and at the same time empathized with her struggles in her relationship. Upon the therapist's recommendation, Monique read a couple of self-help books that focused on Black women's resilience and self-empowerment. Finally, the therapist encouraged Monique to get involved in a women's support group. The group allowed her to hear other women's stories, process her anxiety with others who had similar experiences, and gave her an opportunity to collaborate with them in choosing healthy dietary options. Using a feminist approach provided space for empowerment, change, and growth, and it allowed Monique to better understand and claim the unique identities from which she navigated these complex systems.

CONCLUSION

In order to conduct effective couples work with minority clients, integrative sex and couples therapists must learn about intersectionality and the management of multiple identities. If therapists do not have an adequate understanding of themselves and their relationship with power and privilege, then they run the risk of alienating couples who need support in creating or maintaining intimacy in their romantic relationships.

Identifying and helping couples manage fluid power dynamics in relationships as it relates to varying social identities—including race, gender, class, ability, and sexuality—is a necessary skill. Integrative sex and couples therapists should seek additional training if they are unable to unpack these complex processes for themselves or their clients.

In addition, sexology programs and organizations should consider weaving intersectionality concepts within their training curricula so students and professionals have a grasp on how individuals manage their multilayered identities. Sex and couples therapists need to be introspective, reflective about past professional encounters, and possibly even push themselves to learn about their own intersectionality.

Chapter 8

Relationship Counseling and Sex Therapy with Kinky Clients

Neil Cannon, PhD, LMFT, and
Amanda Holmberg-Sasek, LMFT

WHAT IS KINK?

Kink is an umbrella term for a rich array of sexual practices, including BDSM, fetishes, erotic role-play, and virtually any other kind of erotic behavior. Kink can be defined as "sexual behaviors, sexual interests, or relationship structures not accepted by the dominant culture" (C. Moser, personal communication, 2018). For some kinky clients, kink can be one small part of their sexuality. For others, it can be the predominant way they enjoy sex. Kink can also be the exclusive way that some people express their sexuality and an integral part of their lifestyle and identity.

A prominent type of kinky behavior is BDSM, which is an umbrella term that refers to bondage and discipline (BD), dominance and submission (D/S), or sadism and machoism (SM). Bondage involves the erotic use of physical restraints, such as rope or cuffs, and discipline can involve a broad array of activities including training and punishment. Dominance and submission involves a power exchange in which one partner controls the other partner (dominant) or gives up control to them (submissive) in order to enhance sexual pleasure (Pillai-Freidman, Pollitt, & Castaldo, 2015). Finally, sadism involves gaining sexual and erotic pleasure from inflicting pain on a willing and consensual partner or partners, whereas masochism involves deriving pleasure from having pain consensually inflicted upon oneself. However, for any of these activities to be considered BDSM, there must be consent between all parties involved.

For many, *pain* is a loaded word with many implications. In the world of BDSM, the word *pain* is often used synonymously with sensation. Sensations can be experienced on a spectrum, and each person has different responses to various types of touch. Therefore, it is important for therapists to use clients' preferred way of discussing pain or sensations and to be aware of the varying levels and preferences that will look different to different people. What is painful to some may not be described as painful to others. For most masochists to be aroused by pain, there must be context and intent. For example, there is no pleasure in stubbing one's toe in the middle of the night because it is without context or intent.

There are many ways kinky individuals may identify with BDSM identities, as the same terms can have different meanings to different people. For instance, a client who identifies as a dominant may have a different definition of what that means for them or within their relationship(s) than someone else who also refers to themselves as dominant. Being dominant does not necessarily mean one is sadistic, and being submissive does not necessarily mean one is masochistic. Similarly, being aroused through the use of restraints does not necessarily mean one is submissive. Therefore, clinicians need to be curious and parse out the details and meaning of these identities for each client.

When the clinician is getting to know their kinky clients, the use of reflective listening and mirroring techniques can help clients feel accepted, understood, and heard. The use of an affirming voice and nonverbal messaging is also important. In the beginning stages of treatment, many clients are testing the therapist to determine if this discussion is safe. Therefore, therapists will want to ask questions with a gentle curiosity that will help them get to know their client. Doing so represents a positive step in being able to provide effective treatment and support.

Although there are currently no studies specifically focused on the prevalence of kink, one only has to look at the phenomenon of the best-selling book *Fifty Shades of Grey* to understand the vast public interest in kinky fantasies of dominance, submission, pleasure, and pain. However, this book tends to be viewed negatively by many members of the BDSM community, as it tends to perpetuate myths around BDSM.

In particular, the book's main character, Christian Grey, is described as having been abused as a child, and his childhood abuse is implied as the reason for his BDSM proclivities. While there are BDSM practitioners who were abused as children, no studies demonstrate higher rates of kink in people who experienced childhood sexual abuse. Therefore, it is dangerous for clinicians to assume there is causation between childhood abuse and being a BDSM practitioner (Richters et al., 2008). Nonetheless, the enormous consumer response to *Fifty Shades of Grey* certainly suggests the general public is more interested in kink than one might have previously thought.

Kink Competence

In 1997, the National Coalition for Sexual Freedom (NCSF) was formed by Susan Wright and others. Through NCSF, a list of "Kink-Aware Professionals" became more widely available to consumers, which provided categories of kink-aware therapists and other professionals. Providing this free listing of resources to consumers was very helpful. However, whenever it comes to therapy today, we believe that it is incumbent upon the therapist to be kink competent, not just kink aware. There are no generally accepted clinical standards that define kink competence—and creating one is not the purpose of this chapter—but at a minimum we do suggest considering the following guidelines for being kink competent:

1. Hold a mental health license, such as that held by licensed clinical psychologists, licensed marriage and family therapists, licensed professional counselors, or licensed clinical social workers.

2. Have education and training in human sexuality, including specific education and training in how to work with sexual minorities (e.g., kink and the various types of sexual expression that fall under the umbrella of kink).

3. Have education and training in couples counseling. Working with couples is very different from working with one client in the context of individual therapy. In addition, because so many kinky couples practice consensual non-monogamy (CNM), having education and training in working with individuals in polyamorous and open relationships is part of being kink competent.

In addition, therapists need to be aware of their own erotic countertransference that may occur during treatment, including feelings of arousal, curiosity, disgust, outrage, or fear. A therapist's positive or negative associations with a particular kinky interest can ultimately have an impact on treatment. For example, a therapist treating a client who is aroused by cross-dressing would want to be aware of their own feelings and experiences in response to this particular interest.

A more extreme example might relate to a therapist's own trauma. For example, a therapist may have had an experience with sexual assault and find themselves being triggered by a client who identifies as a sadist or a dominant. Therapists are not immune from their own biases, but identifying those potential biases is a starting point in making sure they are providing the best and most kink-competent care to clients. We encourage therapists to obtain their own supervision, consultation, and therapy for these identified biases to learn more about how they may be impacting treatment.

The concept of erotic countertransference is so important in kink-competent therapy that we encourage clinicians to be curious about their feelings surrounding kink throughout the entirety of their career. A client who identifies as the dominant partner in their relationship may cause little to no reaction from a clinician, but a different client with a different set of identifying characteristics or presenting problems may elicit an entirely different reaction. If a therapist believes their reactions are having no impact on treatment, either positive or negative, then we suggest the therapist look more deeply at themselves.

For example, consider the case of Sarah, who was an enthusiastic, young, sex-positive therapist. Sarah was treating a straight, married couple who had differing interests when it came to sex. The wife wanted to be dominated by her husband, but the husband wasn't aroused by the idea of tying up his wife and was reluctant to proceed. Sarah knew there was nothing wrong with bondage, so she tried to help the wife explain to her husband that what she wanted was harmless and could be fun. Sarah went so far as to make suggestions about using silk ties or scarves to start. The couple did not return for therapy, and the wife sent Sarah an e-mail saying her husband felt "ganged up on." Sarah's story is a good example of how countertransference of sex positivity can negatively impact client outcomes.

With these considerations in mind, this chapter is intended to help clinicians move toward kink competency so they can provide the best possible care when working with kinky clients. We will first discuss the importance of the therapist lens when it comes to client outcomes. We will also touch on several common issues that arise in the context of couples counseling with kinky clients.

Subsequently, we will provide a framework for providing kink-competent therapy for couples, as there are no existing treatment models specifically designed for kinky clients, let alone kinky couples. This treatment approach applies to issues that span the realm of sexuality and kinky behaviors, including BDSM, fetishes, erotic role-play, and virtually any other kind of kink. It is inclusive and applicable to heterosexual couples and LGBTQIA couples alike. Although we primarily refer to dyadic couples when discussing this treatment framework, its principles apply to those who practice CNM as well.

THE THERAPIST LENS

When it comes to working with kinky couples, the lens of the therapist is critical to client outcomes. The therapist is often the first person many clients have ever talked to about their kinky desires. Many clients have never told anyone about what they often self-describe as their "dark side." Therapists can never underestimate how difficult it is for many clients to talk about sex in general, especially kinky sex.

There are many valid reasons for which clients fear telling their therapist about their sexuality. Most notably, many clients do not disclose their kinky interests out of fear that they will be judged by the therapist. Conversely, many clients choose to "come out" quickly regarding their kink as a means of "testing" the therapist and making sure they are sex positive and affirming of such practices (Kolmes, Stock, & Moser, 2006). Clients may have experienced a lack of acceptance or shame by a previous therapist, or they may have heard about negative experiences others have had with mental health or medical professionals. As a result, kinky clients are hypervigilant for signs of disapproval and judgment from their therapist. When clients withhold information from their therapist due to fear of judgment, this can lead to secret keeping, which ultimately impedes effective treatment (Kolmes et al., 2006).

Kink-competent therapists recognize that working with kinky clients is a sacred honor. There is a beauty in learning to hold space for the experiences of these complex human beings in a way that fosters emotional safety, exploration, and above all, acceptance. Kink-competent therapists focus on hope, strengths, endless curiosity, and sometimes solutions. When a therapist gets it right, the positive impact that this can have on the life and relationships of kinky clients cannot be emphasized enough. However, when a therapist gets it wrong, the harm can be long-lasting. Sex-negative therapists and those who are not skilled at treating kinky clients tend to see clients through a lens of psychopathology.

The following case example illustrates what many clients would say is a common experience in working with a therapist who is *not* kink competent. This case example demonstrates how the lens of the therapist directly affects the client's outcome.

Gerald was a 55-year-old corporate attorney who identified as a submissive masochist, and his wife, Sheila, was a 45-year-old artist who identified as predominantly "vanilla."[1] When the couple presented for sex therapy and couples counseling, they reported that they'd had a negative experience in therapy with their previous marriage

---

[1] In terms of kink culture, vanilla is a term used for someone who is non-kinky.

counselor, Dr. Steve. The new kink-competent therapist asked the couple if they'd be comfortable describing what disturbed them about their past therapy experience so she could be as helpful as possible to them now. Kink-competent therapists know past experiences of shame in therapy can be hugely traumatic, so it is important to make sure that one does not re-traumatize clients by doing something similar. The couple agreed to share their experience with the new therapist.

The couple told the therapist that Dr. Steve was helpful and easy to talk to in the beginning. Dr. Steve had assured them that he was nonjudgmental and told them, "Whatever happens behind closed doors is all good with me." This was the first comment that rubbed Gerald the wrong way, as being kinky in certain semipublic spaces was an important part of his sexual expression and was far from "behind closed doors." Gerald went on to say that when they were discussing kink as a general concept, Dr. Steve seemed "fine." However, as they delved deeper into the specific nature of their conflict, Dr. Steve started to make them feel uncomfortable because *he* seemed uncomfortable. According to Sheila, "He was using a bit too much humor about a subject that was intensely personal and intimate for me."

The couple had told Dr. Steve that BDSM was a source of both conflict and connection for them. The conflict was that Gerald wanted to do BDSM scenes more frequently than Sheila did. On the other hand, Sheila wanted more emotional connection and intimacy in order to do more frequent BDSM scenes. Like many self-identified kinksters, Gerald had a very specific sexual script (or "scene") he liked to follow. Gerald's ideal BDSM scene was for Sheila to "punish" him by paddling him for a rule infraction, whether real or exaggerated. The couple's explicit therapeutic goal was to "figure out how to better integrate Gerald's need for more frequent and intense BDSM scenes with Sheila's desire for more emotional connection and intimacy." Sheila was not aroused by the paddling scenes, but she was not bothered by paddling Gerald as long as they were feeling close and connected.

When the couple first began to see Dr. Steve, they were able to communicate well about most aspects of their life. However, conversations about kink had become contentious, and it was often like holding a match over dry tinder. Arguments could flame up at any moment. Outside of therapy, Gerald and Sheila had many previous conversations about kink that ended in fights, so they had decided to wait until they were with Dr. Steve to discuss it.

Gerald had written a letter to Sheila asking for what he wanted sexually. During the third session, Gerald asked Dr. Steve if he could read the letter to Sheila in session so Dr. Steve could help them have a meaningful conversation about kink without it escalating into a fight. Dr. Steve and Sheila both agreed. The following is Gerald's letter:

Dear Sheila,

I can't tell you how happy I would be if you would go deeper into the world of BDSM with me. I would feel even closer to you than I already do. I think if you could just hear what is important to me, then you would want to do it more. I just think I get so nervous that I fumble around and then you get frustrated and think I have not been honest with you. That is why I am writing this down. Okay, here it goes . . .

I would like you to catch me doing something that displeases you. Leaving the toilet seat up for instance. Then tell me I need to be punished. Make me report to you at a certain place at a specific time wearing nothing but a pair of panties. OMG, I am so embarrassed, and being completely honest, I am so horny just writing this to you. Then, while I am standing in front of you, slowly pull my panties down and tell me you are going to give me the paddling of my life. Make me bend over your lap, and then use the ping-pong paddle to spank me until I am sobbing. When you think I have had enough, keep going a little longer. That is what I mean by edge play. You push me slightly beyond the edge of my limits. Then you take me gently by the ear as if I were a child and lead me to the corner. You softly touch my back and tell me how much you love me and that this paddling was for my own good. Tell me everything is going to be okay. Then leave me standing in the corner for approximately 10 minutes.

I hope you don't think I am too weird. Thank you so much for letting me share!

Love, Gerald

Sheila took Gerald's hand lovingly and thanked him for being so vulnerable. She said she had some questions and looked to Dr. Steve for support. Dr. Steve took the lead and said he had questions as well. Dr. Steve asked Gerald, "Why do you feel the need to receive so much pain? Why do you want to cry and sob like a little boy?" Gerald tried to explain himself the best he could; however, he was nervous because he felt like Dr. Steve did not approve of his fantasies. Next, Dr. Steve turned to Sheila and asked, "Where were your children when your husband was crying and you were making so much noise with your paddle?"

Toward the end of the session, Dr. Steve thanked Gerald for being so vulnerable. Dr. Steve said he could fully understand why Gerald felt uncomfortable sharing "such unusual sexual desires" with his wife. Dr. Steve said, "Sometimes, when men have mothers who are either too controlling or too passive, either archetype can affect their sexuality." The couple quietly listened to Dr. Steve and then did what clients generally do when they feel shamed by their therapist: They disappeared quietly and never returned. In fact, it was several months before they worked up the courage to start therapy again due to the shame they experienced with Dr. Steve. Gerald and Sheila reported they were incredibly hesitant to return to therapy, assuming that other therapists would be just as judgmental.

As is illustrated by this case example, the lens of the therapist can have a tremendously negative impact on a couple's therapy outcome. Dr. Steve made several key mistakes that are patterns frequently seen when a therapist is not kink competent. Dr. Steve saw pathology instead of strengths. He led from a place of "knowing" instead of curiosity. He lost focus of the couple's therapeutic goals. He seemed to believe he knew what was best for Gerald and Sheila. Dr. Steve did harm.

In addition, Dr. Steve committed what is considered a "cardinal sin" in couples counseling: He made Gerald the identified patient, which caused an imbalance in the therapy room. Dr. Steve also assumed he knew the cause of Gerald's kink, when kink-competent therapists know the manner in which erotic templates are formed is currently unclear. Therapists who tell clients they know why a client is the way they are, or why they like what they like, risk doing harm. Effective therapists are curious and help clients find their own answers, ones that are true for the client and not necessarily for the therapist.

We will come back to Gerald and Sheila later in the chapter to see how their new therapist continued with treatment after hearing about the couple's experience with Dr. Steve.

COMMON CONCERNS WITH KINKY CLIENTS

When it comes to reasons couples enter therapy related to their kink, every situation is different. However, common themes present with kinky couples. For some couples, it is because one partner is kinky and the other is not. They want help navigating and negotiating their sexual differences. For other couples, both partners are kinky, but they have different kinks or may need assistance communicating. For others, the therapeutic goal may have nothing to do with kink, but their sexual lifestyle may be an important part of their identity, and they are afraid of being judged or shamed by a therapist who is not kink competent.

In the section that follows, we discuss some of the common concerns that couples present with—including issues related to causation, secrecy, and interest discrepancy. We will also present accompanying solutions for each. Regardless of the specific concern, though, it is important to find a solution that allows each partner to get their respective needs met in a way that honors each person's erotic templates and that enhances the overall relationship.

Common Concern #1: Causation

When unusual sexual behavior or kink is the presenting issue, it is not uncommon for there to be an intense yearning to understand causation. In particular, couples will often ask causation questions related to their kinky desires, such as "What caused this?" "Why does my husband want to be dominated?" or "Why does my wife get off on pain?"

For example, When Sally and John came in for couples counseling, John explained that his kink was being an ABDL.[2] In the beginning of couples counseling, Sally only wanted to know one thing and that was *why*. "Why does he like to wear diapers? Why does he want to watch cartoons on Saturday mornings and eat children's cereal? What caused this? Was it the way he was toilet trained? Was it because John's mother was overbearing?"

The problem, of course, is there are so many variables that shape a person's sexuality that knowing the exact cause is not always possible. Having therapy centered around the cause of someone's kink also implies there is something wrong with the kink that must be figured out. When somebody is aroused by a common vanilla behavior,

---

[2] ABDL is an acronym for Adult Baby Diaper Lovers. The ABDL acronym represents a community of people who self-identify this way. Adult Baby (AB) represents those who identify as "adult babies" (those who enjoy role-playing as infants), and/or Diaper Lovers (DL), which are people who voluntarily wear diapers. These behaviors may be sexual or nonsexual in nature (Zamboni, 2017).

such as deep passionate kissing, we don't question causation because it is a majority practice. However, when the sexual behavior is a less common minority, there tends to be a yearning to know why.

In addition, when a spouse discovers a long-held kinky secret of an intimate partner, the new information can feel like a very intense betrayal that is similar to the emotions related to the discovery of an affair. For some people in this situation, "why" presents as a driving question in couples counseling. The betrayed spouse can experience intense feelings, and understanding the cause of the kink can take over the mind of an otherwise rational person whose life has now seemingly been turned upside down.

The following are strategies for couples counselors to consider when working with clients who are stuck in the "why" of the kink:

1. **Caution the client against trying to solve a problem that is not necessarily solvable**. Today's intense question of "why" tends to dissipate over time. Two or three sessions from now, it may never come up again. While we can't minimize the client's desire to know why, it can also be a trap to fan the flame of causation as the primary clinical concern.

2. **Provide empathy, compassion, and gentle curiosity to each client**. Clients often view the therapist as the "expert" in the room. That can lead to questions like, "What caused my husband to have a diaper fetish?" Therapists want to avoid the ego rush of being all-knowing. Instead, we suggest leading with compassion and gentle curiosity. Questions like the following can be helpful:

   • "I can certainly understand why learning about this is important to you. Let's see what we can figure out. What do you each know about this?"

   • "John, you have had a lifetime to speculate on this question that Sally is asking. What are your thoughts on this? What are your first memories? What can you share that will help her to understand your experience?"

   • "Sally, how would it feel to not know exactly how this got started? Equally, what if you did know? How would that impact your life and your relationship?"

3. **Help clients develop a more empowering narrative**. Self-talk has a direct and powerful impact on how people feel about themselves, and this is no exception in sex and couples therapy. Some clients may struggle if they have developed a negative internal narrative about their kinky interests, so it is necessary for the therapist to help them develop a narrative that is more empowering. For instance, John's disempowering narrative was that he was a freak for having a diaper fetish. Through therapy, he was able to create a narrative that was kinder and more compassionate, which made him feel better about his sense of self. Often it is the client's relationship with their kink that can be explored over the actual behavior itself. Helping clients with the story they tell themselves can be healing and empowering.

   At the conclusion of therapy, John's new and empowering narrative was that he was aroused by something that is more common than most people are aware of. His relationship to diapers made him feel calm and peaceful. He couldn't fully explain it, *and that was okay* because he was now at peace with this part of himself. For her part, Sally was able to develop a more positive narrative as well. Sally told herself that she didn't need to know exactly why John was so intensely aroused by diapers or why they brought him so much peace. Instead, Sally focused on her new narrative, which involved being honored that her husband now felt accepted by her and trusted her with the biggest secret in his life.

Common Concern #2: Secret Kink

Sometimes, couples seek counseling because the kinky partner has kept their kink a secret. When their spouse learns of it, they can have immense feelings of betrayal.

For example, Jan was stunned when, after 30 years of marriage, she came home early from a business trip to find Bob wearing a cheerleader's outfit. Both partners were 50 years old at the time, and Bob had kept his secret fondness for cross-dressing from everyone, including Jan, for almost 40 years. Jan was heartbroken and felt a deep sense of betrayal. She wondered if their "entire marriage was a sham." When Bob's fetish was discovered, he felt such intense shame that he experienced suicidal ideation for the first time in his life.

When Bob and Jan first presented to couples counseling, they entered with the goal of saving their marriage. However, they were also considering a divorce and asked if they should separate. Most therapists know that it is generally not best practice to tell clients what to do when it comes to major life decisions. In most cases, clients need to determine the direction of their life. In this case, though, there was no evidence that a separation would increase Jan and Bob's chances of saving their marriage. There was no domestic violence or severe substance abuse issues. They had no therapeutic reason for separating since saving their marriage was their goal. Therefore, the therapist asked many questions about what *they* hoped to gain by separating and how separation would impact their ability to heal. The couple was able to see they were more likely to divorce if they separated, which was not the outcome they wanted, so they decided to continue living together while in therapy.

The therapist first helped the couple work toward healing from Jan's felt sense of betrayal. The therapist also normalized cross-dressing as a common interest, which was helpful for Jan to hear, as this was something she had never considered before or discussed with her friends. A tremendous amount of work was done with the couple to build empathy and help each other feel truly heard and understood. From there, the couple was able to collaborate on an agreement whereby Bob would wear women's clothing only while Jan was traveling. Jan didn't want to see Bob dressed as a woman. However, she was perfectly happy if he did so when she wasn't around. Like many couples who feel successful in therapy, they both wanted each other to be happy and were willing to collaborate on solutions.

Common Concern #3: Interest Discrepancy

Another reason couples seek counseling is because one partner is longing for a specific kinky behavior with their partner who has no interest in the kink.

For example, Jayla and William presented to couples counseling after having been married for 10 years. When discussing their concerns, Jayla explained how she longed to have William spank her. She explained that when they were dating, William spanked her as a prelude to intercourse and he promised to spank her even more often once they were married and lived together. However, after getting married, the frequency with which William agreed to spank Jayla actually decreased.

During couples counseling, William explained he had come to realize he was not comfortable spanking Jayla because his mother had taught him that *good* men don't hit their wives. He talked about how much he loved and admired his mother and his grandmother, and there was something about those childhood messages that made it hard for him to spank his wife despite her consent. William also did not want to cause Jayla any pain. The couple had now reached a stuck point with Jayla's desire to be spanked.

After some time in therapy and a great deal of psychoeducation about BDSM, William came to see that spanking Jayla was not experienced by Jayla as being hit or harmed. Rather, Jayla's experience of being spanked was associated with an intimate expression of love. William also came to understand that the spectrum of what he considered "pain" represented varying degrees of sensation for Jayla. For her, spanking was not painful in the traditional sense. Rather, it allowed her to experience a variety of more intense sensations during lovemaking that she would otherwise not experience. These sensations intensified sex for Jayla, and it made her feel closer and more connected to William since he was the one providing her with these sensations. Once William came to understand that on a deep, heartfelt level, he was able to participate willingly in spanking scenes that inevitably also ended up in very passionate sex (which he also enjoyed).

When working with kinky couples, there are also times when therapists will find that one partner appears to be highly emotionally activated by the other person's kink. In these cases, one partner's kink may be triggering the other partner's trauma experiences. Although the treatment of trauma is outside the scope of this chapter, when this occurs, the therapist can explore the possibility of a trauma history by asking some of the following questions with a gentle curiosity:

- "You seem to be experiencing some deep emotions about this. What is coming up for you? Have you felt this way before? When?"

- "Does this topic bring up something else for you? A different memory perhaps?"

- "Have you ever engaged in something like this before, either consensually or nonconsensually?"

If the client answers yes to any of these questions, then it is important to refer the client to a kink-competent therapist who is also competent in treating trauma. We caution against attempting to do individual therapy in these cases and, instead, recommend that the client be referred to a different therapist for individual therapy. In some states, providing concurrent individual and couples counseling is considered a dual relationship and, therefore, possibly unethical.

TREATMENT FRAMEWORK

Our treatment framework for working with kinky clients has five primary guidelines: (1) build therapeutic alliance, (2) create clear understanding, (3) foster empathy and compassion, (4) collaborate on solutions and boundaries, and (5) check in with ongoing communication. These guidelines are not intended as steps or stages that therapists must follow in a prescribed manner. Rather, they are intended to be used in a fluid and flexible manner, depending on the direction of therapy. Generally, therapy is never as neat and tidy as we might like. It is okay to roll around in the mess that can come with complex cases as long as therapists have a path in mind and keep their eye on the client's goals.

Build Therapeutic Alliance

Effective therapy starts with the formation of a therapeutic alliance. The strength of this therapeutic alliance accounts for a large portion of success in therapy (Blow, Sprenkle, & Davis, 2007; Rogers, 2007), and this is particularly true when working with kinky clients. Kinky clients often experience many layers of shame in relation to their sexual interests. The fear of stigma is almost always present for kinky clients. As a result, kinky clients are often fearful of being judged by their therapist. Therefore, building and maintaining a solid and safe therapeutic alliance is at the foundation of success when it comes to working with kinky couples.

There are many nuances to maintaining a strong therapeutic alliance with kinky couples, and this cannot be stressed enough. When one partner is reluctantly drawn into kink by their partner, it is critical for the therapist to assure the reluctant partner that the therapist is not going to pressure them in any way to get involved in anything they do not want to do. If the reluctant partner feels like the therapist is trying to convince them to get involved in kink, then the therapist has failed.

Being kink competent means having a framework that creates emotional safety for a process that inherently feels unsafe to many clients. Talking about sex is hard enough for many clients, let alone talking about kinky sex. To build a strong therapeutic alliance, a kink-competent therapist will often subcontract with the couple, seeking permission to go slowly. Subcontracting is a process that happens many times throughout the course of therapy wherein the therapist seeks permission to discuss certain topics or to take therapy in a certain direction. Subcontracting empowers clients and provides a model of good communication skills for the couple. It is a parallel process of identifying vulnerabilities and cocreating a plan that helps the couple feel safe and supported. Returning to Sheila and Gerald's case example, subcontracting in their case is illustrated via italics:

Therapist: "I am so sorry you didn't feel supported and accepted by your last therapist. Thank you so much for sharing that experience with me. *Given your past experience in couples counseling, would it be okay if we go extra slow so I can really get to know you?*"

Sheila: "Yes, for sure."

Gerald: "Definitely."

Therapist: "Thank you. I think that will help you ease into complex discussions more easily. I want to make sure I know you and see you. I really want to learn about all of the amazing strengths you undoubtedly have because we can use those to help you achieve your goals. In therapy, going slower actually turns out to help things go faster. If we take that approach, I feel confident you will come to feel emotionally safe during our sessions, and that is a critical component of effective therapy. *Would it be okay with you if we work together to slow down a bit and focus more on being thorough than being fast?*"

Sheila: "Yes."

Therapist: "As I hope you will quickly come to see, my intentions are always to help you. *If I ever say anything that bothers you in any way, would you be willing to share that with me?*"

Gerald: "Absolutely. We appreciate this. Thank you."

In order to build a strong therapeutic alliance, the therapist should also take time during the first session to help couples relax into therapy and talk about their lives and concerns. Toward the end of this first session, it is also particularly helpful for the therapist to take a strengths-based approach in asking the couple to discuss their love story (e.g., "Would you be willing to share your love story with me? How did you meet? How did you know your partner was *the* one?"). Finally, the therapist can conclude the session with a request for change or a commitment to change. For example, the therapist might say, "In individual therapy, a lot of the change occurs right here in this room. However, with couples, most of the improvement is directly dependent on how you treat each other between sessions. Given everything you know about yourselves and each other, what is one simple request for change you would like to ask of your partner that might make you feel a little better between now and the time I see you next week?"

Introducing the concept of sexual templates—which are also referred to as erotic templates and peak erotic experiences (Morin, 1996)—is another powerful way to help clients start to trust that the therapist won't judge them about their sexuality. Erotic templates reflect the sexual fantasies and behaviors that turn us on and turn us off. They serve as our sexual "accelerators" and sexual "breaks" (Nagoski, 2015). In many ways, erotic templates are like thumbprints. No two thumbprints are alike, and no one thumbprint is better than the other (Cannon, 2011). For example, some people like to kiss passionately, while others do not. Some people are aroused by having their nipples pinched during sex, while others are not. Neither is better or worse, just different. Kinky sex may be less common than vanilla sex, but unusual or even rare forms of sexual expression are not inherently better or worse.

Introducing the concept of erotic templates early in therapy gives kinky clients permission to be different, unusual, or even rare. It normalizes less common forms of sexuality and is a step toward de-shaming. It assures clients that the therapist is comfortable with all forms of human sexuality. For example, as trust was built with

Sheila and Gerald, the therapeutic alliance was strengthened, and they came to trust that this therapist would not judge them. This allowed the couple to be vulnerable with each other and to engage in the complex conversations required to help them achieve their therapeutic goals.

In addition, it can be particularly helpful to connect kinky clients with a kink-safe community, particularly if they are trying to heal from shame. Kinky clients are sexual minorities and can experience what is known as "minority stress." Sometimes, it helps clients to know about various communities with people with similar interests given that group support and group identity can protect against minority stress (Meyer, 2003). For example, Fetlife.com is a social networking site dedicated to kinky people. At the time of this writing, there are more than seven million members. There are also thousands of special interest groups that meet in person or chat online. For some sexual minorities, being part of a community is an important part of normalizing their kinky behavior, lifestyle, and identity. For other clients, though, joining a community is not desired, and that is to be honored as well.

Create Clear Understanding

Once the therapist has collaborated with couples to create a safe place for complex conversations about kink, sex, intimacy, and relationships, it is time to take those complex conversations to the next level. During this stage, the therapist helps each person become clear about their wants and needs, gain insight, and speak their truth. The therapist also helps the couple clearly understand what each other is seeking. Many sexual discussions have gone awry due to false assumptions and a lack of clear understanding about what each person actually wants.

For example, consider the case of Ted, who wanted his wife, Georgia, to engage in anal play with him. She had heard and assumed that meant Ted wanted her to penetrate him anally with a strap-on dildo, like in a porn she had seen with him. Anally penetrating Ted with a strap-on was a "turn off" for Georgia, and it was not part of her erotic template. As a result, the discussion was shut down and Ted became resentful.

Several years later during sex therapy, it came to light that Ted would have been just as happy with any kind of anal play. Once Georgia was able to gain a clearer understanding regarding Ted's wants, she learned to penetrate him anally with a small vibrator guided by her own hand. She had no problem with doing so and actually came to enjoy seeing how aroused Ted became. It was specifically the strap-on dildo to which she objected because in her words, "I'm not a man, and only men have cocks."

Similarly, for Gerald and Sheila, part of therapy involved helping the couple gain a clearer understanding of how to increase Gerald's desire for more frequent BDSM scenes while also maintaining Sheila's desire for emotional connection. By speaking her truth, it became clear that Sheila was worried about doing more frequent scenes with Gerald because it bothered her to see him wearing the pink panties he generally selected for each scene. Sheila didn't mind at all that Gerald wore panties as part of the scene, but the pink color bothered her a great deal. It reminded her of when her older brother got caught stealing a pair of her pink panties when she was a teenager. When her father found out, he slugged her older brother in the face and called him a "fucking pervert." She loved her big brother, and it was a very disturbing memory.

When Gerald came to understand Sheila's discomfort with the pink panties, he was taken aback. Although the couple had been together for seven years, he had never heard any of this before. Gerald said that the color of the panties didn't matter to him. He liked pink for the humiliation aspect, but it was panties in general that aroused him, not the specific color. By having this conversation in therapy, they discovered Sheila would be willing to have more frequent scenes if Gerald selected panties in a different color. It is often little things like this that come out by delving deeper into each client's experience. The devil is in the details.

Curiosity is one of the most powerful tools that therapists can have in their therapeutic toolbox during this process. Not only does curiosity help couples gain greater self-understanding, but it also saves therapists when they feel stuck. There is great clinical effectiveness in taking the stance of not knowing. Therapists can maintain this curiosity by asking questions like, "BDSM and kink mean so many things to different people. Would this be a good time for you to help me really understand what it means to you? If so, tell me more. How do you identify within the scene? What turns you on and what turns you off? Do you have a scene name? What is it that you love about kink? Walk me through one of your ideal scenes." When therapists ask questions in this manner, they are also joining with the client. They are sharing in the client's joy, which allows clients to feel accepted and supported.

As clients' stories unfold, therapists want to be attuned to any assumptions couples make about each other so they can gain a greater understanding of each other's experience. These topics are often so intensely charged for clients that the therapist needs to slow things down to make sure everyone feels heard and understood. Comments that one partner may have said many years ago—but no longer hold true—could still be alive for one or both of them.

Helping couples develop a clear understanding also involves unpacking how their inner dialogue impacts their desire to participate in kinky activities. This inner dialogue may have been influenced by messages from their childhood, church, family, or society; fear of others finding out; fear of their children finding out; or other factors. Working to understand clients' inner dialogue and any accompanying shame points will help therapists understand each client more fully as a person. One way to help couples understand their shame points is to ask them, when it comes to being kinky or sex in general, who is—metaphorically—at the foot of their bed. Sometimes, clients will stare blankly at this question, and the therapist will need to explain further. For others, however, the answer comes immediately.

For example, when the therapist asked Sheila to think about who was metaphorically at the foot of her bed as she thought about engaging with Gerald in this scene, Sheila responded immediately: "Oh dear. I had never thought about it, but it is my grandmother. My mom's mom. She told me repeatedly that, 'No decent man will want you if you aren't pure...Good girls keep their knees together.' She also told me that my dad's mother, my paternal grandma, was a hussy for getting remarried after my grandpa died." Having that understanding opened the door to an eye-opening discussion about how Sheila's shame points impacted her feelings about sex in general. It also helped explain why she experienced intense feelings when it came to thinking about BDSM scenes with Gerald.

There are many ways to help clients express themselves during these complex conversations. Help clients use kind and gentle language. Teach them to avoid judgmental words. If a client feels judged by their partner, simply doing the kinky behavior will often feel shallow at best. To help couples navigate kink, it is valuable to help them grow to accept themselves and then feel accepted by their partner for their sexuality. For instance, at the beginning of therapy, Sheila referred to paddling as a perversion. After a sufficient therapeutic alliance had been established, the next time she referenced perversion, the conversation went as follows:

Therapist: "Gerald, how does it feel to hear the word *perversion* used to describe this part of your sexuality?"

Gerald: "It makes me feel bad about myself, like I'm sick."

Therapist: "Where do you feel that sick feeling in your body?"

Gerald: "In my upper stomach and my heart."

Sheila: "I'm sorry, Sweetie. That wasn't my intention."

Therapist: "I wonder what it would be like to just use the specific words that describe what you are speaking about. For instance, if you are talking about the paddling, just say paddling. If you are talking about the part of the scene where you lead him to the corner by his ear, just say you took him by the ear, and so on. How would that feel to each of you?"

Both Gerald and Sheila said that it would feel much better. This discussion was successful because the therapy room was a safe place where they could collaborate on solutions without feeling ashamed. The therapist also avoided getting triangulated and fostered a space where Gerald could share his feelings (as opposed to explicitly telling Sheila not to reference Gerald's kink as a perversion).

Foster Empathy and Compassion

Empathy is the ability to understand and relate to the feeling of another person. When therapists lead with empathy and compassion, they help the couple move the conversation from their head (thoughts) to their heart (feelings). It is only when couples can genuinely and deeply feel their partner's emotions about a specific conflict that sustainable change can occur.

There are many ways to help couples get to a place of deep empathy. Imago Dialogue is one effective approach, and the Gottman-Rappaport Method is another. When working with couples who have conflict or find themselves in an emotional gridlock, we find it effective to utilize the Heart-Felt Hearing (HFH) approach, which was developed by coauthor Dr. Cannon (2011). Emotional gridlock occurs in a relationship when one person's preferences, such as kink, block what the other person prefers to do (or not do). Like many other techniques used to help couples communicate, the HFH approach is a method of communicating in which one person speaks while the other person listens. This approach is highly structured in the beginning, but as couples become more skilled, certain principles can be flexibly used to help them communicate well on a day-to-day basis. The following example illustrates how HFH was used when treating Gerald and Sheila:[3]

Therapist: "I love the way you two have been able to share so much and be so vulnerable. Today, I think you would benefit by shifting our approach away from you talking to me so much and, instead, having you start to talk to each other. How does that sound?"

Gerald: "I'm game."

Sheila: "Me too."

Therapist: "Go ahead and turn toward each other. You are welcome to hold hands if you wish. This is going to be very structured in the beginning until it comes naturally to you. One of you is going to be the speaker first, and one of you is going to do the listening first. Gerald, since you have a big request for change, how would you feel about speaking first?"

Gerald: "Sure."

Therapist: "I would like to roll my chair in so I'm a little closer and centered right between the two of you so I can support you equally. Would that be okay?"

Both: "Of course."

Therapist: "Okay, Gerald. What I would like you to do is think about your request for change and then express it in this language: 'When it comes to my desires for kink, this is how I feel about it, and this is what I want.' When you talk about your feelings, you can always tap into one of the five feelings we have discussed: mad, glad, sad, scared, and ashamed. You know Sheila better than anyone on the planet. Use language that is kind and gentle so she can hear you. Speak from your own experience. Use 'I' statements. Avoid the word *you* because that might make her feel blamed and defensive. Use your voice and your facial expressions to express yourself. Keep it bite-sized. In other words, give her just the right amount of information to chew on. You will have all the time you need, so take your time. Sheila, for now, your only job is to listen deeply and then reflect back what you hear. It is critical to know in your heart that listening does not mean you agree. Listening is just listening. I will help you both as we go.

---

[3] The following transcript is a shortened version of an exercise that took 45 minutes.

	Okay? All right, Gerald, go ahead. This is what's going on, this is how I feel about it, and this is what I want."
Gerald:	"Well, my desires for kink are beyond anything I have words for. I can't explain why it's so important to me, but it is. The way I feel about it is sad and scared. What I want is to have paddling scenes more frequently than once per month. I also want to feel like you want to paddle me, not that you are doing it because you have to."
Therapist:	"That was great, Gerald. Kind, considerate, clear. And Sheila, you did great listening. Your facial expressions said you really wanted to hear what Gerald had to say. Sheila, go ahead and reflect back to Gerald, 'What I heard you say was . . .' After you have done that, ask him if that is what he wanted you to hear."
Sheila:	"What I heard you say was that you are sad and afraid. You want to do scenes more frequently, and you want me to participate willingly and lovingly. And that kink is a big deal for you. Is that what you wanted me to hear?"
Gerald:	"Yes, thank you."
Therapist:	"Okay, Sheila. Now comes the magical part. You are going to get curious with Gerald. Ask him open-ended questions. Questions that start with 'what' and 'how.' Questions about how he feels. Lean into the things you think might be the most difficult to hear. Avoid closed-ended questions that start with 'do' or 'does' because those tend to end with one-word answers that are 'yes' or 'no.' And remember again, listening isn't agreeing. Listening is just listening. Also, when you are curious and lean into Gerald's pain, he will feel heard and accepted by you in new ways that can produce magical results."
Sheila:	[*Turning toward Gerald*] "What are you afraid of?"
Gerald:	"I'm scared you will never be into this. I'm afraid I am going to have to go the rest of my life settling and not getting my needs met. I'm afraid the best I can ever hope for is that you paddle me out of obligation. I'm afraid you think I am a freak."
Sheila:	"Sweetie, I don't think you are a freak."
Therapist:	"Go with that. Ask Gerald how it feels to suppress this part of himself that you have been resistant to."
Sheila:	"How does it feel to long for something so much—something you can only get from me—and have me be so resistant to it?"
Gerald:	[*With tears welling up in his eyes*] "It's so hard. When you turn me down, I feel like a freak. I feel like what I want is not okay, not just with you,

but with the world. I feel like you are the only person I have trusted enough to share this part of my life with, and you hate this part of me or you would do it more."

Therapist: "Sheila, you are doing great listening. Are you curious about his possible resentments?"

Sheila: "I imagine you must be resentful by now. Would you tell me about that?"

Gerald: "I am resentful. It is such an easy thing for you to do, and it only takes 15 minutes of your time, yet you withhold this from me. I don't understand it. I have tried everything, and you always find a reason not to do it. It makes me so angry, and I feel myself getting increasingly resentful. It makes me worry about us as a couple because this is so painful for me to squish down all the time."

Sheila: "I'm sorry, Sweetie. Do you actually think about divorce when I turn you down?"

Gerald: [*Looking down*] "Sometimes. I just feel so hopeless and rejected."

Sheila: "What does it feel like to squish it down?"

Gerald's energy shifted to sadness, and he couldn't speak for 30 seconds. Tears started flowing down his cheeks.

Gerald: "It feels like I can't breathe. Like there is no sunshine. I feel like there is something wrong with me."

Sheila: "Sweetie, I want you to be able to breathe. Are you saying that when I turn you down, you're not only upset about being denied spanking, but it also feels like I am rejecting you as a person and saying that you are a freak for wanting to be spanked?"

Gerald: "Yes, that is exactly how I feel."

Sheila: "I am so sorry. That was never my intention. I don't think you are a freak, and I don't think what you want is wrong to want. You like what you like. Being spanked turns you on. I get it. I just happen to like vanilla ice cream, and you like spanky road!" [*They both laughed.*]

Therapist: [*Bringing the couple back into tenderhearted space*] "Sheila, you are doing great. Ask him how he feels on the days leading up to a spanking."

Sheila: [*Smiling slightly*] "How do you feel on the days before and after I spank your naughty ass?"

Gerald: "The days before we have a scene planned, I feel so bright and happy. The worries from work seem easy to handle. I feel loved and accepted. I feel like I am okay and that you love me."

Sheila: "How about the days after I spank you?"

Gerald: "I feel connected to you. I feel loved by you. I feel light, like a weight has been taken off my shoulders. I feel relieved. And then I start to worry that I won't feel his way again for at least another month."

Therapist: "You have both done brilliantly. A good way to wrap up these kinds of conversations, Sheila, is for you to ask him if there is anything else he wants you to know."

Sheila: "Is there anything else you want me to know, Sweetie?"

Gerald: "Just that I love you very much!"

Therapist: "Gerald, how did Sheila do listening to you?"

Gerald: "Amazing! I have never felt so heard and accepted."

Therapist: "Sheila, how did Gerald do expressing himself?"

Sheila: "Really well. Much gentler than in the past when he was coming from anger. And he didn't blame me for the first time ever. That allowed me to listen to what he had to say."

Therapist: "Are you ready to switch roles of listener and speaker?"

Both: "Yes."

Therapist: "Okay, Sheila, this is what's going on for me, this is how I feel, and this is what I want."

Sheila: "When it comes to me paddling you more often, I feel sort of hopeful about the future, but I also feel a combination of feelings, mostly scared. I feel scared because I don't know if I can paddle you once a week because if I could, I already would have. And I feel afraid that if I don't paddle you every week, then you will be miserable and leave me."

Gerald: "I heard you say that you are afraid you can never paddle me as much as I want because if you could have, you would have."

Sheila: [*Anger building*] "That is not what I said. I did not say the word *never*."

Gerald: "I'm sorry. Tell me what you are afraid of."

Sheila: "I am afraid I'm not enough for you. I'm afraid that even if I did paddle you once a week most of the time, you would only notice the weeks I miss, instead of the weeks I do it."

Gerald: "How does it feel when I get that way?"

Sheila: [*Starting to cry*] "It makes me so sad. I feel like I can never get it right. I feel like I am never enough. If I don't paddle you just the right way, you make me feel like I did it wrong. Then I feel like I never want to paddle you again, so I avoid the whole goddamn thing."

Gerald: "You have never told me that before. Why not?"

Therapist: "Gerald, ask her what it feels like to paddle you, only to feel like she is doing it wrong time and time again and that she is never enough."

Gerald: "What he just said."

Therapist: [*Gently smiling*] "Gerald, see if you can ask her in your own words."

Gerald: "What's it like when I complain about your technique?"

Sheila: [*Crying with more intensity*] "I feel like such a failure. I can't even spank you right. Every single time, you tell me it was really great and next time it would be even better if I did something different. You have never once said it was perfect just the way it was. It makes me never want to do it again."

Gerald: "Honey buns, I am so very sorry. That was never my intention. I truthfully didn't even know I was doing that so often. If it wasn't for me being such a knucklehead, and the pink panty thing we talked about a few weeks ago, is there anything else you don't like about spanking me?"

Sheila: "I know it is cathartic for you to cry, but sometimes it is hard for me to see you cry after I paddle you. And I don't always want to have sex after you are done standing in the corner. Sometimes I do, but not always, so I always feel pressure for sex as well."

Gerald: "Did you think we have to have sex every time you paddle me?"

Sheila: "Yes, I always feel your raging boner on my thigh when you are over my lap."

Gerald: "How would you feel about watching me masturbate after I stand in the corner for a few minutes?"

Sheila: "Seriously, you would be happy with just jerking off?"

Gerald: "Not just yes, but HELL yes!"[4] [*Everyone giggled*]

Therapist: "Gerald, check with Sheila and see if there is anything else she wants you to know on this subject."

Gerald: "Honey buns, I am so sorry I made you feel inadequate. What else would you like this knucklehead to know?"

Sheila: "That I love you and I think you are going to have trouble sitting down now more than you ever imagined! Be careful what you ask for, naughty boy!"

---

4 Note: The couple had fallen into a negotiation, which generally isn't the idea at this stage, but the dialogue was working and they were being playful. Therefore, the therapist thought it best to let them go with the direction they were heading on their own.

Through the process of HFH, Gerald and Sheila were vulnerable with each other and softened their hearts. They spoke their truth. They uncovered new understanding. They both felt heard and accepted. They were now ready to collaborate on solutions and set boundaries.

Collaborate on Solutions and Boundaries

In the world of kink, boundaries are often referred to as limits. No matter how hard-core or extreme somebody says they are, everyone has limits. Part of the job of the therapist is to help couples understand their limits and honor each partner's limits with loving acceptance.

We suggest inviting couples to join in the spirit of collaboration as opposed to negotiation. Although *negotiation* is the generally accepted term in the kink community, the term has an adversarial feel to it. We prefer to help couples focus on collaborating with each other, as doing so elicits a more positive and aligning feeling. Words matter. Intentions matter. Is one partner here to get everything they want, or are they here to equally help their partner get what they want?

A good place to start when it comes to collaborating on solutions is to ask the couple what they have already agreed on. Many couples have had exhaustive discussions or previous counseling, so they may have already resolved some of their issues. The next step is to see where they have disagreements or are in a relationship gridlock. Due to the work that has already been completed, each person at this stage should have already developed tremendous empathy for their partner. In turn, issues that were previously considered unresolvable are more likely now to be within reach of a collaborative solution.

For couples who continue to find themselves stuck, a good way to loosen things up is to start by helping them see what they do agree on. First, help them categorize their differences into two groups: inflexible and flexible. Then lead the couple in a collaborative discussion to accept the limits that each partner has set or to resolve these limits in a more creative way. Couples must realize that most people in life do not get every single thing they want. Helping couples have gratitude toward each other for all they get, rather than what they don't get, is important as well.

It should be noted that transitional solutions are sometimes necessary to deal with existing issues and concerns before there is the development of deep empathy between partners. This process may look something like a partner saying they are willing to keep an open mind when it comes to a nonnegotiable boundary for their partner but that they aren't willing to engage in this particular need at this time.

Another intervention at the collaboration stage is to help couples discover themes to their kink. A theme describes what the individual gets out of that particular kink. For example, Gerald's kink is associated with themes of humiliation, masochism, and edging (lengthy masturbation with orgasm denial). During this stage, the therapist might help Gerald explore other ways to meet the needs of his identified themes, particularly those that Sheila has a hard time with. For example, since Sheila previously reported having difficulty with the humiliation aspect of the BDSM scene, she might be more amenable to participating if, as mentioned earlier, Gerald was not wearing pink panties. Collaborating on solutions for particular scenes in this manner can be very helpful, and we often find that people are willing to negotiate if that means their partner goes from being "okay" with a scene to "excited" or "intrigued" to try it out.

One way to help couples navigate their interests and limits is through a simple communication exercise. We have found that playing "Always, Sometimes, Never" is effective. When we use this method in our practice, we like to send couples out on a date for each step as they navigate through this three-step process:

1. **Brainstorming:** Have the couple make a single list of all the kinky behaviors, fantasies, situations, places, equipment, role-play ideas, and clothing they can think of. There are no bad ideas. This is not a negotiation, just a brainstorming session. There are also many lists on the Internet created by kinksters that can provide a helpful framework for brainstorming. To locate the most current lists, do an Internet Search for "yes, no, maybe BDSM lists." Many couples report this brainstorming session is very arousing, and they end up having great sex when they get home, or on more than one occasion before they even get home.

2. **Categorizing:** Have the couple go out on a second date. This time, have them each bring their own pad of paper, on which they draw three columns representing "Always, Sometimes, Never." Then they take each item from the brainstorming list and place it in the corresponding column as it pertains to them. Hopefully, the couple now has a list of things they are both *always* willing to do, so we encourage them to start there. The "sometimes" column is often where some of the most intense sexual experiences are to be found. Similarly, the "never" list isn't never forever, and we encourage them to consider that it is just never for now.

3. **Planning for kink:** In today's world, so many clients are simply too busy for vanilla sex—let alone kinky sex, which can take time and energy to orchestrate. Therefore, we encourage couples to plan for kinky sex. Put it on the calendar and take turns. If somebody has to cancel, both people need to take responsibility to reschedule it. Failing to reschedule hurts trust, especially if there is a history of unmet needs or false starts. Some couples are resistant to plan sex and argue it should be spontaneous. In response, we often say, "Spontaneous sex, plus planned sex, adds up to more sex. It's just math!"

Check In with Ongoing Communication

Another important part of kink-competent therapy is ensuring that there is ongoing communication happening between couples, as well as with the therapist. There are two important elements to check-ins. The first involves inviting couples to structure regular check-in sessions with each other. Weekly is a common frequency that works well for many couples. Couples need to lovingly hold each other accountable to follow through and meet as planned or reschedule if something comes up. We also suggest a maximum time limit for check-ins because, otherwise, the more communicative partner may go on for a long time, and the less communicative partner will come to dread these check-ins.

We suggest the following structure:

1. **Step 1:** Take turns expressing gratitude (e.g., "I really appreciated how you turned your phone off when you came home from work this week").

2. **Step 2:** Take turns sharing how they feel about their relationship (e.g., "I am feeling very close to you. The time we are taking to do little things together has made a big difference to me" or "I am feeling distant because our schedules are not matching up").

3. **Step 3:** Take turns expressing how they feel about the kink part of their relationship that brought them to couples counseling (e.g., "I am feeling very grateful for the way you have been doing anal with me, and I miss it when we go two weeks without it like we did this week").

4. **Step 4:** Take turns expressing what they want related to any aspect of their relationship or sex (e.g., "What I want is for us to spend Saturday afternoon together doing something connecting, and then either Saturday night or Sunday morning, I would love it if we could do anal play").

5. **Step 5:** Take turns expressing love and gratitude for being listened to (e.g., "Thank you so much for going on this journey with me, listening to me, prioritizing me, and being open to new possibilities for us").

The second part of checking in has to do with the sex and couples counseling process itself. We have seen too many couples change behaviors and then suddenly stop counseling because they start to feel better. Unfortunately, we see many of those couples three to twelve months later and they are back in crisis again—only often it is now worse. Once couples feel like they are close to achieving their therapeutic goals, we encourage them to gradually phase out of therapy, rather than just stopping abruptly. In our experience, the couples that do the best on a sustainable basis gradually go down from once per week or twice per week, to once per month, and ultimately down to once per quarter.

CONCLUSION

If you are reading this, and you are interested in working with kinky clients, then we want to commend you for your efforts in making sure these clients feel heard, safe, and accepted not only by their partner but by you as the therapist. Remember this can mean everything to the client. If you ever feel stuck, go back to the basics of the therapeutic alliance and look for empathy. In addition, please don't go at it alone. Find a community of like-minded therapists who work with kinky clients so you can stay connected. Keep abreast of the latest research, and be aware of countertransference.

Chapter 9

The Mind-Body Connection: Couples, Sex, and Somatic Therapy

Deborah Fox, MSW

"I'd really like to feel wanted by you. But when you invite me to have sex, it seems more like a chore for you." Steve looked directly at Kate as he spoke.

"Yeah, I don't know why it's so hard for me to be more playful about it," Kate responded, briefly tucking her chin down to the side.

Kate and Steve sat in my office facing each other, their knees touching each other's chair. They had been in therapy for two months. They described their problem as a lack of sexual connection due to Kate's low desire.

I asked Kate to put her chin in the same position as before, tucking it down to one side exactly as when she had said, "It's so hard for me to be more playful." Then I asked her, "Is there any feeling or image that shows up?"

What emerged was a memory of being made fun of by her siblings when she was a child, and this memory manifested through her body's movement patterns whenever she was in a position of vulnerability. Kate's revelation made sense to me. Our bodies communicate directly without words. Our bodies allow us to express the residual impact of our past stressors and traumatic memories through our facial expressions, posture, gestures, bodily sensations, skin color changes, and muscle tension. The reality is that traumatic memories are not just stored in the brain; they are also stored in the body (van der Kolk, 2014). The bodily sensations associated with past traumatic experiences and cumulative stress can become trapped in our physiological system. In turn, these sensations provide valuable access points to identify and explore emotional conflicts that are "beneath words" (Levine, 2010). What words can't find, the body often can.

Therefore, integrating somatic interventions into sex and couples therapy can add a valuable layer to treatment. The goal of traditional sex and couples therapy is to deepen the connection between partners so communication becomes easier, understanding increases, and sex is more satisfying and less fraught with conflict. However, for this outcome to be realized, I have found that learning the language of the body is a valuable skill set to have in one's therapeutic toolbox.

WHAT IS SOMATIC-FOCUSED PSYCHOTHERAPY?

Somatic-focused psychotherapy consists of interventions that work to release what the body is holding. These interventions may be as simple as directive techniques to release the tension carried over from gridlocked traffic or as complex as therapist-directed interventions to resolve past childhood trauma. Examples of these body-based treatment modalities include somatic experiencing (Levine, 2010), sensorimotor psychotherapy (Ogden & Fisher, 2015), accelerated experiential dynamic psychotherapy (Fosha, 2000), and body-centered psychotherapy (Kurtz, 1990).

Somatic-focused psychotherapy uses the language of the body (e.g., facial expressions, posture, muscle tension, gestures) to increase awareness of buried emotional conflict and facilitate its resolution. While clients may be consciously aware of painful memories of their past, they often don't realize the impact these memories are still having on their current life and relationships. For example, clients may well remember how much they hated their parents yelling at each other when they were a child, but they don't realize there's any connection that underlies why they want to run and hide when their partner raises their voice. This is because the bodily sensations associated with unresolved traumatic memories are recorded and held in the body's implicit memory system. In contrast to explicit memories, which require conscious recall, implicit memories are stored as patterns of movement that allow us to remember things without consciously thinking about them. For example, implicit memory allows us to ride a bike, even if we haven't ridden one in many years.

Similarly, when a traumatic event occurs, the distress that accompanied the event gets stored in our implicit memory system as a "body memory" that is not readily accessible to conscious recall (Rothschild, 2000). This explains why someone may flinch when they are exposed to a certain smell or the feel of a fabric, without knowing why. That same scent or fabric might have been worn by an abuser from the past and is now stored as a body memory. What becomes trapped in the body may be a feeling of helplessness because there was "no way out" and no resolution at the time.

At times, intense emotional or physical reactivity may erupt because these trapped feelings of helplessness are triggered by some current circumstance. For example, a client may become instantaneously scared in response to their partner's raised voice because as a child, they were helpless to calm their own fear and no one came to their aid. In this case, the memory of the trauma has become trapped in the body, which subsequently triggers the autonomic nervous system to respond as it did at the time of the event. In other words, the nervous system physiologically responds as if the traumatic event were still occurring. The section that follows provides a deeper understanding of the nervous system response, including how it can influence individuals' behaviors, their sense of safety, and their ability to connect with others.

UNDERSTANDING THE NERVOUS SYSTEM

When couples come into my therapy office, they are frustrated, hurt, angry, and at a loss. Communication has broken down. Each partner has a narrative that contains misunderstandings, faulty assumptions, and blame. This disconnection occurs because when we are highly emotional, our nervous system becomes charged, which compromises our ability to clearly absorb what others are saying.

The illuminating work of Stephen Porges's Polyvagal Theory (2001) offers a sophisticated understanding of how our autonomic nervous system responds under threat and how these responses interfere with our ability to effectively engage socially with another human being. According to the Polyvagal Theory, our autonomic nervous system consists of three subdivisions that influence our ability to physiologically and emotionally regulate ourselves: the sympathetic nervous system, the dorsal vagal system, and the ventral vagal system.

The sympathetic nervous system functions as our gas pedal. It engages when we are in action and sends us into fight-or-flight mode when we sense danger. In contrast, the dorsal vagal system immobilizes the body in response to threatening situations, which leads us to freeze, dissociate, or shut down emotionally. It functions as an emergency brake to dramatically slow down all body functions. Oftentimes, victims of violence find themselves in this state when they are unable to fight or flee their perpetrator. Finally, the ventral vagal system is activated when we feel safe. It is for this reason that it is commonly referred to as the social engagement system. It represents a state of relaxation where we can easily communicate with other people.

At the core of Porges's theory is the concept of neuroception, which refers to an unconscious process that we use to assess for potential risks in our surroundings. Our autonomic nervous system is always attuned to the degree of safety or threat we feel in our environment. It is for this reason that social cues can have such a dramatic impact on our behavior. Social cues associated with safety, such as a smiling face or a soothing tone of voice, help calm us by activating the ventral vagal system, whereas being ignored or criticized can cause us to lash out (via activation of the sympathetic nervous system) or shut down emotionally (via activation of the dorsal vagal system) when we perceive we are in extreme danger.

It's neuroception that allows us to distinguish between someone who seems friendly and someone who seems threatening. It is through this lens that we perceive everything about our world. People without a history of adverse experiences can easily bounce back and forth between feeling safe and feeling wary. For example, if they are sitting at an outdoor café and a disorderly, belligerent person comes near their table, their sympathetic system will temporarily engage. If that person continues walking by, they will relax and start talking again with their lunch companion.

However, people who have had traumatic life experiences have a much harder time feeling safe. These individuals experience what is called faulty neuroception, in which they overestimate what is dangerous in the environment and have a more difficult time relaxing and socializing. In the context of relationships, this tendency to be on high alert interferes with their ability to feel safe with their partner and can result in them misinterpreting a facial expression or tone of voice as threatening.

Through my experience with body-oriented therapies, I became aware of how important it was to focus on settling the nervous system of each partner to develop a feeling of safety during the therapy session. Feeling safe in session is a prerequisite for any therapy to succeed. When the nervous system is in a settled or calm state, the ventral vagal pathway is engaged. In this state of social connection, people can hear—seemingly for the first time—what their partners have been trying to communicate, sometimes for a long time. By integrating Porges's understanding of the nervous system with corresponding body-oriented techniques, both partners can begin to truly hear and connect with each other and further unlock emotional pathways. When individuals feel safe with their partners, their tendency to fight or flight or emotionally shut down is sharply reduced. And their ability to listen and effectively communicate with each other dramatically increases.

BEFORE THE CONVERSATION CAN BEGIN

After a history of much angst and debate about sex, it can be a relief for couples to finally arrive at a therapist's office, which is an oasis from their drama around sexuality. They have either been talking endlessly, arguing, or retreating to their silent corners, hoping the conflict about sex will magically resolve.

For example, Jake and Melanie were a distraught couple who came to see me after spending several years battling over how often they had sex. Two years of couples therapy with another therapist had not helped them resolve this issue. Their goal for therapy was to have a sexual relationship that they both enjoyed and to feel emotionally connected to each other. What got in the way was their difficulty understanding and accepting that they each had different paths to get there. Jake tended to feel emotionally connected only after they'd had sex, and Melanie only wanted sex after she already felt emotionally connected. They had not been able to work together toward a resolution because Jake had yet to understand that Melanie's path to feeling sexual was a legitimate one, just different from his. Being able to *hear* Melanie was an essential first step on the road to a resolution.

Therefore, I began the process of preparing Melanie and Jake to have this conversation. Preparing a couple for a conversation is as important as the conversation itself. I could argue that it is almost the most important part of the session. A feeling of safety in session is what best ensures this special and rare opportunity for couples to communicate effectively, particularly around strained areas in their sex life. The more engaged the ventral vagal system is, the more productive the conversation is likely to be. This preparation process involves four steps: (1) engaging in a calming meditation, (2) sharing an appreciation, (3) describing the relational space, and (4) beginning the conversation.

Engage in a calming meditation: When couples first enter my office, I tell them we will do a short meditation exercise to help them "fully arrive" in my office from wherever they have been and to help them be present with each other. This short exercise uses the following script:

> *Close your eyes.*
> *Feel your feet on the floor and your bodies in the chairs.*
> *Notice any sensations in your bodies.*

Take several slow breaths.
Notice any changes in sensations.
Now just pay attention to your breathing.
When you feel ready, slowly open your eyes.

Share an appreciation: After the meditation practice, I ask each person to share something they appreciate about their partner, which can be the smallest and simplest of things. I also ask them to describe why this gesture is important to them and how it makes them feel.

I encourage both partners to express their appreciation in the "language of abundance," which is a perspective I learned early in my career from a wonderful couples therapist, Hedy Schleifer. Expressing appreciation with negativity doesn't count. For example, if one were to say, "Thanks so much for bringing me a cup of tea because I don't think you've done that in 20 years," or "I appreciate your listening to the problem I'm having at work without interrupting me as you usually do," then any sense of appreciation would be canceled out. Rather, simply saying, "I appreciate that you brought me a cup of tea" conveys a pure sense of gratitude.

Even if a couple exhibits a palpable degree of tension when they come into session, sharing an appreciation helps them both to visibly relax, perhaps even with a slight smile. Knowing that something they have said or done has been appreciated by their partner goes a long way toward feeling more connected.

Describe the relational space: Next, I ask both partners to think about how the atmosphere feels between them and to name a few words that describe it. These could be words such as safe, tense, toxic, empty, sunny, or disconnected. The following is a list of words I often give couples to help them describe the relational space:

Safe	Full	Light	Clear
Tense	Stressed	Cloudy	Heavy
Toxic	Loving	Warm	Fractured
Empty	Dangerous	Cold	Chaotic
Sunny	Joyful	Indifferent	Cozy
Disconnected	Connected	Scary	Volatile

Once they have shared some descriptive words, I explain that this space between them has everything to do with how they each feel. If the space feels safe, inviting, and warm, then they are each likely to be more open and receptive, as well as drawn to each other. If the space feels toxic, then they are more likely to feel guarded and ready for battle, and more likely to want to keep their distance. Their tone of voice, the expressions on their face, and everything they do, say, or choose not to say all affect how the space feels. I remind couples they are the guardians of the space between them, and the more they take care of their mutual space through the choices they make when interacting with each other, the more connected and safer they'll feel. With safety, working together toward resolution has a much better chance.

Begin the conversation: When it is time to finally begin the conversation, I tell the couple to think about what they want their partner to understand about them. Then I encourage them to use active listening techniques to hear their partner, in which only one person talks at a time, and each person listens without interruption and then mirrors back what the other partner has said. The process of mirroring is powerful in promoting safety because when we are clear that we've been heard correctly, we quickly feel calmer and our nervous system can settle.

Before responding to their partner, I encourage the person listening to ask questions to clarify anything they do not understand (e.g., "Help me understand . . ."). If at any time during this process either partner exhibits signs of autonomic nervous system activation that threatens to interfere with clear communication (e.g., tone of voice becomes harsh, speech becomes louder or faster, facial expressions become dismissive), I instruct them to pause the conversation. I then invite that partner to tune in to their physiological system, noticing any bodily sensations they are aware of (e.g., tightness, heaviness, tingling, rapid heartbeat), and breathe slowly into that area several times.

If they are able to put their thoughts and feelings aside and listen to their partner again—knowing they'll be able to express themselves later—I invite them to return to the conversation. If they are not able to do that, I instruct them to let their partner know they will return to the conversation at a later time when they are once again able to listen. I then continue to focus on what is interfering with their ability to listen to their partner, asking them again to tune in to their physiological sensations with the intention of being able to return to a calmer state. Ultimately, the goal is to help them be present again for their partner.

Once I had gone through this four-step process with Melanie and Jake and enlisted the help of body-oriented techniques to regulate their highly activated nervous systems, the following interchange took place:

Melanie: "Jake, one thing I'd like you to understand about me is that I am very interested in having sex when I feel emotionally connected to you."

Jake: "Can you help me understand what you mean by emotionally connected?"

Melanie then explained that although she *did* want to have sex with him, she felt like in order to do so, she needed more attention, time spent together, and nonsexual affection. Jake responded, "Ah, this is the first time I've understood what you've meant." After two years of therapy, Jake had finally been able to hear a crucial point Melanie had been trying to make.

GOING DEEPER

The sexual difficulties many couples struggle with are often driven by deeper emotional conflicts. These conflicts stem from past experiences, as well as from negative messages individuals have received about sexuality early in life. Therefore, once the therapeutic work is underway, clients will inevitably hit an impasse when these deeper emotional conflicts become triggered.

When strong reactions show up, it is likely something significant is afoot. In order to help couples explore these conflicts—and come to a place of healing and connection—it is helpful to use somatic approaches. Keeping the ventral vagal system engaged and promoting a feeling of safety between partners is crucial for deeper psychological exploration and for growth and resolution to occur.

Sometimes, the psychological conflicts between couples are so deeply hidden that more common methods of talk therapy are unable to unearth them. Emotional conflict is not always accessible through words and conscious memory. In this case, the physiological system provides a different access point to deeper layers of experience and conflict. For example, Kate was able to access her memory of being made fun of by her siblings when she spontaneously tucked her chin to express discomfort at inviting Steve into a sexual encounter. Kate's discomfort with feeling vulnerable around Steve stemmed from her family history. Developing an awareness of this embodied memory opened the door for her to explore the vulnerability she felt in even imagining inviting her husband in for sex in a soft or welcoming way.

It was a relief for both Steve and Kate to understand that although Kate's way of inviting him into a sexual experience was very task-like and transactional, it was born out of an attempt to protect herself from feeling this intense vulnerability. Steve was able to empathize with her and see this dynamic between them was not a reflection of Kate not wanting him sexually, but more about her response to her own fears. For Kate to be able to make Steve feel desirable by issuing a flirty invitation, she needed to increase her comfort with feeling vulnerable. This understanding made them both feel more connected to each other and less divided by what had up until now been so confusing.

TRACKING THE BODY

When a facial expression, tone of voice, or word choice escalates a mild disagreement between partners, it is likely that a painful experience from the past has been triggered and that person is reacting as if the experience were happening right now. This painful experience may have occurred earlier in the relationship or long before they even met their partner. These instantaneous and repetitive escalations are what keep the couple from being able to effectively understand each other, resolve issues, feel connected, and engage sexually. When an escalation such as this occurs in a couples session, it represents an opportunity to help the couple understand the underlying source of the emotional conflict. Being able to intervene somatically can enable a deeper dive into what emotional struggles are causing tension.

For example, Kevin and Jackie were a couple I worked with who often argued about getting the household chores done. Although the couple had agreed to do the dishes on alternate nights, the dishes were often in the sink the morning after it was Jackie's night to wash them. Her tidier husband was frustrated. They had repeatedly discussed how to resolve this issue, and yet the discussion had gone nowhere. Whenever Kevin would express his frustration, they would start to argue. In turn, Jackie would retreat and try to avoid the conflict. They would stop talking, and their sex life would stop as well. Kevin knew that trying to invite Jackie for sex would be met with rejection, and Jackie knew that initiating sex would likely make Kevin feel better, but she just couldn't bring herself to do it.

When the day of their therapy appointment arrived, they were still raw and disconnected. They had been unable to repair their argument or figure out how to stay intimately connected when arguing, even over things like the dishes. They reported their goals in therapy were to (1) develop rules to fight fair, with the hope that this would help them argue more civilly; (2) repair any disconnections; and (3) find their way back to being sexual without dragging their conflict into the bedroom.

During the initial session, Jackie was perplexed by her own struggle with chores. "Doing the dishes doesn't seem to be that burdensome," she said.

"Turning to our bodies for answers can be enlightening," I said to both of them. "Our bodies 'talk' through the sensations we feel, our gestures, the physical positions we hold, and the movements we make." Their autonomic nervous systems seemed to be settled, so I addressed Jackie.

"Jackie, visualize yourself facing a sink of dishes. What sensations do you notice in your body?"

With her finger, Jackie drew a line down her torso, dividing it into unequal parts of about one-third and two-thirds in size. Jackie then said, "This smaller part just wants to be free and have fun. This bigger part doesn't approve and keeps pushing for more space."

I said, "If you imagine an emotional thread that starts in the smaller part of your torso and travels way back in time to your childhood, where do you land? What image pops up?"

I asked her to connect back to her childhood because she had already said she was puzzled by her struggle with the dishes, so I wondered if the source of this struggle was in her childhood story. What followed involved a description of images and stories from her childhood that pertained to her relationship with her mother. One vignette involved her mother demanding that she dry the dishes with a towel, instead of allowing them to air dry as Jackie wished.

Jackie said, "I could've just dried them with the towel, and that would've been easier, but I felt like I was fighting for my life." By not giving in to her mother's insistence, Jackie had felt that she was able to hold on to some measure of her own autonomy.

While Jackie had always been aware of her struggles in not succumbing to her mother's will—with one example being their battle over dishes—she had not consciously connected how it related to her current conflict with her husband. Her body created the bridge. Tuning in to her bodily sensations allowed Jackie to get to the source of her intense feelings that she hadn't otherwise been able to identify. As the witness to this process, Kevin came to quickly understand that although this battle between them was taking place in current time, it was just as much an unresolved battle from long ago that represented Jackie's ongoing fight for autonomy.

Once this became clear to Jackie and Kevin, they were able to problem solve ways in which to resolve this frequent argument. Neither of them felt like having sex when tensions were high. Being able to go through this discovery process together allowed their feelings of blame, shame, and rejection to recede. It enabled them to reconnect and paved the way for them to be sexual with each other again.

In sex and couples therapy, partners are a witness to the somatic and emotional experience of the other, which contributes to a deeper empathic understanding and connection. Being able to drop into the experience of what the other is feeling can help each partner regulate each other (instead of triggering each other) by engaging their ventral vagal system. When couples are in this state of connection, it is easier to solve problems and connect sexually.

DEEPER INTO SEXUALITY

For many couples who are trying to get their sexual relationship back on track, a key treatment component involves shifting the focus of sex so that it is pleasure-driven instead of orgasm-driven. Although the use of sensate focus exercises can be incredibly helpful in changing this focus, impasses may remain. One partner may be uncomfortable inviting the other into a sexual encounter. Another may feel under pressure to have sex. Another may be anxious when sexual arousal increases in intensity.

For many therapists, a reasonable question to ask is, "What makes you uncomfortable or how do you feel when _____ [*your arousal begins to build or your partner invites you into a sexual encounter*]?" However, I find that directly "asking" the body tends to be the most fruitful in being able to identify the sources of the discomfort. This somatic discovery can be accomplished by asking a question such as, "At that moment, or in imagining that moment here in the office, what sensations do you notice in your body?" Once the sensations are described, there are several avenues to follow.

For example, you may follow up by asking, "As you pay attention to the tightness in your chest, what emotions do you feel?" or "If that knot in your belly had a voice box, what would it say right now?" Or you might ask, "Tuning in to the tension in your calves, what does your body want to do right now? Are there any images that pop up?" I find that these types of inquiries almost universally elicit far richer answers than a direct question such as, "What do you feel when…?" They can be instrumental in moving the conversation to a deeper level. Accessing the information held in the body can do so much in identifying the emotional struggle underlying the current stuck point.

There are somatic therapy models that can take these inquires even further, such as somatic experiencing, which is a therapeutic approach designed to reset the nervous system when it has become unbalanced in the course of experiencing trauma. Our first biological imperative is to survive. When we feel threatened, we attempt to protect ourselves. But when our attempt to protect ourselves is interrupted, that thwarted energy remains trapped in the body and creates a myriad of symptoms that can last a lifetime.

Somatic experiencing seeks to release that trapped energy by teaching clients to increase their tolerance of any uncomfortable sensations and emotions that remain trapped. Through a rhythmic system of pendulation, the client experiences a titrated amount of exposure to these difficult sensations and emotions and then returns to a state of calmer nervous system activation. This is a finely tuned process in which it is critical not to allow clients to pass their threshold of tolerance, as doing so could cause them to become overwhelmed and re-traumatized. Over time, this process eventually restores the autonomic nervous system to a more balanced and functional state. The following case example highlights the powerful potential of somatic experiencing in helping a couple work through desire discrepancy driven by an underlying history of trauma.

Among other conflicts that brought them in to therapy, Mark and Sonia were struggling with desire discrepancy. So far, therapy had helped them understand more about each other and fight less. Overall, they were feeling much closer to each other, but their sexual struggle remained. Mark wanted sex twice a week and Sonia just couldn't imagine sex twice a week, every week. Mark had engaged in several well-intentioned attempts to help Sonia feel desirous—such as encouraging her to get a massage or a manicure, or to go to yoga—but all these attempts fell flat.

With therapy, Mark and Sonia came to understand that Sonia's desire was more responsive than it was spontaneous, meaning that her desire for sex often showed up only after she engaged in touching, not before. Getting a manicure was not going to create spontaneous desire, which is what Mark assumed was missing in Sonia. Along with the recognition that Sonia's desire was more responsive in nature, Mark came to understand that fatigue, the stress of having young children, and frequent conflict were central factors in her not being open to sex as much as he wanted. Although this new understanding was enlightening, it still wasn't helping Sonia feel like she really wanted to engage in sex. Sonia mostly felt pressured by Mark to be more sexual.

In one particular session, Sonia tilted her head back in a noticeable way as she was speaking about trying to find a physical posture that didn't make her feel smothered when she was hugging Mark. Just as with Kate and Steve, this physical gesture was an opening to explore what her body might have been expressing in its nonverbal language. I asked her to tilt her head back in the same physical manner as when she had hugged Mark and was looking for space. Working in the rhythmic manner of pendulating back and forth between uncomfortable sensations and a calmer nervous system state, Sonia was able to release some of the energy trapped in her body. Some of these sensations brought her in touch with the trauma involving her childhood experiences with her parents.

Both of Sonia's parents were self-absorbed, so she had grown up without either parent being attuned to her. Sonia had frequently been shouted at for hours on end by her father while trapped in his presence. Although she was very conscious of her family history, the feeling of being trapped was still held in her body. Being trapped is what she felt when Mark approached her for sex. This somatic work was the beginning of being able to separate her past feeling of being trapped from the unease that she would once again become trapped and overwhelmed.

What followed was a lovely sexual experience that Sonia initiated, in which she felt fully present and engaged. Working with Sonia's initial body gesture had opened a door to release some of the residual impact of earlier adverse experiences that her body was holding.

CONCLUSION

When couples enter therapy, they are rarely open and eager to hear what each other has to say. They are more likely to have rehearsed their own narratives on the way in, feeling defensive, angry, or hurt. They enter with their nervous systems in a state of fight-or-flight or in a state of emotional shutdown. Through the use of somatic-focused psychotherapies, individuals can settle their nervous system, find a place of safety and connection, and increase the possibility that emotional growth will occur.

Therapists who learn to converse in the language of the body can facilitate psychological growth at a level of inquiry that is beneath words—one that goes deeper than the verbal complaints often heard in session between partners. The body offers a beautiful access point when words are inadequate or unavailable. In these cases, a somatic focus is instrumental in guiding couples from disconnection to connection.

Chapter 10

The Nutri-Sexual Health Model

Janet Brito, PhD

CURRENT SEX AND COUPLES THERAPY MODELS

At present, no therapy models integrate nutrition into the treatment of sexual and relationship difficulties in the context of couples counseling. Rather, existing models focus primarily on utilizing CBT, psychodynamic, or EFT methods to treat those suffering from sexual dysfunction (e.g., Bergeron et al., 2018; Betchen, 2009; Johnson, Simakhodskaya, & Moran, 2018). In addition, current sex therapy models focus specifically on alleviating sexual symptoms, such as the sexual dysfunctions listed in the *DSM-5*, and less on enhancing healthy behavior, such as employing a regular sleep schedule or exercising to improve sexual health. Moreover, far less is known about the efficacy of encouraging nutritional habits—like eating leafy greens, fruits, lean proteins, complex carbs, and staying hydrated—in the treatment of sexual difficulties and how it may improve sexual functioning, mood, and overall relationship satisfaction.

Although there is a general lack of research in this area, a few studies have identified connections between nutrition and sexual health, prompting the need for further research. For example, research has found that following the heart-healthy Mediterranean diet can reduce the incidence of erectile dysfunction among men (Di Francesco & Tenaglia, 2017; Esposito et al., 2010) and improve sexual dysfunction among women (Giugliano et al., 2010; Maiorino et al., 2016). In addition, there is an observed relationship between improved dietary habits and increased self-esteem or body confidence, which are both factors that often contribute to sexual health (Eddy, Novotny, & Westen, 2004). Indeed, it is well understood that body image and self-confidence play a large role in sexual satisfaction, and it is important to consider the role that nutrition plays in this equation.

Therefore, this chapter investigates the benefits of adopting a more balanced diet in the treatment of sexual difficulties. In particular, my intent is to provide an integrative Nutri-Sexual Health Model for therapists so they have the knowledge needed to consider the role of food and its impact on mood, relationship, and sexuality. I also provide suggestions for a variety of exercises that can prompt self-reflection in clients and help therapists explore different nutritional and health-related factors that impact sexual satisfaction.

THE NUTRI-SEXUAL HEALTH MODEL

Couples who seek relationship and sex therapy often do so for concerns related to mismatched libidos, performance anxiety, mental health challenges, sexual avoidance, and negative body image (e.g., Gehring, 2003; McCarthy, Ginsberg, & Fucito, 2006; Rosen, Leiblum, & Spector, 1994). When sex and couples therapists treat these sexual concerns, they often conceptualize the presenting problem by inquiring about mental health status, substance abuse habits, and familial or genetic factors. However, they may neglect to consider how sexual difficulties may be impacted by nutritional habits. If therapists instead inquired about healthy behavior, the couple could begin to understand the underlying connection between nutrition, mood, and sexual satisfaction.

It is here that the Nutri-Sexual Health model can come into play. This model adopts an integrative approach to the treatment of sexual difficulties by addressing concerns rooted in lifestyle and relational factors, particularly with regard to nutritional habits that play a role in a couple's sexual challenges. The model focuses on using exercises to increase bodily awareness and allow individuals to understand hunger cues, identify eating habits, and pinpoint daily triggers. These triggers can be foods, feelings, thoughts, or environmental prompts that contribute to sexual difficulties. The model also works to identify strengths in the relationship, specifically the unmet emotional needs that prevent couples from working together. The basic steps of the model are as follows:

Step 1:   Establish rapport and identify sexual health challenges.

Step 2:   Assess current knowledge regarding sexual health and nutrition.

Step 3:   Provide basic sex and nutrition psychoeducation.

Step 4:   Identify vulnerability factors that lead to decreased self-care.

Step 5:   Frame lifestyle and current nutritional status from a strengths-based perspective.

Step 6:   Form a SMART goal.

Step 7:   Discuss possible roadblocks.

Step 8:   Establish a support system.

Step 9:   Assess individual autonomy with regard to healthy living choices.

Step 10:   Suggest integrative interventions.

By going through each of these steps, therapists can help clients identify their nutritional strengths, long-term dietary goals, and barriers that stand in the way of a healthy sexual relationship. In the section that follows, I go into each of these steps in greater detail and discuss their application in the context of the Nutri-Sexual Health model.

Step 1: Establish Rapport and Identify Sexual Health Challenges

The Nutri-Sexual Health model works best when it is introduced to couples as a way of understanding the link between nutrition, mood, and sexual satisfaction. However, to establish an environment of openness and a sense of comfort with sharing intimate details about their sexual lives, and to build receptiveness in the client, the therapist must firmly establish rapport. In this context, building rapport is understood as the establishment of a harmonious and mutually trusting relationship, where the therapist trusts the client to be honest and open without omitting important details and information, and the client trusts the therapist to maintain confidentiality, avoid judgment and provide guidance that will help to resolve concerns around their sex life (Leach, 2005; Tahan & Sminkey, 2012).

During the first session, rapport is established by asking exploratory questions in a neutral, nonjudgmental tone and demonstrating sincere interest through intonation, facial expressions, and encouraging body language, like leaning toward the client and nodding to show understanding. Therapists can begin this process by exhibiting genuine curiosity as they ask exploratory questions that focus on the sexual challenges couples are experiencing:

- May I ask you detailed information about your sexual challenges and how they impact you and your relationship?

- How long have you experienced this problem?

- When does it tend to happen?

- What makes it worse or better?

- How do you manage the stress that arises after the event?

Therapists can ask additional follow-up questions until they feel they have a complete understanding of the core sexual concerns at hand.

Step 2: Assess Current Knowledge Regarding Sexual Health and Nutrition

In the second step, the therapist focuses on helping the client build cognitive connections between sex and nutrition. This starts by promoting understanding of their body, eating habits, and preferences. Before starting, therapists need to make sure that their clients have granted proper permission to explore this topic and that they are interested in exploring their nutritional and sexual health. Similar to talking about sex, clients may feel embarrassment or shame when sharing their nutritional habits. Therefore, it is imperative to first establish a therapeutic alliance in step 1 by asking open-ended questions and then gradually introduce the Nutri-Sexual Health model. Here are some potential questions the therapist can ask to jump-start the conversation about nutri-sexual health in the second session:

- What does nutri-sexual health mean to you?

- How do you feel about your body?

- Where in your body do you experience joy?

- What does pleasure mean to you?

- What foods are pleasurable for you to eat?

- What are the body parts where you experience the most pleasure?

- What does your partner need to know about your body?

- What is your flavor profile? Do you enjoy spicy or mild food?

- How important is it to you to eat together?

- Do you have access to nutritious foods?

- How easy or difficult is it for you to purchase healthy foods and engage in healthy behaviors?

- What gets in the way of living your best life?

After obtaining information from the couple, the therapist can allow for a discussion between the couple where the therapist acts as a mediator. While later stages of the model involve the promotion of healthy eating habits over less-healthy eating habits, in this initial stage, it is important that therapists refrain from making value judgments or dictating a food plan. Rather, the role of the therapist is to help the couple decide what feels good and to let them be the judge of their own bodies. Therefore, the therapist focuses on identifying themes and understanding the meaning each partner assigns to certain foods. The therapist can be curious and explore at length (e.g., "What do you notice when you eat _____ together?"). Once these initial questions have been tackled and discussed, the therapist can introduce the Nutri-Sexual Health model. The therapist should describe the goals of the model, outline the process and expected outcome, and provide the couple with the opportunity to ask questions and seek clarification on any aspects they misunderstand.

Step 3: Provide Basic Sex and Nutrition Psychoeducation

The next step involves assessing the couple's understanding regarding the link between sexual health difficulties and nutrition. Ultimately, therapists want to encourage clients to explore the role of nutrition and related lifestyle factors on their sexual functioning. Therapists can provide clients with the following sentence stems to help gather this information:

- "I feel healthy when _____."

- "My feelings in those moments are _____."

- "I am uncomfortable in my body when _____."

- "I avoid sexual activity after eating _____."

- "After eating, I feel _____."

This discussion can help clients see whether their current nutritional habits are impacting the way they feel about their bodies, their self-esteem, their libido, and their sexual functioning, or if they are pressuring themselves to perform based on societal expectations of beauty and body type. After assessing clients' knowledge and understanding of the links between nutrition and sex in their own lives, therapists can offer clients basic psychoeducation on the impact of food and lifestyle choices on sexual and relational health. The food guide at the end of the chapter can be helpful here, as it provides a list of foods that promote physical and mental wellness (e.g., whole foods, grains, fruits, and vegetables), as well as those foods to eat in moderation. Many of these foods are common to the Mediterranean diet, which has been shown to prevent erectile dysfunction (Di Francesco & Tenaglia, 2017; Esposito et al., 2010). It is thought that since the Mediterranean diet improves cardiovascular health, it promotes blood flow to the penile region and, in turn, helps maintain sexual functioning. Similar studies have also shown its benefit in improving sexual health among women with type 2 diabetes (Giugliano et al., 2010; Maiorino et al., 2016).

At the same time, therapists should refrain from explicitly prescribing meal choices or special diets. Allowing clients to make decisions about their meals is a core part of the therapy. Therefore, clients should be given the freedom to engage in meal planning, ingredient selection, food shopping, and food preparation with their partner. When clients feel autonomous but are still able to make joint decisions about food with their partner, their relationship may improve (Aarseth & Olsen, 2008; Bove et al., 2006; Höijer, Hjälmeskog, & Fjellström, 2014).

Step 4: Identify Vulnerability Factors that Lead to Decreased Self-Care

After therapists have provided basic sex and nutrition psychoeducation, the next step involves identifying factors that lead to decreased self-care. Lack of self-care and self-compassion are associated with lower self-confidence and reduced libido (Germer & Neff, 2013; Salyer, Schubert, & Chiaranai, 2012), so identifying current self-care practices (or lack thereof) is a necessary component of the model.

In this context, it is important to note that healthy eating behaviors are considered part of self-care. For example, some clients may have a busy schedule that prevents them from leading a healthy lifestyle. They may consume an excess of sugary drinks and fatty foods, skip breakfast, and avoid sexual topics with their partner. Especially among dual-income or dual-career couples, the pressure associated with their busy schedules can contribute to an increased consumption of convenience food and reduced time devoted to sexual activity (Neault & Pickerell, 2005; Tye, 2013). All of these factors can negatively affect clients' emotional and physical well-being, including their sexual health.

Some questions and discussion prompts sex therapists can ask their clients to identify vulnerability factors to self-care include:

- You mentioned that you tend to eat _____ when you feel _____. Do you feel this impacts how you feel about yourself?

- Do these eating behaviors occur often?

- What food choices would help you feel better about yourself?

- Do your partner's self-care practices have an effect on how you view them?

- What are some factors in your lifestyle that lead you to make those food choices?

Step 5: Frame Lifestyle and Current Nutritional
Status from a Strengths-Based Perspective

The Nutri-Sexual Health model is a strengths-based approach in that clients' skills and resources are identified alongside their goals and barriers. Therefore, after identifying the lifestyle and nutrition factors that interfere with self-care, the therapist shifts the focus from one of deficits to one of strengths. For example, if a couple has identified a busy lifestyle as a vulnerability factor, then the therapist might say something like, "It sounds like you have a very busy schedule, which limits your ability to remain active or plan breakfast. This is expected for a modern couple like you. The positive aspect is that you are aware of your challenges and curious about how your lifestyle factors play a role." It is important to highlight the strengths, resources, and abilities clients bring to the table when addressing their difficulties.

In addition, therapists can encourage the couple to adopt a "we" stance in discussing their current challenges, as doing so increases accountability and enhances mutual support for each other. When clients describe their experiences using a "we" stance, they acknowledge their mutual role and responsibilities as part of a couple, as well as their locus of control over proactivity toward change. For example, instead of saying, "I'm just too busy to make a full meal from scratch," encourage couples to say, "We can work together to find a way to make sure that cooking a healthy meal fits into our schedules."

Step 6: Form a SMART Goal

The next step in this process involves helping clients create a SMART goal they are willing to put into practice in order to improve the quality of their sexual health. This goal should involve lifestyle and nutritional changes that clients can make to feel better about themselves, as well as to help them feel more connected to their partner. A SMART goal is one that is:

- **S**pecific: The goal should be clear and focused. Specificity can be achieved if clients ask themselves what they want to accomplish, what their motivation is, and if there are any perceived limits or restrictions.

- **M**easurable: A measurable goal is one where clients can track progress. Mentioning time frames, meal portions, and frequency of the target behavior all help make a goal measurable.

- **A**chievable: The goal needs to be attainable for both partners. This means it should involve effort but also remain clearly within reach.

- **R**ealistic: The client should be able to exert control over the actions needed to achieve the goal. For instance, establishing a goal that depends on the actions of another person will not be realistic.

- **T**ime-based: This involves establishing a target date by which the goal should be achieved or the length and frequency with which an activity should be performed.

For example, if a client's goal is to increase connection with their partner, feel less anxious about sex, and improve their lifestyle, then their SMART goal might be:

- For the next month, I will walk around my block daily for 20 minutes, with or without my partner, in order to increase my energy.

- I will add one item from the suggested foods list (found at the end of the chapter) each week over the next three months.

- I will engage in mindful and pleasure-based touch once per week for 30 minutes with my partner to increase bodily awareness and enhance intimacy.

- I will engage in all of these identified healthier lifestyle and nutritional behaviors for the next six months.

Usually, SMART goals are tailored to each partner in the relationship so they can both address individual issues with self-care and eating habits. However, in some cases the goals will be established as a couple. When working with clients to identify a SMART goal (or set of goals), it is helpful to brainstorm how their significant other can help them stay on track. By developing a mutual accountability between partners, the couple is better able to work together and feel more like a team.

Step 7: Discuss Possible Roadblocks

After developing SMART goals, the therapist works with the couple to identify what might get in the way of realizing their sexual health goals. For example, what personality or lifestyle factors would help them work together, and what might hinder their progress? What boundaries could they establish to help them feel empowered and better equipped to stay motivated and accountable to each other? How can they encourage each other to improve their nutritional habits?

The therapist asks these questions and encourages the couple to focus on elements over which they have control. For example, they do not have control over the behavior of ex-partners, other family members, work requirements, or job expectations, but they do have control over what they eat and how much, the way they speak to each other, how early they get up in the morning, what they buy at the supermarket, and their attitude toward cooking.

Encourage the couple to use positive and supportive language rather than language characterized by judgment or blame. For example, consider a client who believes their progress will be hindered because they tend to keep an excess of junk food in the home. In describing this barrier, the client may place the blame on their partner by saying, "My partner has the horrible habit of filling up the grocery cart with junk food. We'll never be able to meet our goals this way." In this case, the therapist can encourage the client to word their concern in a way that demonstrates mutual support. Instead, encourage them to say, "We might be tempted to buy and eat lots of junk food, or we can find a way to maintain our goals instead." The second statement doesn't put the blame on any one person in the relationship. Both partners have a role in creating the barrier, so both need to work together to overcome it.

Step 8: Establish a Support System

Given that clients will start implementing several lifestyle changes in the coming weeks related to their SMART goal, they need to create a list of people they can go to for support during this time. The goal is for clients to be able to reach out to these supportive allies when they need to or when their partner is not available.

First and foremost, the couple must look to each other as the primary support person to achieve their individual SMART goals and their couple-based SMART goals. After that expectation has been established, each partner can begin to look at their social network and choose two to three people they can count on to hold them accountable and support them in times of stress. The therapist can suggest that the couple choose people with whom both partners get along. Clients can be encouraged to talk to these selected supports ahead of time and to specifically ask them for assistance in achieving their goals. These supportive allies should have an understanding of why the clients are working on these goals and how they can motivate them to stay on track.

Step 9: Assess Individual Autonomy with Regard to Healthy Living Choices

After the couple has set SMART goals and identified a support system, the therapist should take a step back to assess each client's sense of independence and power with regard to decision making in and out of the relationship. Clients are more likely to experience success in implementing dietary changes if they feel they have the autonomy to do so (Lange, Corbett, Lippke, Knoll, & Schwarzer, 2015), so it is important for therapists to assess the extent to which each partner feels they can make choices that differ from their significant other.

For example, how confident does the client feel in experimenting in and out of the bedroom? Who tends to take more risks? Does the client feel comfortable expressing their needs and desires to their partner, including setting boundaries? How do they make decisions? How do they determine what they are going to eat or when they will be physically intimate? Does the client feel like they depend on their partner to make decisions about daily activities, the direction of the relationship, their home, how to raise their child, or how to take care of their pets? Or does the client feel confident making decisions on their own, and saying yes or no to their partner?

This discussion regarding autonomy should only occur after the therapist has discussed goals, barriers, and support systems with the couple. These earlier discussions will have provided the therapist an opportunity to observe the couple's power dynamics at play, and this information can be used to corroborate or dispute what clients report in session with regard to healthy living choices.

If the therapist finds that one partner does not feel autonomous in their ability to make these decisions—as evidenced by their self-report or the couple's interactional patterns—then the therapist should directly address these issues of autonomy before moving forward. Ask about different decision-making situations (e.g., decisions regarding home, work, finances, social life), and uncover at least one where this partner does not feel autonomous. Probe this partner about the root cause of their discomfort. Use rephrasing techniques to ensure that their point is clear and that both parties understand what is occurring. Explain that this situation will impede their ability to successfully make mutual changes to their lifestyle. Finally, have them express—in their own words—solutions to the situation. And once the couple agrees, ask them to commit to creating an environment that promotes autonomy moving forward.

Step 10: Suggest Integrative Interventions

After the couple has mastered the previous nine steps of the model and spent time implementing healthy nutritional and lifestyle changes, they may be ready to more mindfully engage in sexual activities. Typically, couples may spend as long as four to nine months (depending on clients' level of motivation) before reaching this stage of the model, though the specific time frame can vary widely among clients.

At this point, the therapist can introduce sensate focus as an exploratory touching tool. This step is meant to complement the Nutri-Sexual Health model and encourage the couple to set aside time to physically connect. Given that couples who seek therapy for the treatment of sexual concerns often spend minimal time being physically close, it is likely that clients will have had difficulties with intimacy before changing their nutritional and lifestyle habits. Now that they—hopefully—feel more energized after having adopted a healthier lifestyle, sensate focus exercises can be used as a way for them to reconnect.

Sensate focus involves a series of mindful touch exercises where the couple takes turns giving and receiving touch for a designated amount of time (Weiner & Avery-Clark, 2017). In sensate focus, the point is to increase awareness of what is pleasurable to the giver of touch, as opposed to the receiver of touch. Instead of getting caught up in whether one's partner is enjoying the experience (which can increase performance anxiety), the point is to increase one's own awareness of what feels pleasurable and to later communicate this to one's partner. This practice helps couples shift their mindset around sexuality from one that is performance-based to one that is pleasure-based. In turn, couples can begin to reduce performance anxiety, increase body awareness and sexual communication, and feel present in the moment with each other.

After describing the process and theory behind sensate focus, the therapist can help the couple identify their "high peak" time, which refers to the time of day when both of their physical energies overlap. At the outset, clients do not need to worry about feeling aroused or being ready for sexual touch during this overlapping time (though that is ultimately the goal). Rather, therapists want to encourage clients to start developing an awareness of each other's natural rhythms. Couples can use this information to their benefit by intentionally choosing to spend time with their partner in a manner that increases connection.

For instance, knowing their overlapping high peak time will help couples know the best time for grocery shopping, meal prep, and physical exercise. Eventually, it also allows them to be aware of the most opportune times to connect with their partner and engage in sensate focus. Like meal prepping, it is essential to plan times for sensate focus in advance to increase the chances of success. Therefore, once the couple has identified a mutual high peak time and become more in tune with each other's rhythm, they should plan time for sensate focus exercises while also scheduling in skills from the Nutri-Sexual Health model that promote health and well-being. Planning to practice mindful touch will give them a new opportunity to connect with each other while also prioritizing nutritional habits.

NUTRI-SEXUAL HEALTH MODEL: A CASE EXAMPLE

Miguel and Ana, both 26, had been together for five years and lived together for one year. They sought out sex and couples therapy to address concerns related to their waning sex life and decline in physical intimacy over the past several months.

Miguel's chief complaint was erectile dysfunction, though he also reported a history of anxiety and anger management problems. His symptoms started one year prior to entering therapy, after a period of relationship difficulties with Ana during which he experienced significant insecurity. Miguel reported he was able to obtain and maintain an erection through self-pleasure, but he complained of trouble maintaining an erection during sexual intercourse. He did not report low sexual desire, problems with orgasm, or ejaculation. He reported overall good physical health.

In describing her concerns, Ana reported feeling as if her libido was much stronger than Miguel's, despite having gained weight after being promoted at work. She also felt Miguel was unable to maintain an erection with her because he no longer found her attractive. Her weight gain, coupled with the perception that this was the reason Miguel could not maintain an erection, caused her to have low self-esteem, but she avoided the topic of weight gain with Miguel altogether.

When asked about their current lifestyle and nutritional habits, Miguel reported being under high stress and having a busy schedule, and he did not engage in any meal planning. For example, he generally skipped breakfast, ate a rushed lunch, consumed sugary drinks in the afternoon, and ate meat and potatoes in the evenings. Ana reported that with her promotion at work, most of her meals involved fast-food eaten at irregular times, and she would eat whatever Miguel prepared for dinner. On the weekends, they would usually get together with family or friends for a potluck lunch, and they would eat leftovers the rest of the weekend. Neither of them exercised, and although they both voiced a desire to get active, they never made plans or a commitment to do so together.

With regard to his role in the relationship, Miguel acknowledged that he avoided the topic of erectile dysfunction altogether—even when Ana voiced concerns that he was no longer attracted to her—because he felt inadequate and embarrassed. He described feeling insecure when it came to matters of romance in general. He attributed this insecurity to developmental factors, such as his strict upbringing by an authoritarian father. He also reported feeling left out and lacking in self-confidence when it came to his social life.

It became clear that Miguel was experiencing situational erectile dysfunction, most likely associated with performance anxiety, rooted in the emotional insecurities within his romantic relationship. Ana, in turn, was experiencing severe self-esteem issues that affected how she felt about herself and how she interacted with Miguel. Both Ana and Miguel's problems were likely compounded by both of their poor lifestyle and nutritional habits, especially their lack of awareness regarding the association between high stress, nutritional deficiencies, and sexual functioning. This was exhibited by their lack of meal planning, rushed food choices, Miguel's disinterest in varying dinner options, Ana's perceived lack of autonomy with regard to food choices, and an overall negative cycle of self-care.

I introduced the Nutri-Sexual Health model and worked with the couple to increase their awareness of the role that nutrition plays in emotional, physical, and sexual well-being. I explained how the foods they eat could affect the way they felt about themselves on a conscious and subconscious level. I introduced them to the basics of the Mediterranean diet and discussed how this way of eating could significantly improve their sexual and overall health. I also helped them identify vulnerability factors to self-care, many of which revolved around their busy schedules.

Once they were in a mindset where they were more aware of the connection between their bodies, their arousal, and their diet and nutrition, I encouraged them to start putting their strengths into action by constructing SMART goals, some individual and some as a couple. For example, one of their SMART goals was: "We aim to take turns cooking seafood and vegetables for dinner every weeknight and to make extra portions to take for lunch the next day."

At this point, Ana and Miguel seemed motivated and optimistic, which was a significant change from the state in which they arrived at my office, so I shifted the discussion to identifying potential roadblocks that would keep them from achieving their goals, and how they would address them. For example, if Ana got home late from work on the night it was her turn to cook, she acknowledged that she might be tempted to pick up burgers on the way home. They decided that they could overcome this barrier by keeping some frozen meals they had prepped in advance, which they could thaw in case of an emergency. They were also able to identify another couple they could lean on for support whose lifestyle choices and ability to work together they admired.

At this point, I already had a sense of the lack of autonomy Ana felt in the relationship, but it was important for them to express it as a couple. In having this discussion, Ana realized that her perceived lack of autonomy came from a sense of guilt at arriving home late so often. To make up for it, she let Miguel make the decisions regarding what to do with the time they were together. This included when they were going to have sex. Even though Ana felt she had a much stronger sex drive than Miguel, her lack of autonomy made it so that she rarely made the first move. As a result, she was sexually frustrated. Miguel was surprised at Ana's thought process and assured her that he did not want her to feel bad about coming home late every now and then. On the contrary, he was proud that Ana's work ethic had landed her a promotion that benefitted the couple financially. He also expressed that he felt aroused when Ana made the first sexual advance. Through this discussion, the couple committed to creating an environment of respect and autonomy in their home. At this stage, I introduced them to sensate focus to help them physically connect. After having gone through the previous steps of the model, they both expressed their excitement at trying it as soon as they got a chance.

Ultimately, the Nutri-Sexual Health model was able to increase Ana and Miguel's awareness of controllable healthy behaviors, like nutritional decisions that could help improve Miguel's sexual health and boost Ana's self-esteem, and allow them to feel more connected to each other. With treatment, they were able to understand the importance of nutrition as a stepping-stone toward increased energy and sexual intimacy.

ADDITIONAL SUGGESTED INTERVENTIONS

The Nutri-Sexual Health model can help clients increase awareness of nutritional and lifestyle habits that impact their sexual health and overall well-being. With a better understanding of ways to improve their health and dysfunctional relationships, clients can play a major role in their own treatment and begin to feel more connected with significant others. However, clients may often feel unmotivated or doubtful about making changes to their nutritional or lifestyle habits. The following are some interventions that therapists can use with clients to help them stay motivated and keep on track during this process:

- **Identify their *why*:** Helping clients develop a better understanding of their motives can make it easier to incorporate new behavioral changes. For example, perhaps they are making these changes to feel more energized, to have more sexual activity, to have a better relationship with their partner, or to enhance their sense of self. Ask clients to write down a list that summarizes their "why." What makes them interested in engaging in new nutritional and sexual health behaviors? Why are they doing this in the first place? What is driving them? Writing down their internal motivation now can serve as a source of inspiration later.

- **Create and keep a dream journal**: Before clients go to sleep each night, ask them to write down their "why" in a journal. Then have clients ask their dreams for clues, guidance, and next steps in this process. Clients can write down whatever they find out the next morning. To enhance relational intimacy, they can share this dream journal with their significant other.

- **Keep a synchronicity notepad**: Ask clients to keep a notepad linking events that happen throughout the week with their inner needs. Clients can review their notes at the end of the week to search for themes, explore meanings, and identify counterproductive behavior. For example, a client might note, "I was feeling frustrated with my husband, so I treated myself to a bottle of wine." By identifying the triggering situation and the counterproductive behavior that ensued, the clinician can encourage the client to identify alternate ways of having dealt with the situation that didn't involve alcohol or food.

- **Explore emotional hunger**: If clients find themselves hungry when they are not physically hungry, they should ask themselves what they are really hungry for. Are they hungry for attention, love, adventure, comfort, or something else? By exploring their emotional hunger, clients can uncover clues regarding their unmet relational needs.

- **Use metaphors**: Ask clients if there are any metaphors they can use to describe how they feel about their nutritional habits and sexuality. For example, "I feel like I am on a roller coaster," "I feel like throwing in the towel," or "I am over the moon with our new habits."

- **Wave a magic wand**: If clients had a magic wand, what would their relationship and sexual life look like? What types of nutritional habits would they embody? For example, would they cook meals together using only fresh produce? Would they adopt a vegan lifestyle? Would they refrain from ordering pizza on the weekends? Ask clients to list three things, rank them in terms of desirability, and share them with their partner.

- **Create a vision board**: In order to close the gap between where clients are and where they want to be, ask them to create a vision board that illustrates their goal. For example, if they like running and would like to incorporate that activity into their daily routine, then they might include a picture of a jogger. Then have them create a second board that illustrates their current status. For example, if they are feeling sluggish and disconnected, then they might include a picture to illustrate that. Ask clients to bring both of these boards to the next session so they can discuss their desired future and compare it with the images of their current state.

- **Follow a "culinary plan"**: Encourage couples to share foods with each other that bring them joy as well as to promote opportunities to cook together and increase emotional intimacy. The following are some ideas that can help couples encourage each other and keep them working toward improved sexual and relational health:

  - Ask couples to maintain photos of meals that nourish them and bring them joy, and to share these photos with their partner.

  - Instruct clients to write down healthy recipes and agree to make one together.

  - Have clients attend a healthy cooking class as a date night and discuss what healthy eating means to them.

  - Encourage clients to adopt the viewpoint that there can be body acceptance at every size and to let go of cultural and societal expectations.

  - Work with couples to help them understand the meaning behind their cravings and to share them with their partner.

■ Have couples track pleasurable activities they do individually and with their partner, and then share them with each other.

In addition to these suggested exercises, the following page contains a log clients can use to gain greater awareness regarding the impact of nutrition on their health and sexual lifestyle, followed by a list of sample of assessment questions therapists can use to gather information about clients when implementing the Nutri-Sexual Health model in their practice.

CONCLUSION

Sex and couples therapists have a unique opportunity to introduce nutritional interventions into the treatment plans of couples with sexual difficulties. When it comes to nutrition, like sex, individuals tend to be private for fear of judgment. However, instead of shying away from the challenges at hand, therapists should explore how food choices impact sexual functioning. When helping clients through this process of self-discovery, it is important to remember there can be good health regardless of body size. Individuals are so diverse in their behaviors and beliefs in relation to food that they might not be willing to adopt one prescribed meal plan, nor should they. Instead, individuals are encouraged to listen to their bodies and increase awareness of foods that promote energy and inspire joy. By encouraging clients to develop a greater awareness regarding the role nutrition and lifestyle choices play in their sexual and relational health, they can ultimately work to improve sexual functioning, mood, and overall relationship satisfaction.

Nutri-Sexual Health Log

The following log can help clients increase awareness of energetic versus sluggish foods and its impact on their health and sexual lifestyle. Clients should use this log when beginning a Nutri-Sexual Health program so they can maintain accountability and increase awareness of harmful patterns of behavior.

Time	Type of Food	Before I ate, I felt...	While I ate, I felt...	After I ate, I felt...	My energy level is...	My body feels...	I feel motivated to be sexual (Y/N)	I am worried about my sexual difficulty (Y/N)	I feel connected to my partner (Y/N)	My unmet need is...	What type of sexual activity would I be willing to engage in?	My partner's response is...

Nutri-Sexual Health Model Assessment Questions

1. How do you think your nutritional habits contribute to your sexual difficulty?

2. What about your daily routine prevents you from eating foods that energize you? Does this slow you down?

3. What nutritional, lifestyle, or health factors caused you to lose track of your sexual health goals?

4. What lifestyle factors bother you the most?

5. What does your partner think about your eating habits and lifestyle routines?

6. How do you feel about working together with your partner on creating and following a nutri-sexual health plan?

7. How do you believe working together on your nutritional habits could help you meet your sexual health goals?

8. What about your nutritional, lifestyle, or health habits are you worried about?

9. What about your nutritional, lifestyle, or health habits are you willing to change to meet your sexual health goals?

10. What do you believe could hold you back from reaching your sexual health goals?

11. What are some things you can do individually (and together) to ensure you are supporting each other?

12. What resources do you already have to support your nutri-sexual goals, and what resources do you need?

13. How can your partner support you?

14. What do you believe about the role nutrition plays in sexual health?

15. What have you learned from your partner about nutrition and its impact on their sexual health?

16. How do you feel when you think about changing your nutritional habits to meet your sexual health goals?

17. How would you feel if your partner was not on board with supporting your nutri-sexual healthy lifestyle?

18. How might you add more fruits, complex carbohydrates, vegetables, or lean protein into your routine?

19. What are your feelings about physical activities, such as yoga or walking? What are your thoughts about engaging in these physical activities with your partner?

20. How do you imagine your relationship might change from making nutritional changes to improve your mood and your sexual relationship?

Nutri-Sexual Health Suggested Food List

Star Foods for Better Sex

These star foods contain a particularly high amount of sex hormone-boosting substances, heart-healthy promoting antioxidants and healthy fats, digestion-promoting fiber, and nutrients that promote sexual health.

Almonds	Ground flax seeds	Pumpkin seeds
Avocados	Oysters	Watermelon
Chocolate	Peaches	Walnuts
Eggs	Pomegranate seeds	

Foods Consistent with the Mediterranean Diet

The following table describes foods that are common to the Mediterranean diet, including which foods to incorporate more of, which to eat in moderation, and which to limit or avoid altogether. The diet is highly plant-forward, with an emphasis on the daily consumption of vegetables, fruits, whole grains, and healthy fats, and the moderate consumption of poultry, dairy, and eggs.

Foods to Eat Sensible Portions of	
Vegetables	Examples include artichokes, arugula, asparagus, bamboo shoots, beets, bell peppers, bok choy, broccoli, brussels sprouts, carrots, cauliflower, celeriac, celery, collard greens, eggplant, endive, fennel, garlic, green beans, kale, leeks, lettuce, mushrooms, okra, onions, parsley, parsnips, peas, radicchio, scallions, shallots, spinach, squash, sweet potatoes, swiss chard, turnip, zucchini
Fruits	Examples include apples, apricots, bananas, blackberries, blueberries, cantaloupe, cherries, grapefruit, grapes, honeydew melon, kiwi, lemons, limes, mango, nectarines, oranges, papaya, peaches, pears, pineapple, plantains, plums, pomegranates, raspberries, strawberries, watermelon
Legumes	Examples include black-eyed peas, butter beans, chickpeas, kidney beans, lentils, lima beans, soybeans
Whole Grains	Healthy whole grains include amaranth, barley, brown rice, bulgur wheat, couscous, farro, oats, quinoa, spelt products, whole wheat products
Healthy Fats	Fats to incorporate more of include extra virgin olive oil, avocado, olives, nuts (e.g., Brazil nuts, cashews, hazelnuts, macadamia nuts, peanuts, pecans, pine nuts, walnuts), and seeds (e.g., caraway, chia, pumpkin, sesame, sunflower)
Seafood	Fish (salmon, tuna, mackerel, sardines), mussels, octopus, oysters, shrimp, squid

Foods to Eat in Moderation	
Poultry	Limit chicken, duck, turkey, and quail to 3 servings per week
Dairy	Avoid whole-milk dairy products and limit cheese, yogurt, and milk to 3 servings per week. Aim for low-fat dairy or Greek yogurt when possible.
Eggs	Limit whole eggs to 3 servings per week. No limit on egg whites.
Foods to Limit	
Red meat	No more than 1 serving per week of beef, lamb, pork, or veal
Foods to Avoid	
Processed meats	Deli meats, hot dogs, sausages
Refined grains	White bread and white pasta not made with whole grains
Refined oils	Soybean oil, canola oil, cottonseed oil
Highly processed foods	Examples include cookies, crackers, cereal, pre-prepared meals (e.g., frozen, microwaveable), packaged soups, and other foods that contain many added ingredients
Added sugars	Soda and sugary drinks, pastries, candy, cookies, ice cream

Chapter 11

Art Therapy and Sex Therapy: Infusing Couples Work with Creative Tools

Einat S. Metzl, PhD

Couples therapy can be some of the most complicated, layered, intriguing, and challenging work. In my experience, infusing couples therapy with creative interventions is the key to bringing about clients' relational transformation. Traditional couples therapy is predominantly verbal, and it can somehow feel like an added complication to add art to an already complex therapeutic process.

However, creativity—both in terms of creative thinking and creative production—is uniquely tied to our survival as a species, as well as our connection to our communities, our loved ones, and ourselves as we recover from life's challenges and traumas (Chapman, 2014; Dissanayake, 2012; Metzl, 2009). By integrating art in the context of couples therapy, therapists have an opportunity to provide couples with tools that lean on their "creative knowing"—their unique, intuitive, and expressive sense of core issues, feelings, and meanings—that immediately come to the foreground through art making.

Art making and art products help couples connect in a way that promotes exploration of their experiences, both separately and together. When combined with sex therapy assessments and psychoeducation, the use of art can depathologize sexual conflicts and integrate the couple's physical, sexual, emotional, spiritual, and cognitive experiences. It allows work to move in a manner that is deeper, less burdensome, and characterized by less secondary conflict. The containing *and* expressive nature of the creative process facilitates the processing of emotional experiences by each partner.

For example, when using creative interventions, I have found that couples do not respond to anger directed toward them in session, but to anger that has been expressed and contained through an image. The artwork reduces each partner's need to defend themselves, and it also prevents them from minimizing or deflecting their partner's pain. Insights become more integrated and are no longer simply intellectual, verbal, or even emotional in nature. Each partner's experience takes on a visual and sensory-motor quality, and this experience can be stored in an image that has rich cognitive-emotional-relational meanings attached.

Clients are able to symbolically voice their challenges from a productive, containing, and expressive stance that contributes to their own resilience building. I am forever inspired, engaged, surprised, and deeply attuned by couples' creative engagement with art and with each other through it. Therefore, this chapter is a glimpse into my integration of creative tools in sex and couples therapy.

Infusing Art in Couples Work: A Brief Literature Review

Over four decades ago, the use of dyadic art making within the context of sex therapy was explored, and it was found to be beneficial in getting couples to feel comfortable in releasing and recognizing their attitudes, emotions, and fantasies, as well as the interpersonal aspects of the relationship (Barth & Kinder, 1985; Sarrel, Sarrel, & Berman, 1981).

However, until very recently, efforts to systematically evaluate the couple's dyadic creative process have been minimal, and all assessments and interventions have been based either on standardized psychological tests (which yield limited data and have low to medium validity) or anecdotal case studies.

Recently, though, a more systematic exploration regarding the use of joint drawings in couples work supports previous anecdotal reports. In particular, research has found that the use of joint drawings—both in terms of process and product—can be an effective, supportive, and psychologically sensitive tool to assess relational dynamics, attachment needs, conflict management, and emotional needs (Snir & Wiseman, 2010, 2013, 2016). The use of SexSmart Body Maps[©] is another example of a drawing task that can help couples explore and communicate where they would like to be intimately touched (Zoldbrod, 1998).[1]

In addition, other forms of creative and expressive therapies have been found to be of benefit in assessing and treating relational challenges. For example, using music and role-playing with props can be helpful in couples treatment by representing relational processes, memories, and themes while encouraging the couple to connect with their emotions, examine their communication patterns, and focus on the interaction itself rather than on the verbal content (Hinkle, Radomski, & Decker, 2015).

In my own practice, I have found that the formal elements of art (e.g., the use of space, color, shape) are useful in the clinical assessment of the relational dynamic. For example, joint drawings that do not have a unifying frame or composition can be indicative of anxious-ambivalent attachment in the relationship, whereas joint drawings in which there is spatial distance between each partner's art (i.e., coexisting but without much interaction) can be evidence of anxious-avoidant attachment (Snir & Wiseman, 2013).

Similarly, artwork that is characterized by a coherent visual narrative and reciprocal relationships can signify a secure attachment relationship (Bat Or, Ishai, & Levi, 2015; Goldner, Gazit, & Scharf, 2017). In this respect, the use of art can help therapists

---

[1] A more in-depth description of SexSmart Body Maps can be found at http://www.sexsmart.com/sex-advice/sexsmart-bodymaps.

explore individual attachment styles that may influence current relationship dynamics, affect communication between partners, and interfere with emotional well-being (Kaiser, 1996).

CASE EXAMPLES

The following vignettes are inspired and informed by my work with couples over the last five years. Out of respect for my clients' particular experiences and circumstances, each case example represents a compilation of client narratives, rather than being taken directly from a single narrative. Therefore, the artwork included throughout these case examples is a loose replication of clients' responses to directives, or themes I have often witnessed, rather than a representation of actual art made in sessions with me.

The Use of Art to Assess Couples' Needs

In my first session with couples, I often introduce a joint verbal and nonverbal task, which was originally formulated by Helen B. Landgarten (e.g., Harriss & Landgarten, 1973). In particular, I ask the couple to choose one color marker each and invite them to draw together on a relatively large piece of paper, which is arranged between them on a drawing board. They are first invited to draw whatever they want, freely, using lines, shapes, and colors, without speaking (nonverbal joint drawing) and then, on a second piece of paper, to draw together while being allowed to speak.

During and after the drawing, we explore each partner's separate drawing experience, as well as how it felt to draw together. Doing so allows the couple to value their own unique process and their interconnected here-and-now process. It grounds them in the moment and brings their conflicts and interactions to the forefront of the session. The art they create offers a new perspective to look at their interactions and reflect on the process—who did what, when, and what happened after—which connects both the journey and final outcome to the meaningful experiences they often have with each other outside of therapy. This simple, creative task offers a wealth of information about the couple's relational dynamic, attachment styles, and communication (Metzl, 2016). The following two figures illustrate the dynamic between a married man and woman, Ryan and Sabrina.

Figure 1 illustrates the utility of examining both the process and product in uncovering the meaning for each individual, as well as the couple's dynamic. Ryan and Sabrina were not speaking to each other or to me when they created this image during one of their first sessions. They stated they would be happy to engage in a creative exercise and told me they were both artists. Sabrina was multitalented and had many expressive hobbies. She was the main breadwinner in their relationship, working primarily in an administrative field, and her husband was a drummer.

In their image, Sabrina chose a black marker and Ryan chose a green marker. Sabrina immediately started drawing what looked like a surreal woman figure but stopped below the neck to draw a prominent (floating) eye and heart. During this time, Ryan looked attentively at what she was doing. He seemed both distracted and fascinated. Then he started drumming with his fingers on his chair. She gave him a harsh,

Figure 1: The Couple's Nonverbal Joint Drawing

Figure 2: The Couple's Verbal Joint Drawing

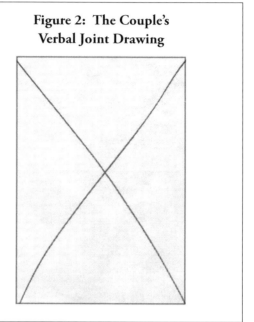

silent look, and he stopped and looked down sheepishly. She gave him another angry stare, and he picked up his marker and—with a different orientation on the paper—drew a drum set, a beat, and a few notes. Sabrina took one look at his drawing and with a look of utter dismay and a sigh, she added a scar and a tear to her heart.

In examining their process, the couple helped me understand their symbols and explained how, even without words, their dynamic with one another showed up. For example, Ryan noted what "critical responses she gives me" and how immediately and effectively he attempted to respond. At the same time, Sabrina expressed feeling alone, unseen, and untouched. She commented how Ryan had gradually moved toward her as he drew, but "he never took the initiative to actually connect, and it took him forever to even join me on the paper."

Through the lens of EFT, this dynamic is often referred to as a pursuer-withdrawer dynamic, which had lasted until the pursuer (Sabrina) became highly reactive toward the withdrawer (Ryan), and the withdrawer gradually came toward her (too little and too late in her experience). When Ryan met Sabrina's anger and frustration, he then went back to withdrawing into himself.

Figure 2 illuminates the exacerbation of that same process, although it is not typical in how overwhelmingly one-sided it is. The couple's directive for this exercise was to work together and create something, but this time they could communicate verbally. Speaking often changes the dynamic, and the difference in engaging with and without verbal language is almost always worthwhile from my experience. Nevertheless, it is rare to see what happened here: Sabrina literally took over the page and drew a big "X" on it—thus effectively expressing her frustration and, at the same time, blocking any possibility of cocreating something together. Ryan moved back and said to me, "How can I create something with her?" I reminded them that they could talk together and see what they could do. Ryan attempted to express his disappointment that they now had to start with the "X." He told Sabrina he wished they would have planned the drawing together. In response, and with a slightly calmer demeanor, Sabrina said, "Well, I guess it is time you deal with my anger."

Exploring these two figures with Sabrina and Ryan, separately and in conjunction, allowed me to begin formulating a working hypothesis about their struggles, needs, and relational cycle. It allowed me to witness with them their relational tendencies to move toward, away, or against each other at different moments and to discuss possible underlying attachment needs and emotional responses (e.g., Gottman, 2004). For example, drumming was so central to Ryan's identity and attempts to connect, which Sabrina had strong ambivalence toward. This ambivalence was reflected in her drawing of the surreal woman—who was looking for a second eye to see her and a second heart or a connection to her heart—and when that connection didn't come, her pain and anger took over. These powerful metaphors anchored the explorations of their experiences with one another from a humanistic, compassionate, and curious space.

Another beauty of making art in session is that the product becomes, in itself, a lasting anchor. For example, a few sessions later, when a big attachment injury came to the foreground, I could see some of Ryan and Sabrina's same responses being played out. I took out these two images, and we all acknowledged the similar dynamic that was being replicated. From the beginning of our time together, these images anchored the couple's processes and helped us objectify their conflict and look at and shift their shared reality.

Exploring Sexual Attitudes, Values, Sexual History, and Desires

Prior to seeing me, couples have usually attempted more traditional couples therapy, and many report never having been asked to explore their sexual connection, desires, challenges, or wants. However, intimacy and romantic connection are core issues for couples. In my own experience, I can report that there has never been a couple—regardless of whether they came to see me for sexual issues or another relationship problem—for whom sexuality was irrelevant in understanding their connection and conflicts. I cannot imagine how restrictive therapy must feel for clients who want to connect to their partners, and who are in therapy due to the challenges of intimacy, but who cannot find the space to discuss the topic of sexuality.

There are taboos in our society around the discussion of sex, which can impact both clients and therapists alike by making it hard to broach the topic. Many people have had the experience of sexuality combined with shame, fear, and reactivity. When clients come into couples therapy, not only are they dealing with the overwhelming impact of societal taboos, but they are also navigating their own layered experiences with intimacy (e.g., with the partner that is in the room and other sexual relationships predating that partner), as well as the potential anxiety about their partner's reaction to processing their sexual experiences and needs. However, I have found once couples know they can discuss and work on issues related to sexuality, they feel liberated to discuss their sexual relationship. It is also here where I find it particularly useful to use creative tools to explore sexual experiences, values, and desires.

Depending on the couple's needs and communication styles, I may use a less or more structured visual-expressive anchor during this process. For example, I often use visual psychoeducation charts, such as the Circles of Sexuality model created by Dennis Dailey (1981), to begin.[2] I briefly review the model to clarify any terms—such as definitions of sensuality, sexualization, and sexual identity—and then ask each client to create their own chart, modifying the circles to show their importance and symbolically naming their wants, needs, sensitivities, and history. The following vignette provides a good illustration of the use of psychoeducation within the context of creative couples work.

A married couple, Janet and Chris, began therapy to help resolve their relational issues. Janet identified as a "conservative, Christian woman who wants to trust this holy bond with my husband." She reported that she and Chris had "communication issues" and fought frequently. When we began discussing the issues they fought about, Chris said, "Well, I just do not want to have as much sex as she does these days." Janet looked embarrassed and admitted she was not as comfortable talking about sex, although she acknowledged that it was an issue for her. I suggested we explore their sexuality through a drawing task, and they very hesitantly agreed to try. They both prefaced this agreement by stating they were not artists and had not drawn since elementary school—which is a typical comment that clients make—so I chose a very structured task, in which there would be little experience of failure or frustration, yet there would be some opportunity to express themselves creatively.

In particular, I asked them to adapt the Circle of Sexuality diagram using colors, shapes, and words to illuminate what was important to them regarding their sexuality and to respond to the different aspects depicted. Janet's response (Figure 3) was completed rather quickly. She seemed to enjoy thinking and drawing about the different aspects of her sexuality, and while she was changing colors and text, she often made comments such as, "Hmm, I guess we never talk about this" or "I can see this is connected too." When exploring her piece, she expressed feeling relieved by the term "skin hunger" that was on the handout, which refers to the human need to be physically touched. Janet noted this term effectively expressed her desperate desire to physically connect with Chris.

Janet also became aware of how her age (she was 42) played a role in that desperation. For example, she noted she was getting older and "maybe the hormones now are also part of what's going on. These are also my last years to have another baby, and while we haven't really talked about it, I really want one!" This realization opened the door to a bigger dialogue between the couple about their shared vision for their family; their physical, romantic, and sexual connection; and how all of these issues resided within the context of their identity (apart and together), their values, and their faith.

---

2 An adapted version of Dailey's model is available at https://www.health.state.mn.us/people/sexualhealth/circles ofsexuality.pdf.

Figure 3: Illustrated Response to the Circles of Sexuality

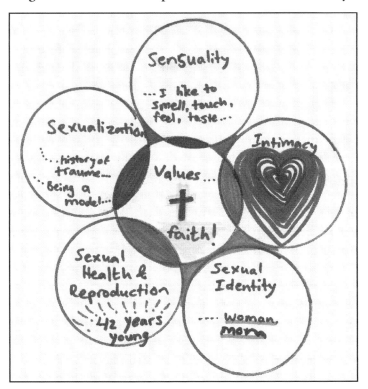

Assessing Challenges and Sensitivities While
Making Corrective Experiences Possible

Body mapping is a specific art therapy directive that involves responding to an outline of the human figure in order to explore sexual and somatic narratives that impact a couple's ability to connect as they desire. There are a variety of existing protocols that use this directive, such as the SexSmart Body Maps (Zoldbrod, 1998) and the BodyMap Protocol (Lubbers, 2017). While each specific protocol uses different materials, sizes, and directives, and their objective differs slightly, each exercise assists clients in facing sexual and somatic traumas creatively.

In my own clinical practice, I similarly offer couples a body mapping exercise in which they use figure outlines to symbolically tell me and their partner about their needs, boundaries, body, and the stories their body holds. This exercise offers a concrete visualization from which clients can clearly express what, when, and where they can be touched or responded to, and it creates clarity around those expectations. Body maps offer a literal map for their partner to consider, and they provide a starting point for discussion.

Figure 4 illustrates the way a body map can assist couples in understanding each other's somatic and emotional challenges and sensitivities. This image of a woman was drawn by Libby, a client who identified as a Japanese-American lesbian feminist woman, who came in to see me with her partner of two years, Kelsey. The couple had enjoyed their first year and a half together "on all levels," but their sexual interest had drastically decreased over the last six months.

Figure 4: Mapping Possible Connections Through Body Mapping

The women both agreed part of the issue was that Libby was very particular regarding where she wanted to be touched and that "she wanted almost no foreplay." Because of this, neither of them felt like they could have satisfying sex anymore. By using a simple body map, both women visually described which areas they were willing (and wanting) to have their partner touch. Each woman depicted those areas in orange—noting areas that were "sometimes okay" to touch during intimate play—and then added green arrows with check marks to depict which areas were "always okay."

The process of making the figure was very meaningful for Libby. She seemed self-conscious at first, but as she became engaged, she noticed that her feet and hands (the "okay" parts to touch) seemed disconnected. When Kelsey asked her why she didn't indicate anything in her face that was okay to touch, Libby initially replied, "Oh, I forgot . . ." However, she then corrected herself and said, "I do like when we have sex, but I have a hard time with kissing. I know it is not because of you but because of my previous relationships. In fact, now that I think about it, this might be some of my issue with our foreplay!"

The art process and product here helped the couple explore with curiosity an issue that was otherwise too painful to talk about and that they had fought over when they tried to discuss it in the past. The art also allowed Libby to gain new insights about her needs—insights that could later be explored in more detail, which were connected to previous sexual traumas—and helped us work through sensitivities and barriers to sexual joy for this couple.

Attachment Injury and Reconciliation

Attachment injuries are one of the more common reasons individuals seek couples therapy, which can be related to a wide range of experiences, such as betrayal, infidelity, and abandonment (Johnson, Makinen, & Millikin, 2001). These cases have some shared challenges, as therapists must navigate the devastating experience of loss of an attachment bond and the accompanying posttraumatic symptoms of intense emotions and disrupted functioning, which may or may not be clear to the partner. Most therapists working with attachment injuries share an understanding that in order to move to reconciliation, the couple has to be guided through an empathic dialogue so they can process the individual experiences of trauma, grief, and loss; understand the factors leading to infidelity; and begin to reestablish a sense of trust and safety.

Few therapeutic tools take people straight to the heart as well as creative expression. An art piece can offer couples a different way to view their relationship, and it physically contains strong feelings (e.g., anger, sadness, fear) without projecting those feelings onto the partner. Art can offer both the partner who is attempting to describe their pain, and the partner who is witnessing it, a way to do so without accusing, defending, or deflecting. Although this process still requires that the therapist provide enough safety and care for the emotional content to be held, once that is part of the therapeutic space, the art draws the partner in through its visual cues. It allows the partner to experience the shapes, colors, and spaces that the other is dealing with internally.

The following vignette and accompanying artwork illustrate the visceral pain inherent in attachment injuries. Andrew and Jill were a couple in their sixties who had been living together for five years. They had been friends since high school but became romantically engaged after their previous relationships had fallen apart.

Jill created this particular image (Figure 5) when she and Andrew came to a session furious at one another. Both expressed feeling deeply hurt and misunderstood. I tried to explore their conflict with them verbally but could immediately tell they were not going to be able to engage in a thoughtful dialogue. I suggested we draw a bit "about

Figure 5: Attachment Injuries Reflecting Visceral Pain

what was going on" and then talk. Although initially reluctant, they both chose oil pastels and became absorbed in their art. I could tell that by simply being close to each other and calmly drawing, some of their heightened emotions were contained. Because art is inherently expressive, they were still processing their own thoughts and feelings in a nonverbal manner, with the clear promise that the images would be shared and talked about further. After 10 minutes or so, they both reached what felt like a natural stopping point.

Andrew shared his drawing first, which depicted a big question mark over the head of a person aiding another in a wheelchair. He explained that he had been spending more time caring for his aging mother and recently had to stay there a few nights a week. He did not understand why Jill was so angry with him for doing so and was hurt by her not being more supportive. Then Jill spoke tearfully. She shared how frightened and abandoned she felt on those long nights when Andrew was not there. She described being sad because she did want to support him and often tried to ask if she could come with him or if she could stay at a friend's house. Jill reported that whenever she would ask Andrew this, he would just tell her, "Come on, you are a big girl. You can spend a few nights by yourself, no?"

Jill spoke quietly and quickly, and then they both stared at her drawing together. She had depicted herself curled up on a bed, naked and alone, with a looming, fuzzy dark figure hidden underneath. Andrew asked about the figure looming underneath the bed and reached out for Jill as he said, "I'm so sorry. I really didn't understand. I know you told me before, but I just don't see you as fragile and fearful, ever. But in this picture, I see you differently. I'm sorry I left you alone with that." Jill's artwork helped communicate her underlying pain in a way that Andrew could resonate with, while also containing their secondary feelings of anger and frustration. Art is not magic, but it paves the way for people to face their deepest hurts in a new way, and when they are able to do so together, magic does happen.

Discrepancy in Sexual Desire or Expression

Another common challenge that brings couples to therapy, and specifically sex and couples therapy, is a felt discrepancy in sexual desire or expression. In these cases, using art to help couples explore their desires and their sexual expression (or lack thereof) can be surprisingly helpful. Through the use of art, individuals are able to explore—first individually as they work side by side—their own understanding of their needs and wants, and how they act on those creatively. This process is often experienced as empowering, as it liberates them from the "stuck place" they have reached. It offers a wealth of insight through the art-making experience itself, as well as through the subconscious aspects of the self that can show up in the created images. Then the couple is invited to explore the art each of them has made so they can consider any similarities and differences in their work, explore possible meeting spaces, examine the potential for change, and consider how they might respond to one another sexually.

Figure 6 is an image depicting the experience of Paul, who lost his first wife in a car accident when his kids were young. He raised the kids as a single parent until his mid-thirties, when he finally began to date again. It was then that Paul met the woman to whom he was now married, Julie.

They came to therapy because now—four years after they met and two years after their marriage—their relationship, as Paul described it, was miserable. He commented, "We always fight, we have nothing in common, we don't enjoy anything, my kids do not get along with her, and I do not want to waste the rest of the life I have with a woman who never wants to have sex." In response, Julie explained that over the last few years, she had been experiencing physical changes related to menopause and, on top of that, had recently hurt her back. She understood Paul's frustration but did not see why their connection had become "all or nothing, and all or nothing about sex."

During the session, I had placed several art materials in front of them and suggested they use them throughout the session when they felt called to do so. The figure Paul created depicted a cognitive schema he was consciously, and to some extent subconsciously, contending with. He explained, "If life is the sum of the Yes you get over the No, then my life feels like a small fraction of Yes's." In this particular case, a collage image I had in my office (which stated "Yes over No equals LIFE") helped Paul connect to an existential question he had regarding the overall purpose and quality of his life. Exploring the underlying feeling behind his equation allowed him to express some of the unprocessed pain over his first wife's death, the current empty-nest syndrome he was feeling, and how much he wanted Julie to help this part of his life feel more like a yes. After Julie

Figure 6: Exploring Felt Discrepancy in Sexual Desire and Expression

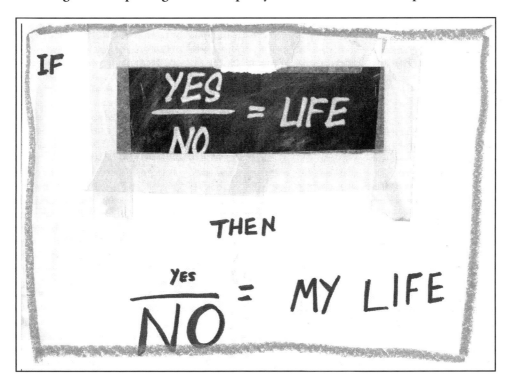

responded with care and understanding, he was then able to contextualize the rejection and frustration he felt about not making love to her in a way she could hear more deeply.

In this particular case, Paul's intuitive use of collage work allowed him to express a conflict he was originally holding at a purely cognitive level. Through the process of becoming physically engaged in making and exploring his artwork, he was able to connect to his underlying emotional and sensorimotor experiences. The context of the couples session allowed his wife to be part of this revelation, which allowed her to connect to his needs on a cognitive-emotional-relational level and reexamine her place "in his equation."

CREATING A CREATIVE SPACE

When encouraging clients to tap in to their creative and expressive abilities, it is important for therapists to create a nonjudgmental space where clients can approach anything that comes up with curiosity and compassion. We all intuitively know that when we feel judged, fearful, or ashamed, we are much less likely to take risks, try new strategies, or openly explore "what was just formed," whether that be psychologically, artistically, or relationally.

Although I consider myself an eclectic therapist, I am strongly informed by an EFT approach when working with couples (Greenman & Johnson, 2013). I find that by creating a more accepting, non-pathologizing space—one in which both partners can begin to trust each other, me as their therapist, and the art as a meaningful tool—clients can begin to see that their problem involves their "cycle" with one another. It also allows them to understand that this cycle is a really a result of their desire to connect with their partner and not be hurt while desperately trying to do so.

In order to create a bound yet nonjudgmental space, I generally rely heavily on choices, such as choices of materials and cocreation of directives. I also place a strong focus on the process involved in making the art and verbally exploring its meanings instead of focusing on the final product. I intentionally avoid power struggles (e.g., "I really think you should use this material or directive"), and I try hard to move away from my own learned reactions, whether positive or negative, as these can infer judgment and aesthetic expectation (e.g., "Oh, what a beautiful piece"). Instead, I remain curious about the choices and responses clients have to their own work, reminding them that they are the expert of their creations. In addition, I model how they can engage in a shared exploration of individuation and psychological separateness, as well as relational and empathic connectedness. I ask them to treat each other, and their creative experiences and products, similarly.

When considering whether to create a space for art-based interventions in the context of sex and couples therapy, therapists must first explore their own training and familiarity with art materials, art directives, and explorations thereof. It is important for therapists who are not trained in art therapy to understand they cannot and should not offer "art therapy" to their clients. Rather, they should frame it as an intentionally selected creative intervention that couples can use to explore or process an issue, and therapists may want to seek out further training and consultation from a registered art therapist if the creative intervention does not produce the reaction they anticipate.

In addition, therapists should always consider the scope of their practice and the clinical fit when it comes to creative interventions. If a therapist is treating a couple that seems to do better with, or consistently asks for, art-based interventions—and the therapist is at a loss regarding how to do so in a therapeutic manner—then they should always consider referring to an art therapist.

CONCLUSION

The use of art can be a powerful addition to couples work. Infusing traditional talk therapy with creative interventions can immediately transform the space between couples by taking them out of their comfort zone. When there is sufficient trust in the therapist and the intentions of the art interventions, clients are invited to meet their own abilities, limitations, joys, and frustrations. The process and product involved in creating art allows clients to explore their experiences, as well as those of their partner, from a novel perspective that is characterized by intimate curiosity.

Working with LGB(Trans)QIA Couples Using an Intersectional, Psychodynamic, and Gender-Affirmative Approach

Stephanie King, PsyD

Navigating intimate and sexual relationships can be complicated under any circumstance, but it is particularly complex when working with transgender couples, who can have intersecting and sometimes changing identities. In addition, transgender people, like any other population, can have varying sexual orientations. Their partners may also be transgender, nonbinary, or cisgender, and they may share a congruent sexual orientation or identify with a different orientation altogether.

Given these complexities, therapists who are involved in working with couples in which one or both partners are transgender must be attuned to how each individual's personal history and patterns of attachment impact their current relationship, as well as the therapeutic relationship.

While it is usually assumed that transgender people's experiences are similar to the bisexual, lesbian, or gay experience (Bigner & Wetchler, 2012), this is not always the case. Therefore, in this chapter, I have coined the term "LGB(Trans)QIA" in an attempt to exemplify and differentiate transgender people from the other, often intersecting, identities they are often associated with: lesbian, gay, bisexual, queer or questioning, intersex, and asexual. Holding these intersecting identities in mind is essential when working with transgender people.

Overall, this chapter intends to offer therapists—and cisgender therapists in particular—a more accurate understanding of transgender people's needs and to discuss effective ways to intervene in sex and couples therapy. In particular, this chapter explores the importance of engaging in clinical self-reflection, understanding intersectionality, maintaining a gender-affirming and sex-positive approach, and using a psychodynamic lens. Finally, two cases are presented to highlight these modes of thinking. While reading this chapter, keep in mind the following important terms:

Cisgender	A person whose sex assigned at birth or body corresponds to their gender identity. Generally preferred over terms such as non-trans and bio man/woman.
Transgender	An umbrella term that describes a person or people whose sex assigned at birth differs from their gender identity. This is also an adjective, not a noun or pronoun.
Transwoman	A person whose sex assigned at birth was male but who identifies as a woman.
Transman	A person whose sex assigned at birth was female but who identifies as a man.
Nonbinary	A gender identity that is neither strictly male nor strictly female.

SELF-REFLECTION AND THE INTERSECTIONAL LENS

An essential tool for clinicians working with transgender clients is the ability to be consistently self-reflective, and this is particularly true when it comes to cisgender clinicians. It is imperative that cisgender clinicians be committed to ongoing self-reflection and lifelong learning, especially regarding socially commanded gender norms, gender training, and gender socialization.

Part of this process involves unlearning gender socialization and gender training, which is an intentional process that requires time and effort. Gender training is defined as the rigid, pervasive messages that we receive from a young age about what it means to be a boy/man or a girl/woman, including rules about appearance, behavior, emotional expression, preferences, dislikes, and ways of relating to others (Chang, Singh, & Dickey, 2018). At first glance, it may not be clear why it is problematic to categorize people in this manner. However, problems arise when a person does not fall into these neatly organized categories of behavior. They may be mistreated, othered, described as mentally ill, and even demonized. Therefore, it is crucial for cisgender clinicians to unlearn these harmful gender stereotypes and expectations in order to promote a gender-affirmative approach.

Once therapists begin to examine the gender training and gender socialization they have been indoctrinated with, they will begin to see cisnormative, cisgenderist, heteronormative, and heterosexist messages everywhere. These messages reinforce intolerance for gender-expansive expression and reinforce gender roles, which stigmatize those who demonstrate "nonconforming" behaviors or appearances. Developing this awareness is important not only because it allows therapists to know what their transgender clients have experienced in life, but also because it provides them with an understanding of the significant impact of these structures on *everyone's* lives. It also serves another vital function for cisgender clinicians: to help them reflect on their own cisgender privilege, which is often invisible for those who hold it.

Heteronormativity and cisnormativity are reflected in the couples and family therapy literature, which can also be understood as a reflection of public opinion. Between 1975 and 1995, only .006 percent of articles in marriage and family journals directly addressed LGB (lesbian, gay, or bisexual) issues, and between 1996 and 2010, only 2 percent did (Clark & Serovich, 1997; Hartwell, Serovich, Grafsky, & Kerr, 2012). Moreover, when it comes to transgender-specific research, marriage and family journals are just beginning to acknowledge and validate transgender people and their relationships, with only nine articles (0.0008 percent) on this topic having been published between 1997 and 2009 (Blumer, Green, Knowles, & Williams, 2012).

Being both culturally and pedagogically immersed in heteronormativity and cisnormativity can have a tremendously negative impact on a therapist's thinking and therapeutic interactions, which is why working with transgender clients requires constant self-reflection and unlearning. As a therapist, understanding one's clients along with one's own intersecting identities is the best clinical path forward.

INTERSECTIONALITY

Intersectionality, which was first introduced by Kimberlé Crenshaw in 1989, is a theoretical approach that takes into account all of the intersecting identities one person holds at any given time (see Chapter 7). It refers to the interconnected nature of categories—such as age, race, gender identity, sexual orientation, religion, ability, and access to care—that create overlapping, interdependent systems of disadvantage that can lead to discrimination and privilege. This knowledge of intersectionality can help therapists get a broader understanding of a person's experience as opposed to simply categorizing them with a single identity. Transgender people, as do all people, have a multitude of identities, and some might even be actively changing.

For example, a 23-year-old lesbian, Latina, Catholic, transwoman in a relationship with a 29-year-old White bisexual, atheist, cisgender woman will have many identities that will impact the ways she navigates the relationship. The transwoman will need to contend with being a young woman of color who, as a transwoman, has lost her former gender privilege and is spiritually connected to a religion that has been known to oppress and deny people in her community. Additionally, if her transition occurred while in the current relationship, she has gone from the dominant, socially "accepted" sexual orientation of heterosexual to one of less acceptance and privilege: lesbian.

The transwoman's partner is rooted in her privilege of whiteness and heterosexuality, but she is partnered with a transwoman, which can bring scrutiny from family and friends and also has the potential to bring her heterosexual identity into question to herself and others. While being atheist seems fairly neutral, it may be difficult for her to understand the ways her partner may feel spiritually conflicted and isolated. Paying attention to these multiple intersecting identities is vital to all clinical situations. It is also an exercise for therapists to begin to recognize, perhaps for the first time, their own intersecting identities and to become aware of their privilege status if they are heterosexual and White, or to explore how their own identity intersects with the client's.

LAWS AND DISCRIMINATION

More than just receiving specialized training, and being familiar with and grounded in a particular theory, therapists working with the LGB(Trans)QIA population also need to be familiar with the historic and current sociocultural and sociopolitical world we inhabit, which also contributes to one's intersectional identity. This involves staying up-to-date regarding current laws that include or exclude people who fall under the LGB(Trans)QIA umbrella. People who identify as LGB(Trans)QIA, especially those who are transgender, are a less protected class under federal law in the United States and have less protection against discrimination under state laws. Having knowledge of these laws—as well as knowledge regarding access to available gender-affirming medical interventions and potential outcomes of said interventions—is also useful. However, this should not overshadow the wide and varied emotional needs, mental health concerns, and relational realities that arise for this population.

Transgender people have experienced years of oppressive, stigmatizing "gatekeeping" practices taught throughout the mental health field that have created barriers to affirmative care. Gatekeeping is the notion that clinicians determine whether someone is "truly transgender," which is a practice that has created a legacy of harm to transgender people. The following excerpt is from a text that was assigned to this author for American Association of Sexuality Educators, Counselors, and Therapists (AASECT) certification:

> For many transsexuals, particularly female-to-male, life would be much easier for them if they could accept and feel comfortable with a homosexual identity. Sometimes the extreme and rigid rejection of homosexuality reveals a personality that may not fare well after surgery. (Bancroft, 2009, p. 299)

This kind of thinking is problematic: It is akin to conversion therapy and implies gender identity and sexual orientation are somehow interchangeable. The text goes on to direct clinicians not to offer "false optimism" to clients, especially regarding the difficulties that should be communicated regarding whether clients "look the part." This particular kind of thinking and training reinforces gender binary norms and insinuates there are only two prescribed ways to express gender. As a therapist working with a couple or individual, utilizing this misguided belief system can pressure clients to conform to masculine and feminine norms and "values" that will inevitably impact sexual functioning.

The practice of gatekeeping has also inadvertently created a generic transgender script, passed down within the trans community, which is often believed to be the only way an individual can access care. This script consists of a variety of ways for trans people to describe their gender experience that doesn't always hold true for each individual. Most of these statements are now used in the *DSM-5* as symptoms of gender dysphoria (American Psychiatric Association, 2013), which is harmful because it forces individuals to use a script that may not be true to their experience in order to get access to the services they need.

GENDER-AFFIRMING AND SEX-POSITIVE THERAPY

Part of practicing gender-affirming therapy is understanding that language matters and is constantly changing. Clinicians who want to work with transgender people should stay well informed of the evolutionary changes in language, as doing so sends a message to their clients that the clinician wants to be inclusive and use language that does not harm or alienate their clients' experiences. As therapists, we must bear in mind that the words we choose have the power to confirm or deny someone's very existence.

When clinicians are thoughtful with their word choices, the chance that clients will feel safe and affirmed in the therapeutic setting increases. The use of affirming language is especially important when working with trans people in sex and couples therapy. Although gender-affirming language goes far beyond accurate pronouns and names, using correct names and pronouns is always important. The best way to know how someone identifies is simply to ask, "What pronouns do you use?"

There are many ways to describe one's gender identity, and not all trans people identify with binary options. Therefore, it is also important to make space for those with nonbinary or gender-fluid identities. The following are some terms that are no longer considered affirming and their alternative, affirming descriptors. In all instances, it is best practice for therapists to ask when they don't know, noting that they want to be respectful, and then to listen and mirror the language being used by clients.

Not Affirming	Affirming
Male-to-female, "born" a man, biological man, male-bodied, transsexual	Transgender woman, transwoman, transfeminine, transfemme, woman
Female-to-male, "born" a woman, biological woman, female-bodied, transsexual	Transgender man, transman, transmasculine, transmasc, man
"Real" man/woman, non-trans	Cisgender man, cisgender woman
Passing as . . .	Being read as . . .
Stealth	Sharing/disclosing or not sharing/disclosing one's identity with others
"Preferred" pronouns	Pronouns

When it comes to sex, trans people are both overly sexualized (sometimes fetishized) and equally desexualized. One way to understand the sexual treatment and mistreatment of trans people is to look to disability theory, as both communities are plagued by the idea of "normalcy" (Langer, 2019; Oliver, 1996). According to disability theory, an individual's experience of limitation arises from a society built on oppressive systems that do not make accommodations for people with disabilities. In other words, this pathology exists within society, not the individual (Erickson-Schroth & Boylan 2014; Langer, 2019). If this social system were appropriately addressed and abolished, there would be less discrimination and increased access to resources. This is an important distinction to note, as much of the literature and social attitudes about trans people purport the opposite.

Pathologizing trans people in this manner can lead them to internalize thoughts and beliefs associated with the feeling they are somehow "impaired," and this is particularly relevant when it comes to sex. Social attitudes have suggested that trans people should focus on "passing" and that it is "too demanding" for them to expect to be sexually fulfilled as well (Langer, 2019). This line of thinking can lead to a variety of challenges trans people may experience and seek therapy for.

A simple, profound intervention to help trans clients feel empowered, connected, and present in their sexual lives leads us, yet again, back to language. The power of gender-affirming language should not be underestimated. For example, if discussing bodies or body parts is relevant, as with any sex therapy client, ask your trans client how they want to hear their body talked about. Ask what words they prefer to use. Encourage dialogue between partners, each sharing words that feel most positive and affirming. Some trans-affirming terms to keep in mind to describe bodies are chest instead of breasts and genitals or private parts instead of penis or vagina. These terms are appropriate until you hear terms from the client that are more preferable. For example, a transwoman who has a penis may report that referring to it as a clitoris assuages her dysphoria. Similarly, a transman may find comfort in using the word "dick" or "cock" when discussing his clitoris. When clients can feel their bodies are their own, they are much more adept at and available to receiving pleasure.

At the same time, discussing bodies and body parts can be emotionally upsetting for some trans people and should be done with the utmost respect and care. It is best practice to never ask a trans client about their genitals unless there is a legitimate reason to do so—and usually not until or unless the person brings up the subject themselves and indicates it is relevant.

In addition to helping trans clients own their bodies, another important sex-positive clinical intervention involves helping clients find ways to feel good *in* their bodies. To do so, many trans clients may have to go through yet another unlearning process, this time regarding sex and the sexual response cycle. The classic sexual response cycle proposed by William Masters and Virginia Johnson (1966) is a model that outlines the stages of excitement, plateau, orgasm, and resolution during sex. Historically, research on models of sex and arousal have not included transgender people, which inadvertently set the expectation that "normal sex" should be similar to cisgender sex. This misconstrual can lead trans clients to set themselves up for disappointment. Instead, help clients focus on how they want to *feel* during sex and how they want to be touched. This should include questions about how a client's dysphoria does or does not impact their sexual functioning or satisfaction.

One step in this process can be to create questions that clients can ask their partners, either in the therapy room or as homework. It is not unusual for trans clients to minimize their own sexual needs out of fear or discomfort related to dysphoria or inexperience in their "new" gender. How will they communicate their specific wants and needs to their partner(s)? How will they challenge the belief that their specific needs might be burdensome to their partner(s)? One way to begin with a couple is to use a "yes, no, maybe" list to get the conversation started, which allows clients to express their desires, needs, and comfort levels related to sex. It acts as an external tool that mitigates anxiety, embarrassment, or fear of rejection. Therapists must be sensitive to these intersecting dynamics, exercise trust, and exhibit a nonjudgmental demeanor when having this conversation. Normalizing fears and vulnerabilities, encouraging eye contact, and using Imago Dialogue techniques are also helpful interventions.

For partners, trans or cis, discuss how they can also have an embodied experience that supports their own identity and that acknowledges their partner's identity and needs as well. Emphasizing the various ways they can experience sexual intimacy in the bodies they each have, whether or not dysphoria is present, can be the pathway to a fulfilling and satisfying experience. Part of this process involves thinking creatively about how sex is defined. It may be obvious to sex therapists that sex does not just involve vaginal penetration by a penis. However, clients who have been inundated with social messages that sex only happens one way—and that it also happens quickly and easily—may believe they are doing something wrong if their sex life does not look the same. Offer psychoeducation on the wide-ranging sexual activities that can happen with different bodies and different body parts. For instance, remind clients that kissing and touching, as well as tickling or paddling, can also be called sex.

Clinicians should be aware of the options available to clients that might assist or enhance sexual experiences, such as the use of prosthetics, strap-ons, vibrators, pumps, trans-positive porn, and trans-positive erotica. This awareness also includes an understanding of precautions that can be taken and time allowed to accommodate for changing physical and emotional needs. Many transwomen on hormone therapy, for instance, experience a decrease in desire and arousal and may need extra time to adjust to their changing bodies, desires, and needs.

For some, engaging in physical intimacy will generate bodily dysphoria and has the potential to lead to a dissociative experience during sex. It is possible to prepare for and circumvent this outcome with the help of a trusted partner, good communication skills, and a safe environment. These communication skills can include before-sex negotiation, during-sex updates, and after-sex check-ins. No matter what kind of sex people are having, good communication is always an important foundation. Sometimes, this requires planning and practice.

Before-Sex Negotiations

Before-sex negotiations can include a variety of discussions regarding boundaries, desires, areas of the body that are off-limits, words that should be used to describe bodies, and a (safe) word or phrase that can be used to stop the interaction if something doesn't feel right. For example, a person may feel that touching the chest is off-limits but that biting earlobes is perfectly fine.

During-Sex Updates

Remind clients that just because before-sex negotiations have been agreed upon, that doesn't mean all will go smoothly. It is important to stay connected throughout the experience and to have partners check in with each other throughout. Depending on how well partners know each other, they can use a combination of verbal check-ins. One way is to ask, "Does this feel good?"

Observing each other and watching facial expressions is also important. Some partners know each other well enough to see a change in facial expression and know that something may be shifting for their partner. In this case, they can quickly intervene and ask if everything is still feeling safe and comfortable. However, not all people will know what is truly going on with their partner just by looking at their facial expression, which is why verbal check-ins are also good practice. Again, this practice requires trust, patience, and good communication.

After-Sex Check-In

After sex can be a lovely moment of relaxation and pleasure. It is also a good time to reflect together about how the experience felt for both people. Even with before-sex negotiation and during-sex updates, more can still be processed. Perhaps one partner went along with something in the moment and in hindsight wishes they hadn't. Or maybe they stopped something from happening and wish they had tried it after all. Now they are feeling regretful and ashamed. The most important thing to remember is that all of these issues can be talked about, learned from, and thought about for future negotiations.

The following is a clinical example of a sex-positive and gender-affirming approach in the clinical hour between spouses: Lisa, a cisgender woman, and Martin, a transgender man.

Lisa:	"I'm really ready for our sex life to come back to life. It just feels like it's flatlined, and I want more."
Therapist:	"Martin, how do you feel?"
Martin:	"I just feel nervous about it. It's weird, we've been together a long time, but I just need things to be a little different now, and I feel guilty for changing it up on Lisa like this."
Therapist:	"Lisa, do you know what Martin wants to be different?"
Lisa:	"I think I can guess, but he hasn't really said much. We will get started, and then all of a sudden, it's like he's not even there anymore, and I can tell. So I just stop and ask 'What's going on?' and he says 'Nothing.'"
Therapist:	"So you get started all right, but then in the midst of getting close, something shifts?"
Lisa:	"Yeah, and I just end up feeling like he's not into me anymore or like I'm not good or something."
Martin:	"That's not it! I've told you that before. Why don't you listen to me?"
Lisa:	"Well, it's pretty hard to believe you! Whenever we start to have sex, you just shut down. I mean, there I am, going down on you, and I'm totally into it, and you just freeze."
Therapist:	"Martin, do you recognize this also? This sort of freezing experience?"
Martin:	[*long pause*] "Yes . . ."
Therapist:	"Do you know what's going on for you in those moments?"

Martin: "I'm not sure. I just start to feel weird, like something is wrong with me, and then I just sort of shut down because I can't explain it."

Therapist: "What do you mean something is wrong with you?"

Martin: "I don't know; it's just that my body, well . . . it feels wrong, I guess. I mean, I know it's fine. It's just that when we have sex the way we've always had sex, it's hard for me to feel like a man, you know? I just sort of disconnect from myself."

Therapist: "It's a common experience to want to have sex differently after transitioning."

Martin: "I think that's what's happening. I just don't know what's going to feel good."

Therapist: "Well, according to Lisa, it sounds like something happens once the two of you get started, and when she's going down on you, I'm guessing there might be something about this that no longer feels comfortable."

Martin: "Yes. I start thinking about my genitals, and it just goes downhill from there."

Lisa: "But, honey, you know I love that part of your body."

Martin: "I know, but I think that's part of the problem. To you it's my pussy, and I hate that. I hate that word associated with my body."

Therapist: "Martin, how do you want your body to be talked about? Do you know?"

Martin: "I want her to notice the changes that the testosterone has given me and relate to those parts of my body."

Therapist: "Lisa, have you noticed the difference since Martin has been on T (testosterone)?"

Lisa: "Yeah, he's hairy and his voice has deepened, and his clit has gotten a lot bigger!"

[*Martin winces at the word* clit.]

Therapist: "Martin, I think that word is hard to hear, is that true?"

Martin: "Yes."

Therapist: "Is there another way to talk about it or a different word to use that would feel better to you?"

Martin: "I guess, but it's just . . . I've only been thinking about it myself."

Lisa: "Tell me."

Martin: "Sometimes, when you say that you want to eat me out, I try to imagine that you really said you want to suck my cock."

Lisa: [*smiling*] "Oh my God! I can totally say that, honey! Why didn't you just tell me?"

Martin: "Because I feel scared!"

Therapist: "Martin, it makes sense that you feel scared, but I think Lisa wants you to feel safe with her. Telling her these things can help."

A Psychodynamic, Relational Attachment Approach

When clients enter into couples therapy, they each bring with them an attachment history that has shaped their way of interacting in all relationships, including in the context of their current relationship (Wallin, 2007). In order to uncover this attachment history, therapists must use a psychodynamic, relational attachment lens that allows them to recognize the underlying cues that are reflective of a client's attachment style. These cues can range from small, seemingly irrelevant gestures made during the session to flat-out dissociative states that arise when the content becomes too overwhelming. Often, the couple will demonstrate these patterns of attachment in front of the therapist without even realizing it.

In this process of paying close attention, therapists need to be mindful of any countertransference happening throughout the session. It is through this process that therapists can learn from the couple, uncover what patterns are being enacted, and formulate how to intervene and shed light on them. For example, the therapist working with Martin and Lisa was aware of the couple's history and knew each of their attachment styles. Martin's family of origin was supportive on the surface when he first shared his lesbian identity with them. They said they supported him but also made frequent homophobic remarks. When Lisa came into his life, the couple was frequently left out of family events. When Martin shared his transgender identity, it was more than his family was willing to accept: They argued that it was just "too much." Since then, he had struggled with the loss of his family's support, even though it was only ever minimal at best, and he continued to worry that this is what would happen with Lisa at any moment. Martin had an avoidant attachment style, and Lisa had a secure, though sometimes anxious, attachment style. This dynamic resulted in a repeating pattern of fear of rejection and dismissal for Martin and confusion for Lisa.

The following dialogue provides an example of how the therapist working with Lisa and Martin maintained a psychodynamic, relational attachment focus in session.

Martin: "It's been really hard to be close, and it's sad because five years ago, it was like nothing could have come between us."

Therapist: "Well, a lot has happened in these last five years. It makes sense that things would change."

Lisa: "It's just really frustrating because I've been through a lot too, and it doesn't feel like that is allowed to be acknowledged. I'm really trying here, and he just keeps giving me the cold shoulder. When we first met, it took him a long time to open up to me—and, in some ways, I feel like we're right back there again."

Martin: [*looking away*]

Therapist: "So there's something familiar about the emotional place you both find yourself in right now? It feels difficult to be close, and you've both experienced this before."

[*Martin and Lisa both nod.*]

Martin: "I think you're right, but I hadn't really noticed it until just now."

Therapist: "What are you noticing?"

Martin: "I remember when we first got together, Lisa was the first woman I'd ever tried to, you know, get close to, and I was just so nervous. I couldn't believe she might actually like me back. I think I was just really cautious, so I would try to limit my contact with her. I didn't want to get involved because I just knew at any minute she was going to say to herself, 'What am I doing with this person?' and then leave."

Lisa: "It was crazy. I was so into it and said as much the whole time, but it was like pulling teeth to get closer."

Therapist: "Martin, I think you've been waiting for the proverbial 'other shoe to drop' ever since you transitioned. It's been impossible for you to believe that Lisa loves all of you, no matter what your gender identity is. But Lisa is sitting right next to you, and from the way it looks right now, she's not going anywhere. She just wants to be close to you and for you to let her."

Martin: "I'm just so scared sometimes."

Therapist: "Tell Lisa what feels scary."

Martin: "I just feel like my life has been a burden on you and that you have needed to take care of me against your will, like I've forced this on you, and I do know how intense it's been for you. I just feel like I don't want you to have to do this anymore. Like, it's okay, you can stop and just go live your uncomplicated life." [*tears*]

Lisa: "Are you kidding me right now? I love you and our complicated life! Yeah, it hasn't been a picnic, but I'm here, and if I didn't want this life, then I wouldn't be here. You have to know that if I really didn't want to be here, then I would leave. You know that about me: When something doesn't work, I find something that does. Like that crap contracting job I was doing earlier this year, remember?"

Therapist: "Martin, can you hear what Lisa is saying right now?"

Martin: "I don't know. I mean, yes, I think so. But it's so hard to believe that I'm not just some pity case."

Lisa: "Okay, now you're making me angry. I wouldn't be here if I thought you were pitiful. I love everything about you. I love the way you know yourself so well and all that you have been able to do to get to this place in your life. It takes massive amounts of effort and courage—and yes, pain as well—but you have stayed true to who you are, and that makes me love you even more! You inspire me to never back away from what I want in my life!"

Martin: "I guess I didn't know that. I mean, maybe I know it in my head, but sometimes my heart tries to tell me something different."

Therapist: "Yeah, sometimes it takes a while to get those two on the same page, but I think you're both on your way. It's hard when your history with your family has shown you a different reality than the one right in front of you, but the one in front of you is unfolding in a completely different and wonderful way. In the past, with your family, you had to protect yourself, but here, with Lisa, you don't."

Holding in mind this couple's history, including their family history, and the ways it had changed in the course of their relationship was a guide to shed light on the ways their unconscious internal working models tried to steer them to repeat patterns of relating—old patterns that did not work in the current relationship.

Referring Out

As important as it is to be aware of the ever-changing landscape of working with transgender couples, this chapter alone isn't nearly enough training to work competently and ethically with transgender people. There are several avenues for continued training, as well as consultation groups available nationwide. Some of these resources include becoming a member of the World Professional Association for Transgender Health (WPATH) and the U.S. Professional Association for Transgender Health (USPATH). There are also several nationwide and worldwide conferences therapists can attend, such as the annual Gender Spectrum Conference in California. Therapists can also search for local providers who are gender specialists who offer consultation or consultation group work. Knowing when to refer out is important so transgender people will get the proper care they deserve.

Chapter 13

Integrative Alternative Mindfulness and Sexuality

Tammy Nelson, PhD

with contributions by Jen Gunsaullus, PhD

MINDFULNESS AS A SEXUAL INTERVENTION

Not much has been written about the connection between alternative treatment and sex and couples therapy. However, research on mindfulness and sexuality by Lori Brotto and colleagues has found that mindfulness practices can improve sexual functioning in a variety of populations, including women with hypoactive sexual desire, survivors of gynecological cancer, and women with chronic pain.

In particular, the use of mindfulness techniques can increase sexual pleasure and decrease anxiety by addressing symptoms of spectatoring and avoidance that interfere with arousal, desire, and satisfaction. Spectatoring is a phenomenon that involves worrying about sex during the act of having sex. It involves "leaving" one's body during sex and shifting the focus of attention away from the sensations of the sexual experience to outward thoughts about the act itself. This type of performance anxiety can take individuals out of the moment, reduce pleasure, and interfere with the capacity for orgasm, especially among women.

Mindfulness addresses these issues by helping individuals intentionally focus their attention to the present moment in a way that is nonjudgmental and compassionate (Kabat-Zinn, 1990). It allows them to reorient their attention to the here and now, instead of getting in their head and ruminating about the past or worrying about the future.

When individuals cultivate an attitude of mindfulness, they learn to be in the moment, accept any feelings they may be having, and then let those feelings go. They notice their thoughts, emotions, and bodily sensations, and accept them without judgment. By observing their experiences instead of just reacting (e.g., lashing out, shutting down, distracting, or numbing), individuals start to slow down and reflect on what makes them unhappy, anxious, angry, sad, uncomfortable, lonely, or fearful.

Since mindfulness involves developing a nuanced awareness of one's emotions, sensations, and beliefs, it is well suited for breaking through stuck patterns around sex. In particular, when mindfulness techniques are applied to sex and couples therapy, the focus of this mindful awareness is shifted to the giving and receiving of pleasure. One recommendation for couples specifically struggling with low desire is to apply mindful awareness to two aspects of this struggle.

First, there are many nuances to the somatic experience of sexual desire and arousal. Even if the partner with hypoactive sexual desire does not think they ever feel desire or arousal, using mindfulness skills to observe new subtleties of sensations can help that partner see the ways their body *is* responding and then build from there.

Second, mindfulness can help the couple accept, without judgment, that a desire discrepancy is part of their relationship but that doesn't mean there is anything wrong with either partner or the relationship as a whole. A deep level of self- and relationship-acceptance breaks negative patterns of resistance, guilt, and rejection, and it allows the conversation and interactions to blossom in new directions.

These same two components of integrative mindfulness practice can also assist individuals struggling with a variety of physical concerns, such as vaginismus, early ejaculation, and post-surgical gender transitions. Mindfulness allows individuals to notice the details of their bodily responses—gently sitting with emotional and physical sensations of pleasure and discomfort, instead of resisting, numbing, or running—and to accept (with self-compassion) their current situation. This approach allows the body, mind, and heart to work together in unity, instead of fighting and viewing parts of oneself as the enemy.

Although mindfulness is rooted in Buddhist meditation practices, it was first brought to the forefront of psychotherapy in the 1970s by Jon Kabat-Zinn, who found that a Mindfulness-Based Stress Reduction program was comparable, if not more successful, than other psychological interventions in treating anxiety. The efficacy of mindfulness in the treatment of anxiety explains its utility in the treatment of sexual desire, as anxiety is a common factor in many sexual dysfunctions among males and females alike, including erectile dysfunction, ejaculatory dysfunction, orgasmic dysfunction, and vaginismus.

Given the power of the mind-body connection, it is reasonable that the psychological benefits of mindfulness would extend to issues of sexual satisfaction, desire, and arousal. Indeed, the quality of sexual satisfaction is often measured via phrases that are associated with a typical mindful experience. For example, people often describe great sexual encounters by saying things like, "I was fully alive," "I was completely there," "I was totally in tune with my partner," or "I was aware of every breath and every sensation."

Therefore, the following chapter explores the utility of mindfulness as a treatment intervention for anxiety and avoidance in the context of sexual relationships. Using a six-week erotic recovery protocol, I discuss how couples can use methods combining sex therapy, couples therapy, mindfulness, and sensate focus to achieve connectedness, arousal, intimacy, and increased desire in their sexual relationship.

MINDFULNESS, SENSATE FOCUS, AND SOMATIC THERAPY

In their training, *Sensate Focus: The Alchemy of Touch, Mindfulness, and Somatic Therapy*, Constance Avery-Clark and Linda Weiner provide a contemporary look at the integration of mindfulness and sex therapy with their more modern take on sensate focus. In particular, they weave together three areas in the practice of sex therapy—mindfulness, somatic experiencing, and sensate focus—to create a holistic intervention for sexual dysfunction and desire issues.

In terms of **mindfulness**, the goal is for couples to focus on the sensations of pleasure. The protocol is to create an environment where the couple can connect physically—with limited pressure to have intercourse—and to instead focus purely on touch, both in terms of giving and receiving. **Somatic experiencing** involves developing an awareness of both interoceptive and proprioceptive input during this process. This tactile awareness includes being mindful of what individuals feel inside and outside their body in the current moment. Finally, the use of **sensate focus** exercises involves shifting the focus of sex so it is pleasure-based instead of performance-based. Redirecting that focus means repeatedly refocusing one's attention to the sensations experienced in the moment, whether they are pleasurable or uncomfortable, rather than pursuing some end goal. In a culture that is focused on reaching a "finish line" during sex, which is primarily the male orgasm, it can be culturally significant to look at sex this way.

With these three areas in mind, Weiner and Avery-Clark assign couples progressive sexual assignments over a period of time, helping them to increase their ability to tolerate touch, intimacy, and pleasure. Ultimately, the goal of this integrated intervention is to help couples get their conscious mind out of the way and allow the natural sexual response to occur on its own. It does so by helping couples reactivate and restimulate sexual feelings and reduce pressure, expectations, and performance anxiety. It provides an opportunity for what Weiner and Avery-Clark call the reactivation of close, intimate emotions and the restoration of meaningful sexual interest, arousal, and intimacy.

THE USE OF MINDFULNESS IN SEX AND COUPLES THERAPY: A CASE EXAMPLE

Joan and Sheila came to my office because Joan could not orgasm with Sheila, and she was not sure she ever could reach a climax, even with masturbation. This sexual issue had been plaguing their relationship, both in and out of bed. Sheila felt pressured to help Joan with her orgasm "issue," and Joan was embarrassed and felt like the "identified problem." When Joan described the issues that were interfering with her ability to experience sexual pleasure, the following exchange took place:

Joan: "I'm able to relax just fine for a while, but when Sheila starts to get that look on her face, like she wants me to come, you know, orgasm, I get this anxious feeling, and I worry. I start to think, 'Am I taking too long? Does she not want to be doing this? Is she tired? And what is wrong with me, and I think about how cold the bedroom is, and I get mad because she won't ever turn up the heat. Then I think about our heating bills and how expensive it is to live here in this part of the country, and then I wonder where the dog is . . . and well, you get the picture."

Therapist: "So you are not really in the moment at all. When you are relaxed and you can feel the pleasure of the moment, when Sheila touches you, does it feel good?"

Joan: "I don't know. I guess it feels good for a minute. But I can't stay with it."

Therapist: "If when you notice your mind wandering, do you think you could return your focus to the feeling of Sheila's touch?"

Joan: "It's hard because I feel such guilt, really. I know she's trying so hard."

Therapist: "What about you, Sheila? Do you notice when Joan begins to get distracted during sex?"

Sheila: "I can tell when she stops reacting to me. I think it's working, that I am turning her on, and then whatever I am doing stops working. She doesn't respond to me anymore. She just lies there or stiffens up."

Therapist: "So, Joan, are you still feeling the sensations of Sheila's touch in those moments? Or are you totally in the distracting thoughts? The worries? The guilt? Too much to feel what is happening in your skin in that moment?"

Joan: "I just feel distracted, nervous, and worried."

I then talked with Sheila and Joan about the efficacy of mindfulness on improving their sex life and, in general, the quality of their intimacy.

Therapist: "Mindfulness has been shown to reduce stress and keep you in the moment. Are you willing to try a technique right now, just a small thing, to give you an idea of what I mean?"

Joan: "Sure."

Sheila: "That sounds fine."

Therapist: "Take a look around the office right now and notice one thing that perhaps you have never noticed before. Is there something you can find, even though you have been in this office before, and you have been sitting here now for over 45 minutes, that you have never seen before?"

Sheila: "Yes, I see that yellow notebook there."

Joan: "Yes, I see that shadow on the side of the desk."

Therapist: "Great. This is an example of being mindful, of being totally in this moment. You just used a technique to bring you right into this moment, with us, in this room. Now can you imagine a way to use a technique like this when you want to bring yourself back to the sexual experience, to focus on your partner's body? Back into the moment when you are trying to connect sexually?"

They both agreed this small exercise was a beginning to using mindfulness. I was ready to try giving them both more advanced suggestions as they became more comfortable with this small suggestion. In particular, I introduced them to my Six Weeks to Erotic Recovery protocol (Nelson, 2014), which takes the typical sensate focus approach and modifies it to work within the context of integrative sex and couples therapy. This protocol, which is discussed in greater detail in the following section, is suitable for couples who want to reconnect or create a sexual connection.

SIX WEEKS TO EROTIC RECOVERY PROTOCOL

Many couples who come into therapy still prioritize daily activities in front of their intimate life. It is important to let couples know that when their sex life gets pushed to the bottom of their to-do list, one or both will start to feel like the relationship is unimportant, and in turn, one may feel like they are no longer important. The fun and the intimacy may start to erode when the focus is off the erotic life. I emphasize to clients that it's important to plan sex dates in order to prevent disconnection.

In response, some couples may complain that if they have to plan sex, then it is not spontaneous. I often answer by pointing out that someone is usually planning sex at some point—and, frankly, sex can only be spontaneous if people have time for it. Therefore, spontaneity only happens when and if individuals arrange for it, especially if both partners have a busy schedule, a house to run, children, and jobs. When two busy people try to create and continue a connected erotic life, their day-to-day management of the busyness of their work and their family can get in the way.

If a couple has been through a crisis in the relationship—the loss of a job, an illness, or a betrayal that creates emotional distance—then the Six Weeks to Erotic Recovery protocol can help couples reconnect and become sexual again. If a couple has never had an intense erotic connection to begin with, then this protocol can help them connect in a completely new (and perhaps even better) way.

Introducing the Protocol

When explaining the Six Weeks to Erotic Recovery protocol, it is important to tell the couple to follow the directions closely, without rushing the steps. The weeks are laid out in a way that will take the couple slowly from exercise to exercise, beginning with assignments that lead from gentle touch to more sensual touch, and moving into more sexual touching exercises, designed to get the couples used to approaching each other and adding erotic anticipation to the night. As each week progresses, the exercises move into more intimate and erotic emotional connection, and sexual energy should increase between the partners. I typically introduce the protocol to couples as follows:

Make a date with each other for an erotic evening. Erotic dates are an important part of creating spontaneity and represent a special time in your relationship. It shows commitment and intention to your partner, and it adds a caring and more erotic element to your relationship. These six weeks of erotic dates will help you begin again, start fresh, and build anew.

Each week, your erotic date night should be an agreed-upon night (or day) that you will each be able to commit to on a regular basis. Make an agreement that every week on the same day, you will meet at the same time, regardless of how you feel. You may be tired one week, or angry and frustrated the next. However, commit to each other that you will meet anyway.

The erotic date is not about having intercourse, although it usually leads to that by the end of the six weeks, but each week you may have an erotic experience that far surpasses your expectations. Or one week you may feel disappointed and let down. Don't let that stop you.

Your erotic date night is a special, sacred time the two of you are carving out of your busy week together. It is the time that you can be together, without distraction, where you can focus on each other and your erotic relationship. Your erotic life together is the one place where you are not just roommates and friends or coparents. You are lovers. It is designed to focus on remembering why you came together in the first place. However, take it slow. Start with the commitment to meet each week for one night, for your erotic date night.

Finding a time to meet can sometimes be the hardest part. Find a day, mark it on each other's calendars, and make a promise to each other and to yourself that this is your practice time each week—for your erotic life together. Planning this erotic date does several things. It creates consistency, and it shows your partner that you respect and honor them. It also creates erotic anticipation. Your bodies will start to look forward to the times when you are together, even if your minds are on other things.

When the date night arrives, know that you will have some type of sexual contact, even if you don't feel like it in the moment. Sometimes arousal comes before desire, but don't wait for desire to hit. You are creating an environment where desire can flourish, once it is aroused.

On the date night, try to create an atmosphere in the bedroom that will remind both of you that this is a sacred, erotic space for you to be in together. Light candles, put fresh flowers on the nightstand, and put soft sheets and blankets on the bed. Make an extra effort to pick out music your partner will like.

When the big night comes, keep your expectations open and reasonable. If the evening goes as you envisioned it, then great. If it doesn't live up to your expectations, remember this night is a success if it makes you feel connected to your partner.

In the beginning, each night will include massage and touch, with limited erotic contact. There are many ways to experience erotic connection, including laying naked together, soft touch, massage, touching your partner in a sensual way, or pleasuring your own body while your partner watches. There is no wrong way to have an erotic date night. However, you don't want to push the sexual contact right now. We are going to take that pressure away for now.

Your erotic nights will begin with week one and progress to week six. The following are six weeks of suggestions to follow for each night of your six dates.

Exercise One, Night One

The goal of night one is for partners to massage each other without touching any "bikini or bathing suit" areas. The sender serves as the massager, who gives the receiver the experience of just receiving the massage. The sender can touch the receiver in a soft, gentle, massaging touch, using any way that feels good. The sender can massage the whole body while avoiding any touch of the genitals. Avoiding orgasm is the goal. In fact, orgasm and intercourse are off-limits on night one.

The receiver should lie on a soft bed with a sheet or blanket spread out underneath them (one where massage oil will not damage it), a massage mat on the floor, or a massage table with sheets. The sender should begin massaging the receiver's body, using massage oil that is nonperfumed to avoid irritation. The sender moves their massage to the back of the receiving partner, with firm strokes going from slow to fast, or soft to hard. During this process, the receiving partner works on breathing and receiving, noticing what thoughts and feelings surface. The directions for this first erotic night are as follows:

Starting at the extremities and moving inward, or beginning at the neck and shoulders and moving down to the hands or feet, touch the receiver in a sensual manner, in a way that you think your partner would appreciate. Your moves can be sexual, sensual, or erotic, but keep in mind that your partner's bikini or bathing suit areas are off-limits.

You may be surprised how this restriction takes the pressure off you and your partner and allows you to explore each other's bodies in ways that are simply pleasurable with no other goal. It may also create some nice erotic tension when you realize you can't touch places you might want to touch.

Being the receiver, you might long to be touched in places where there are restrictions. Focus on this lovely feeling of sexual tension and be with it, feeling the energy of it. Do not try to change it, evaluate it, or judge the feelings. Just notice them. Notice what is pleasurable.

If you are the sender, notice what feels pleasurable under your hands. Revisit the landscape of your partner's body, remembering that this is a very generous experience, both the giving and taking.

Feel your partner's skin and the smooth, cool texture of their body. If you are the receiver, feel your partner's hands on your skin, and let yourself stay focused on the moment. Notice if your mind is drifting, and let yourself focus again on the feelings of their hands on your skin. Remember, the only goal is to be as much in the moment as possible.

See how much pleasure you can allow yourself in the moment without worrying about where this is going or what your partner is thinking. Notice any thoughts in your head and let them pass through, without holding on to them. Notice any feelings you may be having without trying to change them. Is there resistance, anger, or frustration? Is there sadness, love, or longing? Let the feelings come through, and do not judge or hold on to a desire to accomplish anything. You may notice there are frozen or resistant parts of your body as you feel the massage strokes, or you may not feel anything at all. Perhaps you are numb. You may resent the strokes or welcome them. Feel and welcome all the feelings without judgment.

At some point, whenever you decide, the receiver can offer feedback, but only using a 5-point feedback scale. Using words can be tricky, as you run the risk of judging, critiquing, demanding, or even saying what you want more of. Use the following scale to describe the experience of the sensations you are experiencing, and try not to use words. Using numbers instead of words will allow you to fully experience the sensations without the added complication of trying to think of words to respond. This will free up your brain to just feel the experience instead of trying to make sense of it, assign it meaning, translate it into language, and speak.

1. A one means that you are not comfortable, or it feels almost painful, and your partner will know to move away from that stroke or touch.

2. A two is somewhat uncomfortable, but by no means is it unpleasant.

3. A three is a very nice but more neutral feeling.

4. A four is very good and feels wonderful.

5. A five means you are experiencing intense pleasure and that you want the touch to continue. It feels marvelous and your partner should do more of it, perhaps even on other parts of your body.

The receiver should only provide the sender feedback using this 5-point feedback scale. Words are otherwise off-limits. By using this scale, the receiver can direct the sender to places that feel pleasurable and away from areas that feel uncomfortable. Working on trying to get the receiver to experience a 4 or 5 is desirable but not necessary. Noticing the feelings internally is more important.

Is there resentment, guilt, or wonder? What is going on inside as the feedback is given about the massage?

As the sender, can you change the strokes so they feel better to your partner? Are you surprised your partner is reacting to the strokes the way they are? Would you have thought otherwise? Without judging your performance or your partner's receptivity, take in as much information as you can and continue your movements, noticing how the stroking feels to you. If you have music playing, try to move with the rhythm of the music. Or move to the rhythm of your breath, breathing in and out as you move your hands back and forth on your partner's body. Try and time your breathing with your partner's breath. Breath is an important part of this exercise.

If you can time your breathing to go in and out as you move your hands, this will give you more power and awareness in the massage, and with your partner. You may feel a deeper and more intense connection with the receiver if you are connected to your own breath and with theirs. If you can connect to the rhythm of their breath as you are inhaling and exhaling, you may feel a unique circular rhythm to the experience. As they breathe out, you breathe in. As they breathe in, you breathe out. At some point, you may feel as if the massage is almost a meditative experience.

You may notice that your partner's heartbeat begins to slow. You may feel their pulse slowing and notice that they sigh. You may feel their muscles relax, and their whole body settles into the bed or the floor. Can you get them to relax even more? What makes them relax? Is it the hard, deep strokes or the light, caressing strokes?

You may notice that you feel some of your partner's emotions as you massage them. If you suddenly feel sad or anxious, ask yourself if this is your emotion or if you are picking it up from your partner. See if you can feel your partner's emotions through their skin, the tilt of their head, their shoulders, or their thighs. What do you think they are experiencing right now? Can you calm them down and shift their emotional space through your touch? Can you be more loving, more holding, more caressing? What do you think they need right now?

Normally when we are making love and focusing on intense sexual pleasure, we don't think about the subtleties we may be missing in our partner's emotional experience, or the many signals their body is sending us. See what you may have been missing by focusing deeply now on their inner selves, right beneath the skin. What can you tell about them right in this moment? You may feel some sexual or erotic feelings coming from them, and you may feel those feelings of desire and arousal yourself. Because you have committed to your partner that this week, week one, there will be no intercourse, you can feel those feelings and just breathe. Notice these feelings and do not judge or act on them at this time.

Let yourself inhale the feelings and feel their power. Feel how you appreciate your partner in this way, and let yourself bathe in the attraction to your partner.

Let yourself love them in this moment, and send them your feelings through your hands. Remember, try not to cross the boundary you have both agreed to, and don't cross the bikini areas.

It can be a very powerful addition to this exercise to hold in your mind appreciative and positive thoughts and feelings about your partner as you touch them and as they touch you. Imagine them surrounded by white light and think only clear and kind thoughts about them. While they are touching you or you are touching them, their energy is mingling with yours.

You want this energy to be clear, loving, healing, and without conflict. By visualizing the energy as white light and thinking about your partner in a positive, loving way, you can clear the energy between you, at least temporarily.

The exercise ends with the slowing down of the sender's strokes and deeper breathing. As the sender, slowly lie on top of the receiver, with your full body, breathing deeply and closing your eyes, to seal the experience. Breathe for at least three minutes, or ten deep breaths. If you can hold your partner's hands or open your palm and lay it flat upon their hand while you do this, it will seal your energies more completely. Taking one last deep breath, move off the receiver, thank your partner for letting you touch them, and let them fall into sleep with no pressure to reciprocate.

It is preferable to have one partner serve as the sender this first night and to save the next date night for them to serve as the receiver. This gives the receiver the opportunity to totally relax and fall asleep without any pressure to reciprocate. Although you can send and receive in one night, note that no overt sexual activity can take place this week, even though you may both feel aroused or desire something more erotic. Remember, there is no breast or genital touching at this time. Stay away from the bikini areas and do not engage in intercourse. Hold on to that desire and sit with it. Honor that tonight is not the night.

Appreciation is also an important part of this exercise. Individuals always get more of what they appreciate, which is why it is so important for couples to integrate this appreciation language into their communication and into their erotic date nights. After the evening of sexual connection and pleasure, each partner should share what they appreciated about the night. Ideally, couples should see if they can each share three things they appreciated about the night and about each other. This sharing and giving of appreciation can be done on the date night itself or the next day.

Couples might share appreciations with each other every time they have a sensual experience, or they can practice appreciations every day. When couples say three things they appreciate about their partner on a daily basis, this can bring the relationship to a whole new level, and it can maintain the connection couples are working to build over these six weeks.

Exercise Two, Night Two

The directions for night two are the same as night one, though the sender may now also touch and massage the receiver's breasts and genitals—making sure to touch these parts with the same amount of attention and direction as the rest of the body. Because this week involves the addition of more sensitive areas of the body, the touch should be gentle, and the massage should be only about pleasure and sensual touch. This is not an erotic massage; it is a sensual massage.

When the sender massages the receiver, they should initially focus their attention to every part of the body except for the breasts and the genitals. They should only move to these more sensitive areas when the rest of the body is relaxed and seems open to the idea of further touch. Then the sender can slowly massage the breasts from the outer edges, moving closer to the nipple area, staying soft and gentle, and then moving away from that area to rest of the body. The sender should *not* focus on the breasts for an excessive amount of time.

It is important for the sender to respect their partner's body and to give them time to adjust to the total body massage. The sender should only move to the genitals if there is no resistance. Resistance would include a number lower than 3 on the 5-point feedback scale. Therefore, if the receiving partner says "2" as the sender begins to massage their genitals, they should move away and come back again later in a gentler and less intrusive way.

The sender should not, under any circumstances, attempt penetration of the vagina or anus at this stage. There should be *no* insertion, penetration, or orgasm. This week is only about massage, and the massage should be for sensual pleasure. The goal is only touch. If orgasm happens accidently or as a matter of course, then it is only polite to stay with the partner while they orgasm and to help them to finish, and to listen to anything they may ask to help them have a pleasurable experience. However, individuals should not coerce, force, manipulate, or trick their partner into having an orgasm, or into giving themselves an orgasm. This should be an experience where there is no threat or worry of crossing the boundaries that were set prior to the exercise.

For this exercise, couples are encouraged to enjoy the sensual touch they each enjoy, both as the sender and the receiver. If the couple wants to switch roles on the same night, then each partner can take turns being the sender and the receiver. If the couple wants to divide the exercise into two separate weeks, then the receiver can relax after the initial exercise, and each partner can drift off into sleep, perhaps even holding each other in their arms.

Exercise Three, Night Three

In this week's assignment, the same directions apply as those in weeks one and two, with an extra focus on the genitals and breasts, or whatever parts of the body are the most rewarding to touch. For example, if the sender enjoys massaging the breasts, then they can spend extra time giving pleasure to the breasts this week.

However, the sender will need to elicit feedback from the receiving partner to know if this experience is rewarding to them. Given that dialogue is still off-limits in this exercise, the sender can encourage their partner to give feedback from the 5-point rating scale by simply asking "Number?" and by listening carefully to their partner's reactions to the touch being given. For example, the sender can pay attention to their partner's breathing and notice whether it gets deeper, faster, or shallower. They can listen for any moans, groans, or other sounds that may indicate the receiver is enjoying the experience of being touched.

The key this week is for the sender to give the receiver as intense a pleasurable experience as possible *without* bringing them to orgasm. The sender can try to bring their partner to that pleasurable plateau right before orgasm, but they should not bring them over the edge. The goal is to stop right before orgasm. It is important that partners do not bring each other to the place of no return, to the threshold of ejaculatory inevitability. The goal is to avoid orgasm but to give a pleasurable experience. And remember, penetration is *not* allowed at this stage.

Similar to the preceding week, couples can decide whether they would like to switch being the sender and receiver on the same night, or split the exercise across two different nights.

Exercise Four, Night Four

When couples are ready to practice the fourth exercise, they have reached a crucial stage in their six weeks of erotic dates. Thus far, they have practiced engaging in sensual touch, exhibiting restraint, and communicating in a new manner using the 5-point feedback scale. This week, they get to add something exciting. In particular, they will repeat all of the previous massage exercises and accompanying steps—and, if both partners desire it, they can also add orgasm but without penetration of any kind. Only non-penetrative orgasm and manipulation are permitted in this week's exercise.

For heterosexual couples, the female should always serve as the receiver first so she can have her orgasm prior to the male orgasm. Using the techniques in week one, the sender should take their time and give the receiver a slow and sensual massage. The sender can focus on the receiving partner's breasts or genitals while listening carefully to their feedback so they know what is working for them and what they are enjoying.

If the receiver is relaxed, aroused, and enjoying the touch, then the sender can continue with a genital massage, starting at the extremities and moving in toward the clitoris if they are touching a woman, and starting with a light stroke and moving to a firmer stoke on the penis if they are touching a man. The sender should bring their partner to orgasm manually and then hold them closely, letting them come down from the heightened sexual experience and letting them feel the flood of pleasure in their body with no pressure to reciprocate or perform in the moment.[1]

When the receiver is ready, the couple may want to switch and begin again as sender and receiver, or they may decide to split this exercise into two separate nights. In the latter case, it is a good idea to drift off into sleep holding one another and letting the pleasure of the moment be what it is, without asking more of each other or of the experience.

---

[1] Ian Kerner provides a good reference for manual stimulation in his two books, *She Comes First: The Thinking Man's Guide to Pleasuring a Woman* (2004) and *He Comes Next: The Thinking Woman's Guide to Pleasuring a Man* (2006).

Exercise Five, Night Five

Once couples reach week five, they can add manual penetration to this sensual and erotic date night experience, assuming they are ready for and desire it. However, penetration at this stage can only involve the fingers, and it can only occur after the sender has given the receiver a massage and has provided enough manual stimulation to ensure that penetration of the vagina or anus is welcome.

This is the week that a good lubricant—one without warming, cooling, heating, smell, or taste—is important. It is preferable to use one that is as plain and gel-like as possible. A water-based lubricant is also best for cleanup. The sender should make sure their hands are clean and that both partners have agreed prior to the date night that manipulation of the genitals is welcome and insertion of fingers is acceptable if there is sufficient stimulation. It is important to ensure there is enough arousal so the vagina is prepared to receive insertion, and if anal stimulation is desired, that there is enough relaxation and preparation. As always, stimulation and insertion must also be desired by the receiver.

Similar to week four, couples can integrate orgasm in this week as well. When the sender is giving the receiving partner an orgasm, they may want to include insertion at the same time. If they want to take the exercise to a whole new level, they can also maintain eye contact throughout the orgasm. During this process, both partners should breathe together and try to keep their eyes locked on each other. If one partner is unable to maintain eye contact with both eyes, then they can gaze into their partner's left eye, as it is sometimes easier to gaze into one eye than both. The energy of the left eye gaze can make both partners feel the moment of orgasm, which can be a shared sensual moment through many levels of connection.

During this experience, the sender is touching, hearing, seeing, smelling, and perhaps even experiencing other senses as well. The focus of attention should be on all of these senses as the sender penetrates their partner. They must be with the receiving partner in as many ways as they can, opening themselves fully to their partner and to their pleasure. Giving and sending pleasure can be as powerful a gift as receiving and being open to pleasure.

If the sender is unable to give their partner an orgasm for whatever reason (e.g., they may be tired, shy, sore, full, frustrated), then the sender has several choices. They can let the receiver bring themselves to orgasm, with the receiver's hand guiding their own genital manipulation and the sender's hand on top. Alternatively, couples can let go of the goal of orgasm altogether. Remember, orgasm is always optional. It is never mandatory. It is never the goal of the exercise. The orgasm can happen or not.

If the receiver is a male partner and he loses his erection, then it is important he not chase it, fight it, or try to force it. He should let go of the need to be hard and let the sender enjoy the feeling of his flaccid penis in their hand. If the receiver is a female partner and she cannot have an orgasm, then she can either bring herself to orgasm as her partner penetrates her manually, or she can let it go and be happy with some gentle massage and gentle penetration. It is important that couples value the moment for what it is and what it has brought them as they maintain eye contact, hold positive thoughts about their partner, and end the experience by holding one another.

Similar to previous weeks, couples can decide before beginning the date night if they are going to switch being the receiver and sender in the same evening, or if they will split the experience into two nights.

Exercise Six, Night Six

Once couples reach this final stage in the protocol, digital penetration, orgasm, touching of the breasts and genitals, and sensual massage are all permitted. The key to this week is that couples have a choice in how they spend the night. The sender can enjoy the sensation of giving, and their partner can enjoy the sensation of receiving. The sender can choose to give their partner a massage, or they can give their partner a sensual massage with an orgasm at the end. However, they should try to avoid or delay genital penetration of the anus or vagina. Intercourse or insertion is not the goal. The idea is to let go of any goal at all except for being in the moment.

In addition, this week adds a new element to the process: emotional disclosure. During this final erotic date, both partners should talk about any feelings that come up throughout the exercise. Couples can check in with each other by asking questions such as, "How are you feeling now?" If at any point either partner experiences an emotion, either positive or negative, then they should try to describe it in the moment. For example, they might say, "Right now, I feel happy and relaxed." Or, if a partner is feeling withdrawn or shutdown, they might say, "I need a time out" or "Can we start over?"

Even if a partner feels unpleasant feelings in that moment, sharing these feelings does not mean the night has to end. It may mean the couple is connecting at a whole new level, and they can combine this new level of emotional disclosure with sensual touch. If either partner needs a break, they can stop the sexual touch and go back to the massage portion of the exercise until their emotions calm down or change. At some point in the massage, that partner may relax and their feelings may shift, allowing them to feel ready for more intensive experiences, like an orgasm or eye contact.

Couples should talk about their feelings before, during, and after the experience. They should try not to judge each other about whether they are ready for intercourse. It is important that they do not attempt to intellectualize their partner's feelings or try to get them out of a particular emotional state. The goal is *not* to "fix" one's partner, so it is not appropriate to make statements such as, "Don't feel sad" or "You shouldn't be angry." Doing so can make the other partner feel like their feelings are wrong.

Rather, it is important for individuals to respond in these instances with validating and empathizing statements. For example, if one partner says something like, "I am feeling stuck. I am unhappy," then a validating response would simply be, "I hear you are feeling unhappy." At that point, they could ask their partner if they need a break and, if so, they could slow down the experience and simply hold their partner. Once both parties are ready to resume giving or receiving a massage, they can return to the exercise and move on to genital massage, penetration, and orgasm, if desired.

AN EXERCISE IN INTIMACY

When I told Joan and Sheila about the Six Weeks to Erotic Recovery, they took an entire week to come to an agreement that they would commit to the protocol. The idea was that they would put off sexual intercourse of any kind during the protocol and follow the directions for each night of the six dates. After deciding to commit to the protocol, they took another week to decide which night would work for both of them, and they finally agreed on Thursday nights. They penciled the dates into their calendars to remind themselves that they were moving forward in therapy and in their sexual commitment to each other. Although the protocol can be completed in six weeks, Joan and Sheila decided to stretch it into a 12-week exercise instead by splitting each week into two nights. This allowed them to concentrate fully on being either the sender or receiver, without having to switch roles on the same night.

When I asked for their feedback at the completion of the protocol, Sheila replied, "It seemed that Joan trusted me more. Our hearts were more in alignment. After one or two dates, I realized there was no pressure to perform and I could just let go. I had no expectation and no judgment. It was freeing."

Similarly, Joan said, "I felt we really connected by the fifth session, which felt new for us. I was able to really stay present, and I didn't try to avoid being with her. I didn't go out of the room in my head. I was able to stay with her the whole time."

When I told them both that they could come back to these exercises anytime they wanted to feel connected or realign with each other, they both agreed that these dates would help their relationship forever. "Oh, we are going to have date nights like this every week!" Joan said.

No matter how a couple works the six-week protocol, the exercises are focused on intimacy, closeness, and finding a way to focus on the moment. Talking and negotiating how to work these exercises is the beginning of preparing for lovemaking. For a practice that begins with a once-a-week erotic date, these six weeks of exercises can guide couples back to a sex life that was previously not working. It provides them with a guide to a lifelong practice of sensuality, intimacy, and connection.

CONCLUSION

In any intimate interaction, choosing to be awake and present with one's partner, both emotionally and sexually, can increase the level of connection, arousal, intimacy, and desire each partner feels. In fact, when people are asked to describe qualities of "great sex" or "optimal sexuality," there is one prominent theme that emerges—and that is being present (Kleinplatz et al., 2009). Regardless of how couples operate in their relationship or with regard to their sexual functioning, being mindfully present ultimately leads to passion and great sex.

Chapter 14

The Future of Sex: What Do Polyamory and Technology Mean for Monogamy?

Tammy Nelson, PhD

THE NEW MARRIAGE: A NEW MONOGAMY

Monogamy as a concept is more fluidly defined than ever before, and there is a wider definition of what is acceptable in relationships. Couples are negotiating monogamy in new ways, one of which includes polyamory, meaning that couples define their fidelity through transparency and disclosure rather than by maintaining sexual fidelity to one partner. People are increasingly identifying themselves as preferring this nontraditional relationship lifestyle, with some researchers estimating that about 4 percent of the U.S. population is involved in a polyamorous relationship (Rubin, Moors, Matsick, Ziegler, & Conley, 2014). That estimate translates to over 10 million people, which means there are enough polyamorous people to fill the island of Manhattan.

Some researchers argue that this increase in polyamory is a reflection of low sexual desire in long-term relationships or a generational response to high rates of infidelity, which can range anywhere from 20 to 55 percent for women and 40 to 65 percent for men (Schmitt & Buss, 2001; Tafoya & Spitzberg, 2007; Vaughan, 2003).

However, according to Helen Fisher—a biological anthropologist at the Kinsey Institute—extramarital affairs have always happened at this high rate and are only now being reported more accurately (Fisher, 1992). If infidelity is not new, then this upsurge in polyamory may be due to the longevity of the human life span that has changed across centuries. In today's society, people are living longer, with an average life expectancy of 78 years, which means people can be married to the same person for up to 50, 60, or even 70 years, all with the expectation of monogamy and sexual fidelity. In turn, couples may be looking for new ways to manage the loss of interest in one partner, which is an inevitable result of cohabitation and long-term commitment.

Polyamorists describe themselves as ethically nonmonogamous and differentiate themselves from couples who have affairs or engage in "swinging." According to polyamorists, swingers enjoy having sex with multiple partners for the rush of new-partner sex. In contrast, "poly" couples define themselves as uniquely progressive. They claim to have discovered that the secret to a long-term partnership is to have multiple partners, to overcome jealousy and possessiveness, and to live in harmony with all of these partners at the same time. The new rules of attachment that characterize open marriage and polyamory involve a more fluid idea of connection to the primary partner. In polyamorous relationships, there is an assumption that the primary partner remains the main attachment, and that secondary, tertiary, and other attachments can happen without affecting the primary attachment. Some poly relationships are nonhierarchical and do not recognize a primary partnership, but see all their relationships as equal in importance.

In fact, polys insist that not only can jealousy be overcome as a baser, less necessary emotion; they say they can actually be happy if their partner finds pleasure with someone else. They call this process *compersion*, which is a word invented in a California commune that means "the desire to find satisfaction in a partner's happiness"—even if that means the partner is having sex or finding emotional fulfillment with someone else. Compersion is the opposite of jealousy, and poly couples believe it is the goal of a mature relationship.[1]

Poly couples come in many shapes, sizes, pairs, triads, quads, and larger groups, which are called clusters (or "polysystems"). Some clusters or poly pods include single lovers that the couples share between them. These are sometimes called "unicorns," which are highly desirable bisexual lovers. Some clusters have lovers that never cross the line of the primary partnership; the married primary partner does not share the lovers, and they perhaps have not even met. Many poly couples practice polyfidelity, which means their system is a closed one that is not open to letting in other lovers. They are committed to each other and to their system.

But are these couples polyamorous or are they just "polysexual"? Are polys seeking pleasure through sexual contact with multiple partners and justifying it under some broader social construct they are calling multiple love? In my work with poly couples and couples in open relationships, I have talked to both men and women, straight and gay, who have described polyamory as a unique way of dealing with long-term commitment *and* sexuality. To some, polyamory may sound challenging, but to others, it is the answer to their questions about long-term monogamy.

Couples who live in open relationships and have a polyamorist lifestyle reflect a cultural swing toward negotiated fidelity, what I call the "new monogamy" (Nelson, 2012).[2] Several of the couples I see for counseling have come into my office not to save

---

[1] Helen Fisher, an outspoken critic of polyamorous relationships, argues that jealousy and monogamy are hardwired into humans and that polyamorous couples are "fighting Mother Nature" in trying to overcome this instinctual response (Bennett, 2009). In fact, for some individuals, a total lack of jealousy and possessiveness in a relationship may not be compersion but, rather, an indication of an underlying problem. It may reflect a pathological inability to attach in relationships. A relationship devoid of reactivity in response to threat from competitive mating may be indicative of sociopathy, a lack of empathy, or the chronically unattached nature of idealism of the single, premarital, non-pair bonded youth.

[2] A TEDx Talk regarding the new monogamy can be found at https://www.youtube.com/watch?v=3JMioYaBJDc.

their marriage but to help negotiate the complicated communication lines of multiple partnerships. They maintain a primary connection and are legally married. On the side, they have a variety of sexual and loving partners.

For example, one couple I worked with, Mark and Laura, had a "V" relationship. There was a third young man in their polysystem, Justin, who was in love with Mark. Justin did have sex with Laura, but he spent every Saturday night in bed with Mark while Laura slept in the guest room. Mark and Justin would play video games and hang out with friends when Justin was sleeping over.

When I asked Laura if she felt lonely, jealous, or left out, she replied, "Sometimes, but only if they don't tell me what they are doing. If I know they're in the next room, then I am somehow involved and, frankly, it turns me on. I am happy for them. And I get to have sex with Mark the rest of the week. I feel like I am giving him a gift. Why would he ever cheat on me when he can have what he wants?"

THE LONGEVITY OF POLYAMOROUS RELATIONSHIPS

What does the increase in polyamorous relationships mean from a cultural perspective? Is marriage changing to accommodate a new definition of fidelity, or is this just a blip on the screen of sexual mores, like swinging was in the 70s? Without the luxury of a longitudinal study, we can make some guesses about the long-term survival of these sexually "open" relationships, but these are only suppositions based on past cultural swings.

During the 1970s, the "swinging" movement eventually led to a rise in sexually transmitted diseases and swung back (no pun intended) to a more conservative sexuality and, in turn, an increase in divorce rates. As divorce rates rose, AIDS increased and there was an increase in serial monogamy. People got remarried at a faster rate than ever, and we saw an increase in drug involvement with sex similar to the "free love" movement of the 1960s.

In the 1990s, the emergence of "roofies"—the date-rape drugs of the new millennium—made sexuality more dangerous, particularly for college-age women. At the same time, education about sexuality and women's rights to pleasure and orgasm have increased in the current era, as it did in the 1970s. We also have a new generation of swinging clubs for couples to engage in sexual freedom with multiple partners. These clubs are different than the swinging groups from past decades in that the focus is on *staying* with one's partner and joining in group sex. The idea of polyamory implies that one can love more than one partner and still be faithful to the primary partner. It is no longer about sexuality but an attached relationship.

Polyamorists are in the news every day claiming celebrity. Regardless of one's personal beliefs about monogamy, fidelity, and marriage, therapists are likely to have at least one person walk through their treatment room door who is either involved in or wants to be involved in an open relationship. Whatever therapists may feel about these relationships, they are happening, and these couples, triads, quads, and systems will need therapy like anyone else affected by relationship stressors—perhaps even more so due to the sheer complexity of their set-up.

Treatment Considerations When Working with Polyamorous Couples

How can therapists be available for this new level of relationship challenge when it comes to therapy? At a minimum, it means therapists working with polyamorous couples should examine the assumptions they are making about how marriage or partnerships are supposed to work. Therapists who are unfamiliar with the structure and philosophy of polyamorous relationships may pathologize or alienate couples who seek treatment, so they must evaluate their own implicit expectations before working with couples who are negotiating more fluid agreements and open relationships. In addition, therapists must remember that the couple—not the therapist—determines the "rules" of their relationship. When rules around infidelity are broached, it is less important what it means to the therapist than what it means to the couple.

For example, Julia was a 36-year-old wife and a mother of two. She sat in my office and talked to me about her relationships with her boyfriend, Jasper, and her husband, Lawrence. She related, "Finding emotional and erotic satisfaction with multiple partners is our birthright, isn't it? Who's to tell us we shouldn't love more than one person? I want an open relationship, and I want to do it for my husband. It's just not easy. But I look at my neighbors, and they are all cheating on each other. So who has it better? Me, who can sleep with whomever I want? I'm not lying to my husband. He knows where I am at night. In our open marriage it's hard, for sure. We get jealous, but we do it anyway. This way it's all out in the open."

I asked Julia directly, "Do you think your polyamorous open marriage is a way to avoid intimacy with your husband?"

Julia looked annoyed. "Why do all therapists judge open relationships? Even you?"

I nodded. "You're right. That did sound like I was judging your relationship. But I know that you and your husband Lawrence have some problems with sharing your feelings."

"Well, okay, that is true," she said.

Even though Julia and Lawrence were committed to each other and to their open relationship, their primary partnership still needed work. I asked Julia if she wanted to bring in her husband for therapy. When they came in together to my office, I asked Lawrence how he was feeling about their relationship. "I feel fine about Julia and Jasper, if that's what you mean. But I feel like Julia doesn't really tell me how she's feeling about things."

I then asked Julia what she wanted to talk about with Lawrence now that we were here in the session.

"I am afraid that since I am with Jasper, Lawrence will find and get involved in a relationship with one of the women he talks to online."

"I am confused," Lawrence said, "I thought you were okay with me finding a girlfriend as long as I don't spend too much emotional time with her. I am confused."

I asked them to revisit the "rules" of their relationship, which they had decided on when they first started to open their relationship. They replied that fidelity was important in their poly relationship, as it is in any committed partnership. If either of them were to "cheat" by going outside their agreed-upon partners, or if they were to have a sexual relationship with anyone and not tell the other, then this would be a betrayal not only to the other, but to the integrity of the marriage.

As Julia and Lawrence's example illustrates, consensual non-monogamy is different than having an affair. It is not sex for recreation or entertainment. It is not sex to improve the erotic connection. It is negotiated non-monogamy between two committed partners. It is a personal decision between two adults. Sex and couples therapy with polyamorists is similar to any therapeutic work with couples, but it allows for an understanding of the negotiation of non-monogamy, perhaps allowing for elements of group therapy as well.

As relationships change and the rules of honesty and disclosure change, transparency becomes the rule. When transparency is negotiated, this affects the boundaries of the whole system. This boundary issue becomes paramount as couples strive to maintain intimacy with a primary or secondary partner, or when there are three or more in a polysystem who are trying to create intimate connection and emotional attachment. Often, there can be a disruption in the system or between the primary partners that can occur as the poly relationship develops over time.

The developmental stages of healthy poly relationships are the same as those of other interpersonal relationships. There is the new relationship stage, or falling in love stage, in which partners are enamored with each other, are compulsively sexually involved, obsess about their time together, and may neglect other family members and responsibilities. This phase generally lasts anywhere from 3 to 24 months. After this phase, the couple (or triad) enters the conflict phase, which can result in distancing, arguing, and triangulation among other members of the polysystem.

Clinically, treatment at this phase may include a group meeting to determine the dynamics of the polysystem and how it is affecting parenting, household management, time spent negotiating, and financial obligations. The primary partner may seek treatment at this point to negotiate keeping or dismissing a secondary partner. Many times, when in the conflict phase, a partner will project their frustration onto their spouse instead of their lover and blame them for the end of the secondary relationship.

For example, Mark and Laura, the polys with the "V" system, eventually ended their relationship with Justin. Laura found that Justin wanted more time with Mark than just weekend nights, and she became resentful that Justin did not have to do household chores like mow the lawn. In therapy, Mark had commented that he didn't like that Justin ate all his food and drank all his beer, and Laura seemed to attach herself to this statement and used Mark's "resentment" of Justin to justify ending the secondary relationship. When Mark learned that Laura had ended the relationship with Justin, he was taken aback that she had done so without consulting him first. She also reported having told Justin that Mark was to blame for the dissolution of the relationship, which caused Mark even further anger and hurt. Therapy worked to process this source of conflict and help Laura take responsibility for her actions instead of blaming Mark for them.

In addition, conflict can arise when one primary partner in the polysystem is not as invested in, or wants to stop participating in, the poly lifestyle. What I frequently see in my office is a couple in which one partner is actively pursuing the poly lifestyle and convinces the other partner or spouse to be involved. Often, it is the male partner who initiates bringing in the first outside partner. Eventually, he may grow tired of the system, become bored or threatened, or grow older and prefer to settle back down with his primary mate. At that time, what I see is the wife or primary female partner—who was at first reluctant but is now fully engaged in the lifestyle after having experienced alternatives to monogamy—refusing to disengage from her outside lovers. This divergence can cause stress and disappointment, and it is sometimes the beginning of what leads to separation and divorce.

For example, Alana and Trent first began a poly relationship when Trent decided he was "not into monogamy" and told Alana he wanted to open up their marriage to include other outside relationships. Alana was resistant to the idea until they had three or four deeper conversations about how they would handle conflict, jealousy, and emotional connection with outside partners. Once Alana believed Trent would stay connected to her and was not interested in finding a replacement wife, she agreed.

Trent dated three women he met on a poly website, and each time Alana waited for him at home while he was out with the other woman. She resisted dating for almost nine months. When she finally met someone at work and started dating him, she told Trent she had feelings for this man and was not interested in dating other people. She was happy with their current arrangement. In therapy, Trent described feeling nervous about her relationship with this man. He was afraid it would destroy their marriage and was no longer as interested in pursuing outside relationships. In response, Alana said, "Too bad. Now that I am into it, it's too late. He opened the door. I didn't want to go through the door. Now I am all the way out of the room, and I can't go back."

THE MONOGAMY CONTINUUM

In the new monogamy, the term *monogamy* is fluid. Monogamy is not one thing but a continuum. It is a description of a relationship that involves making a daily "choice." In other words, monogamy is not a one-time choice that is made at the altar when a couple says, "I do" and the issue is closed, never to be discussed again. That would be akin to saying, "I told you I loved you when I married you, so we shouldn't have to ever say it again, or revisit the idea, or talk about what it means under different conditions or at different times of our lives."

In contrast, *monogamy* is an active word. It is sometimes a verb and sometimes an adjective—for example, to be monogamous, monogamish, very monogamous, or less than monogamous. It is not a noun, a fixed state, or a one-time label that is affixed and permanent. Every day, one has to choose to be monogamous, and the type of monogamy that fits an individual, a couple, and their relationship may change, given the circumstances, on any given day.

Monogamy as a continuum flows from totally closed—meaning no sexual, sensual, or emotional connection with others outside of the marriage—to totally open, with both partners being allowed to fully explore sexual, sensual, and emotional connections with people besides the primary partner, while still making that partner the top priority (hence "monogamy"). The continuum may also include having physically or emotionally affectionate and bonded outside relationships without sex, sexual play with others if both partners are present, or total openness, where both partners are allowed unlimited sexual or emotional relationships with others.

Monogamy Agreements

Monogamy agreements are implicit and explicit commitments individuals make with their partners regarding their expectations of fidelity. All partners who define themselves as "a couple" (and even couples who have outside partners) inevitably come to some kind of agreement about their monogamy—explicit, implicit, or both—whether it is fully realized or not yet expressed.

An *explicit monogamy agreement* is a commitment both partners make out loud that defines the relationship's overt "rules" or structure. This can involve a marriage vow or a partnership agreement that generally assumes and sometimes articulates both a personal and legal oath: We pledge our troth to one other person. It is an agreement a couple makes in front of their families, community, church, synagogue, or mosque. It is a tribal type of commitment that they pass on through their families, culture, and lineage, adapting the words that are customary and personal to them, which may be handed down through the generations. The words have meaning, and they ring true on many levels. They feel right. They feel true. But when they don't, people alter them and adjust. They change them as they grow. For instance, very few couples still include the traditional language of "obeying" in their wedding vows ("I promise to love, honor, and obey . . ."), even though that may have been common practice only 50 years ago in Christian wedding ceremonies.

Couples generally take this explicit monogamy agreement as a contract, and they take it seriously, regardless of whether they end up breaking it or changing it at some point in their marriage or partnership. This contract usually has a time line, and many times the length of the contract persists "until death"—referring to the death of one partner or the relationship itself. Usually, there is the expectation that romantic and sexual involvement with others is forbidden. The couple believes in the agreement, even if they don't necessarily maintain it. They believe in being monogamous and holding true to their agreements.

In contrast, an *implicit monogamy agreement* refers to the unspoken understanding each person has about what monogamy actually means, which might differ from the spoken, explicit monogamy agreement made between partners. This implicit agreement is based on cultural mores, religious beliefs (or lack thereof), traditional sex roles, family background, and personal moral values. These implicit beliefs may never be openly discussed before the commitment ceremony, or even after.

Monogamy means something different for everyone, so each partner may hold a different or even opposing understanding of what they think the agreement means. For example, implicit monogamy agreements might include things like, "We should promise to be faithful until one of us grows tired of the other. Then we should move on and find other partners or break up"; or "I won't cheat, but I might check out people online"; or "I'll be faithful except for strip clubs. They don't count."

Because couples often have different implicit assumptions about what monogamy means, each partner may believe they are being true to their explicit monogamy agreement when they are actually following a different set of guidelines. They may assume their partner is following these same guidelines and never discuss the rules, which can lead to relationship ruptures when one partner crosses an unspoken boundary that the other partner unknowingly had set. Sometimes, people also hold sexist or misogynistic beliefs that underlie their implicit assumptions (e.g., "I'm a guy, so it's okay for me to flirt; it's just what we do. The future of the relationship is up for grabs"), but they don't voice these beliefs to their partner. It's not until there is a conflict in the relationship that these beliefs rise to the surface, after which both partners may be surprised to learn these hidden beliefs are influencing their implicit assumptions about monogamy. Most couples never talk about their assumptions until a problem happens.

To avoid a crisis of misunderstanding, each partner needs to make their implicit assumptions explicit so they can avoid problems of communication, expectation, and disappointment. The couple needs to get clear about what each person is committing to and perhaps consider changing their monogamy agreement. When individuals get married or enter into a partnership, they don't necessarily commit to the other person. They commit to the agreement. Therefore, if a client is having relationship trouble, or doubts that they chose the right partner, it is not necessarily a sign that they've committed to the wrong person. They may have committed to the wrong agreement.

In this case, couples can choose to rewrite their monogamy agreement. This process can work with and for anyone. All it takes is openness, conversation, dialogue, empathy, and understanding. To have a workable monogamy, both partners have to agree on what works for them. This new monogamy agreement can integrate both their explicit and implicit monogamy agreements, thus eliminating the "monogamy gap" that so often exists between what is spoken and what is assumed. This new agreement should lay out specific and mutually agreed upon expectations and limitations that define the relationship, including romantic and sexual involvement with others. It answers questions such as, "Will we have relationships outside of the marriage?" or "Will we communicate with strangers online?" or "Is it okay to have social media relationships?"

The trick is to have couples establish and continually revisit their own rules so they can conform enough to their own set of values. No one can define what it means to be in an "open, monogamous relationship" except for the couple. By defining the boundaries of their relationship, each partner knows where the other stands, while allowing enough freedom for each partner to grow. Individuals need safety to feel attached, and they need freedom to feel that they can each grow within and outside of the relationship. Couples should revisit this agreement over and over again, perhaps once a month, once a year, or at the very least, every couple of years. Maybe even every weekend. What matters is that the monogamy agreement remains a talkable aspect of the relationship.

Has Technology Changed the Way We View Sex?

What about how we view monogamy when it comes to technology? Can individuals stay monogamous when they live in an era that is rife with electronics and robotics? Is technology a new challenge to monogamy or a new form of open relationship?

The increase in technology has changed not only the way we view life but who we are as people. The use of smartphones, computers, smart watches, and other handheld devices has turned us all into partial-hybrid-humans. We have almost become cyborgs, sporting robotic extensions off our own bodies, with our phones really becoming more like high-tech, nonpermanent partial extensions of our limbs. We feel obligated to check in, post, swipe, update, and check out almost all the time. We barely put down or turn off our tech, even when we sleep.

The technology of today has changed us all from simple humans into high-tech digital beings. What if individuals paid this same type of obsessive technical attention to their digital devices when it came to sexuality? It appears that many people do. Pornography use has increased by 75 percent over the past 15 years, and individuals' erotic identity is influenced more by their digitized pursuits than ever before. In addition, with the development of more high-tech teledildonics[3] and perhaps even robotic sex partners, pornography has become more interactive than ever before.

This new form of interaction between a real person and a computer has created a gray area for sex and relationships and more than a little confusion around monogamy, which used to be quite black and white. The rules used to be clear: Don't touch, or you're cheating. However, what does cheating mean now? Can someone cheat on their partner while lying in bed next to them? For many, porn and webcam sex has become a way to maintain monogamy, allowing for variety and excitement with a non-touch partner— like a computerized, digital affair. However, pornography is so accessible and virtually realistic now that individuals can cheat on their partners without ever meeting another real person. It makes porn more interactive and tempting.

For example, Joe and Bob came to my office when Joe was caught on the computer masturbating to pornography. Joe and Bob had an implicit monogamy agreement that included pornography as part of their relationship: They could each watch it, but they had to talk to each other about it, and it could not be used to replace their sex life with each other. However, when Bob walked in on Joe, he had been watching pornography while interacting with someone over a webcam using teledildonics. Bob felt this was much more than purely viewing pornography. It felt like a different form of relationship, which violated their agreement.

Joe explained, "I did realize Bob wouldn't like it, but I got this handheld device free from this company. They sent it to me in the mail, and I wanted to try it. It's like a device that connects to the porn movie. And when someone else is watching it too, you can click on the webcam. I was fascinated by it. I had to try it."

Bob said, "I know that Joe is into the technology stuff, and it makes sense that he would be into the handheld dildo thing. But it vibrated and moved along with this other person. This is like being with an actual person."

"Let's talk about your monogamy agreement," I said. "Is there something you want to update in your agreement?"

---

[3] Teledildonics are sex toys that can be controlled via an Internet connection, providing the technology needed to stimulate another person remotely.

Joe said, "Yes, I think we should open our monogamy agreement and include other people as long as they are virtual, and we are not touching each other physically."

Bob replied, "I don't agree; I don't want anyone else in our monogamous relationship, even if they are virtual."

Bob and Joe met together in therapy for three more sessions before they could come to any agreement about their monogamy. We continued to discuss the effect that virtual reality and technology and pornography would have on their relationship.

New Tech Can Give Users a Fuller Sexual Experience

Virtual reality porn is currently happening. In August 2014, the adult movie streaming service provider SugarInstant (formerly known as SugarDVD) announced they would begin partnering with Oculus to make adult movies in 3D and that these movies would have the added benefit of being extra interactive. At this same time, the adult entertainment industry began creating new life-size sex toys to go along with these 3D movies, called Virtual Dolls. These Virtual Dolls, which are primarily marketed to men, are interactive, technical, and robotic sex partners.

As virtual reality and artificial intelligence (AI) models have been increasingly made available to the public, prices have come down to a reasonable, everyday scale. For instance, Naughty America (a porn site) and Fleshlight (a sex toy company) have combined forces to integrate porn movies with sex toys so the experience of virtual reality porn meshes the visual experience with the physical one.

Similarly, Kiiro, a sex toy manufacturer, is working with video companies to integrate 4D films with a virtual reality headset for a full 360-degree immersive visual experience (and when used with a toy, an interactive experience as well). In addition, the patent on teledildonics has expired, paving the way for more inventors to create more lifelike sex toys that can connect to pornographic content or to a remote partner who has a controller. According to Bryony Cole, the founder of Future of Sex (www.futureofsex.org), these human interactions with tech can (and do) give users the experience of a full sexual encounter. The experience of online sex is moving to a whole new level and will never be the same.

What Does this Mean for the Future of Sexual Relationships?

We have more questions than answers right now about sex and tech. Will virtual reality robots and AI dolls add to a culture of aloneness by creating more isolation and decreasing connection? Are robots a result of a burgeoning loneliness and isolation, or are they a solution? What happens to real intimacy when there is no eye contact, when there is nothing to gaze into or empathize with but a circuit board?

It's important to keep asking these questions, as well as to stay open and curious, in order to evaluate the ethics of what we're doing and where the field of sex tech is going. Perhaps the sex-tech industry will create more connection by providing ways individuals can practice real intimacy. For example, the use of sex and tech can be used to provide sex education for both men and women, gay and straight, trans and intersex, who might need to learn about sex. It can teach them how to orgasm, how to self-cure from sexual dysfunction, and how to act out fantasies or generally improve their erotic lives.

Some robotics companies are already experimenting with these ideas. The best example in the sex and tech market is the company RealBotix, which has created a virtual-reality headset that can be used alongside a life-size sex doll called "RealDoll." You can soon buy their robotic sex doll with AI for about $20,000.[4] Futurists, like Ian Pearson, predict that sex with robots will outpace human-to-human sex by 2050, and David Levy—an expert on AI—predicts we will marry our robots by then. In Japan, this is already happening.

Still, there is an understandable fear that relationships with sex tech will dehumanize us. These fears parallel the concerns we have had as technology has progressed throughout the years. For example, when the telephone was first invented in the late 1800s, we were afraid it would take away eye contact. When texting became prevalent in the late 1900s and early 2000s, everyone feared it would take away our voice. Now, and in the future, the question remains whether sex with robots will take away our humanity.

Our greatest fear is that robots will take over one day, even over our relationships. We fear that they will replace our lovers and our families. That they will replace us. We can never measure up to a "perfect" robot. We cannot help but project human emotions onto lifeless machines. We are afraid of a world where robots look like us but cannot think or feel, as they lack the basic moral fiber of humanity.

Regardless, it is clear that the future of sex and tech will influence a whole generation of couples and how they relate to one another. Instead of fighting the tide of technology, perhaps we can embrace the way we integrate these changing applications and entertain the possibility that *what we fear could ultimately be good for us.*

CONCLUSION

The future of relationships and sex will most certainly include technology. We are all moving into a more innovative and connected world, one in which we have the opportunity for new types of relating, where we can stay connected at a global level and where we will be challenged on a personal level to find new ways to stay intimate and channel our erotic energy into our one-on-one partnerships. We will be exposed to more options for non-monogamy, and yet we will be able to choose to expand our relationships to include artificially intelligent beings and ways to enhance our sexual experiences and performance. This may have implications for helping people with disabilities, the traumatized, the separated, the disenfranchised, and those who want to learn more about what it means to be emotionally and physically intimate but for whatever reason, lack the skills or the healthy sexual education.

It is our responsibility as integrative sex and couples therapists to use these tools as part of the larger landscape, one in which we can assist people who need our help to move into collaborative, more connected relationships and ultimately create a society with less polarization and loneliness and more fulfillment and happiness.

---

[4] A preview of these AI sex robots is available at https://abcnews.go.com/Nightline/video/buy-sex-robot-equipped-artificial-intelligence-20000-54712355.

Conclusion

Integrative Sex and Couples Therapy

Tammy Nelson, PhD

The chapters in this book have covered a variety of practical clinical interventions—as well as case examples and anecdotal stories by real, hands-on professionals—that highlight the use of sex and couples therapy in helping couples heal from relational and sexual difficulties. With the interventions in this book, thousands of couples have been helped through their most intimate sexuality issues.

Although this book has demonstrated how alternative and adjunctive therapies can and should be added when addressing sexual and relational difficulties among couples, this book alone is not enough. There are more techniques and interventions to consider, and continuing research on the psycho-bio-social-sexual approach to sex and couples therapy will lead to ever more theories in this field. In addition, most therapists have still not had adequate training in either sex therapy or relationship counseling, and given all of the challenges that contemporary couples face today, it is clear that we—the experts—need training in both areas.

As a result, I have created a new training institute in Washington, DC, called the Integrative Sex Therapy Institute, which is a developmental program and learning community that provides resources, connections, and integrative training to support therapists in becoming certified sex and couples therapists. It combines the best therapists and experts in the field in one place, both in person and online, in order to meet the needs of psychotherapists in this new and challenging world. The training is drawn from my own 30 years as a therapist, as well as some of the authors in this book, along with the finest researchers, professors, sex therapists, and couples therapists in the field today who contribute their experience and expertise.

Through the Institute, we have developed a new certification—the Certification in Sex and Couples Therapy (CSCT)—which is a designation we feel will be necessary for all therapists in the coming decades. The CSCT is offered only by the Integrative Sex Therapy Institute, and certification proves to the professional community, and to clients, that clinicians are experienced and trained in both areas: sex and relationship therapy. It is my hope that this book and the CSCT program contain the criteria needed to take us into the future of integrative relationship therapy.

About the Authors

Janet Brito, PhD, is an AASECT certified sex therapist who also has a license in clinical psychology and social work. She is a graduate of Pacifica Graduate Institute and completed her postdoctoral fellowship at the University of Minnesota Medical School, one of only a few university programs in the world dedicated to sexuality training. She is currently based in Honolulu, Hawaii, and is the founder of the Center for Sexual and Reproductive Health. Dr. Brito has been featured on many outlets, including *O, the Oprah Magazine; The Huffington Post; Playboy; Healthline; Women's Health* Magazine*; Thrive Global;* and *MidWeek* Publications.

Neil Cannon, PhD, LMFT, is an AASECT certified sex therapist and supervisor in Denver, Colorado. Dr. Cannon is an instructor at the University of Michigan School of Social Work Sexual Health Certificate Program, as well as a Professor of Marriage and Family Therapy at the Denver Family Institute, a leading marriage and family therapy school. Dr. Cannon is a master couples counselor and expert who treats BDSM and kink practitioners.

Pamela Finnerty, PhD, is a psychotherapist specializing in relationship issues and has been in private practice in Washington, DC, for over 30 years. She is an AASECT certified sex therapist and a Certified Sex and Couples Therapist. Formerly, she was a tenured associate professor of counseling and associate research professor of psychiatry at the George Washington University. In addition to her practice focusing on couples and group therapy, she is writing and teaching in the areas of sex, aging, and living vibrantly.

Deborah Fox, MSW, is an AASECT certified sex therapist and a certified Imago Relationship therapist in private practice in Washington, DC. She offers individual, couples, and group psychotherapy, as well as clinical consultation. Deborah conducts seminars and consultation groups on couples therapy and sex therapy. She has presented on these subjects at the Washington School of Psychiatry, the Greater Washington Society of Clinical Social Workers, the Institute for Psychoanalysis and Psychotherapy, the Integrative Sex Therapy Institute, and at the 2018 International Imago Relationship Therapy Conference. Deborah is an AASECT continuing education provider and an AASECT certified sex therapy supervisor in training. She is passionate about taking sex and couples therapy to a deeper emotional level and enabling greater intimacy and satisfaction.

Gail Guttman, LCSW, specializes in the integration of sex and couples therapy. Gail has been a certified Imago therapist since 1994 and an AASECT certified sex therapist since 1984. Gail offers consultation and supervision groups. She has been twice recognized by *Washingtonian* Magazine as a "top therapist" in sex and couples therapy. Gail is also an AASECT continuing education provider, an AASECT certified sex therapy supervisor, and an Imago clinical consultant. She is passionate about helping therapists integrate sex and couples therapy. Gail has presented on the subject of sex and couples therapy at the Integrative Sex Therapy Institute, the Greater Washington Society for Clinical Social Workers, previous Imago therapy conferences, the University of Maryland, and other professional organizations.

Amanda Holmberg-Sasek, MS, LMFT, is a licensed marriage and family therapist and an approved supervisor with the American Association of Marriage and Family Therapy (AAMFT). She is an owner and therapist at the Sexual Wellness Institute in Plymouth, Minnesota. She is a faculty affiliate and adjunct faculty at the University of Wisconsin-Stout Graduate Certificate in Sex Therapy Program.

Stephanie King, PsyD, is a licensed psychologist working in private practice in Marin County, California. She is a gender specialist, a sex and couples therapist, and also works with adult daughters of narcissistic mothers. Dr. King is the current president-elect of the Northern California Society for Psychoanalytic Psychology, a member of the World Professional Association for Transgender Health, and an active member of Mind the Gap—a UCSF consortium of mental health professionals dedicated to the care and advocacy of transgender and gender-expansive youth. Outside of private practice, Dr. King provides trainings to clinicians, educators, and medical professionals on gender-affirmative care with her organization, Transgender Advocacy & Consciousness Training (TACT).

Pebble Kranz, MD, FECSM is a board-certified family physician and fellow of the European Committee on Sexual Medicine. She completed her medical training at the University of Rochester Family Medicine Residency Program, with an area of focus in the psychosocial aspects of primary care. She is medical director of the Rochester Center for Sexual Wellness and has a sexual medicine clinic in the University of Rochester Medical Center's Gynecologic Oncology Department. She has clinical appointments in the departments of family medicine and obstetrics and gynecology at University of Rochester and participates in the University of Rochester Medical School and Residency curricula to improve exposure to sexual medicine.

Einat Metzl, PhD, LMFT, ATR-BC, RPT-S, is a licensed marriage and family therapist, registered and board-certified art therapist, and registered play therapist, with additional training in sex therapy, Emotionally Focused Therapy, and yoga instruction. She is an associate professor and chair at the Loyola Marymount University's Marital Family Therapy and Art Therapy Graduate Program. Dr. Metzl is committed to expanding art therapy research and practice and bridging current paradigms with related disciplines.

In addition to her academic roles, she also maintains a private practice where she works with families, couples, and individuals of all ages.

Wendy E. Miller, PhD, is a clinical psychologist with 35 years of experience treating individuals and couples. She received her PhD in 1985 from the George Washington University and is a graduate of the NYU Postdoctoral Program in Psychotherapy and Psychoanalysis. She is an AASECT certified sex therapist and has worked in the field of sexuality for over 30 years. Dr. Miller is on the faculty of The Women's Therapy Centre Institute, where she teaches classes on human sexuality and consults at The Center for Optimal Living in New York City on issues involving the link between sexuality and drug use. Recently, she became a therapy and research collaborator with Dr. Peggy Kleinplatz's Optimal Sexual Experiences Research Team at the University of Ottawa and is conducting couple therapy groups based on this model.

Tammy Nelson, PhD, is an internationally acclaimed psychotherapist, board-certified sexologist, certified sex therapist, and certified Imago Relationship therapist. She is a TEDx speaker, the host of podcast "*The Trouble with Sex,*" and the author of several books including *Getting the Sex You Want: Shed Your Inhibitions and Reach New Heights of Passion Together, The New Monogamy: Redefining Your Relationship After Infidelity,* and *When You're the One Who Cheats: Ten Things You Need to Know.* She is the founder and executive director of the Integrative Sex Therapy Institute, training and certifying psychotherapists to be sex and couples therapists. She has been a featured expert in *The New York Times Magazine, The Washington Post, The Wall Street Journal, CNN, Rolling Stone* magazine, *Redbook, Glamour, The Sun, The London Times,* and a source in *TIME* magazine.

Malika O'Neill, MS, is a graduate student at Widener University where she is working toward a master of education in human sexuality with a specialization in sex therapy. Her research and clinical interests are devoted to the clinical application of intersectionality and feminism and their impact on negotiating intimacy. In addition, she is interested in investigating the confluence of sexual self-esteem, kink awareness, boundary negotiation, and social justice. As a culturally competent and integrative therapist, Malika's clinical practice serves individuals, families, and groups from diverse backgrounds.

Daniel Rosen, LCSW-R,CST, earned his master's in social work from New York University and became a certified sex therapist in 2014. He chaired the AASECT Ethics Advisory Committee from 2016 to 2018 and has provided local trainings in sex therapy for psychotherapists and medical residents since 2008. From 2016 to 2017, he also served as an instructor at the University of Buffalo teaching a course on sex therapy. As a member of the Rochester Center for Sexual Wellness team, he and Dr. Kranz bring this global perspective on sexual health to western New York. Mr. Rosen and Dr. Kranz trained with Dr. Peggy Kleinplatz to collaborate with the Optimal Sexual Experiences Research Team at the University of Ottawa.

James C. Wadley, PhD, CST, CST-S, is professor and chair of the Counseling and Human Services Department at Lincoln University. He received a doctoral degree in education from the University of Pennsylvania with a concentration in educational leadership and human sexuality education. He maintains a private practice as a licensed professional counselor in the states of Pennsylvania and New Jersey. As an integrative therapist, Dr. Wadley has emerged as one of the nation's best sexuality therapists with a focus on intimacy-building in relationships, addiction, and values clarification. His co-edited book, *The Art of Sex Therapy Supervision*, received the AASECT's 2019 Book of the Year award and his new edited book, *The Handbook of Sexuality Leadership: Inspiring Community Engagement, Social Empowerment and Transformational Influence*, offers a strategic blueprint for success for emergent sexuality leaders. Finally, Dr. Wadley serves as an educational consultant to several agencies and institutions across the Delaware Valley.

Resources

Integrative Sex and Couples Therapy

- **The American Association of Sexuality Educators, Counselors, and Therapists (AASECT)**: Provides training in sex therapy, sex education, and sexuality counseling. For more information, visit https://www.aasect.org.

- **Integrative Sex Therapy Institute**: Provides training for therapists to allow them to become Certified Sex Therapists and Certified Sex and Couples Therapists. Information is available at https://www.integrativesextherapyinstitute.com.

- For more information on integrative sex and couples therapy, clients can visit www.DrTammyNelson.com.

Sexual Medicine

- **International Society for the Study of Women's Sexual Health (ISSWSH)**: With a focus on women's sexual health, ISSWSH creates clinical guidelines, spearheads sexual medicine research in women, and provides excellent education for both medical and mental health providers at conferences and through an annual educational intensive course. A listing of providers is available at http://www.isswsh.org.

- **Sexual Medicine Society of North America (SMSNA)**: While this society has a strong urology focus, its conferences highlight the topics of sexual medicine more generally. A list of providers is available at http://www.smsna.org/V1/index.php.

- **European Society for Sexual Medicine (ESSM)**: With excellent basic and advanced courses on sexual medicine, ESSM trains medical providers in a wide variety of disciplines, including urology, gynecology, primary care, endocrinology, neurology, psychiatry, and oncology. The Multidisciplinary Joint Committee on Sexual Medicine (MJCSM) administers the fellowship exam and certification process. Additional information can be found at https://www.essm.org.

- **The International Society for Sexual Medicine (ISSM)**: ISSM promotes research in the field of human sexuality. Its website has patient information, a list of sexual medicine providers, as well as a growing library of clinical guidelines for medical providers: https://www.issm.info.

General Sexual Medicine Patient Information

- **Sexual Health Matters** (www.SexHealthMatters.org)
- **WomanLab** (WomanLab.org)

Sexual Pain

- *When Sex Hurts: A Woman's Guide to Banishing Sexual Pain*, by Andrew Goldstein, Caroline Pukall, and Irwin Goldstein, is an excellent book about sexual pain with an overview of causes and treatments, both for clients and clinicians.

- *Heal Pelvic Pain*, by Amy Stein, describes the field of pelvic floor physical therapy, introduces methods of treatment, and provides a series of stretches, exercises, and therapy techniques that clients can do on their own. It is a great resource for clients and clinicians alike.

Transgender Clients

- **World Professional Association for Transgender Health (WPATH)**: Formerly known as the Harry Benjamin International Gender Dysphoria Association, WPATH, is a 501(c)(3) nonprofit, interdisciplinary professional and educational organization devoted to transgender health. Their professional, supporting, and student members engage in clinical and academic research to develop evidence-based medicine and strive to promote a high quality of care for transgender and gender-nonconforming individuals internationally. They are funded primarily through the support of their membership and through donations and grants sponsored by noncommercial sources.

- **U.S. Professional Association for Transgender Health (USPATH)**: USPATH and WPATH are international organizations that focus on global issues in transgender health. More local advocacy and policy can often be best accomplished by WPATH-affiliated regional associations. Each PATH has the advantage of WPATH affiliation while being able to focus activity and advocacy on the issues most important to that part of the world.

References

Chapter 1
Sex and Couples Therapy:
Biopsychosocial and Relationship Therapy

Annon, J. S. (1976). The PLISSIT model: A proposed conceptual scheme for the behavioral treatment of sexual problems. *Journal of Sex Education and Therapy, 2*(1), 1–15.

Buber, M. (2010). *I and thou*. Eastford, CT: Martino Books.

Johnson, S. (2004). *The practice of emotionally focused couples therapy*. London, UK: Routledge.

Johnson, S. (2008). *Hold me tight: Conversations for a lifetime of love*. New York: Little, Brown and Company.

Kaplan, H. S. (1974). *The new sex therapy: Active treatment of sexual dysfunctions*. New York: Brunner/Mazel.

Kinsey, A., Pomeroy, W. B., & Martin, C. E. (1948). *Sexual behavior in the human male*. Bloomington, IN: Indiana University Press.

Kinsey, A., Pomeroy, W. B., Martin, C. E., & Gebhard, P. H. (1953). *Sexual behavior in the human female*. Bloomington, IN: Indiana University Press.

Masters, W. H., & Johnson, V. E. (1966). *Human sexual response*. New York: Bantam Books.

Masters, W. H., & Johnson, V. E. (1970). *Human sexual inadequacy*. New York: Bantam Books.

Schwartz, R. C. (2001). *Introduction to the Internal Family Systems Model*. Oak Park, IL: Trailheads Publishing.

Chapter 2
Sex Therapy and Sexual Medicine with Couples:
The Collaborative Sexual Wellness Model

Annon, J. (1976). *The behavioral treatment of sexual problems* (Vol. 2). New York: Harper & Row.

Bitzer, J., Giraldi, A., & Pfaus, J. (2013). A standardized diagnostic interview for hypoactive sexual desire disorder in women: Standard operating procedure (SOP Part 2). *Journal of Sexual Medicine, 10*(1), 50–57.

Engel, G. (1977). The need for a new medical model: A challenge for biomedicine. *Science, 196*, 129–136.

Goldstein, I., Clayton, A., Goldstein, A., Kim, N., & Kingsberg, S. (2018). *Textbook of female sexual function and dysfunction: Diagnosis and treatment.* Hoboken, NJ: John Wiley & Sons.

McCarthy, B. (2015). *Sex made simple: Clinical strategies for sexual issues in therapy.* Eau Claire, WI: PESI Publishing & Media.

Miller, S., & Donahey, K. (2012). Feedback-Informed Treatment: Improving the outcome of sex therapy one person at a time. In P. J. Kleinplatz (Ed.), *New directions in sex therapy: Innovations and alternatives* (pp. 195–212). New York: Routledge.

Moser, C. (1999). *Health care without shame: A handbook for the sexually diverse and their caregivers.* Emeryville, CA: Greenery Press.

Ruddy, N., Borresen, D., & Gunn, W. (2008). *The collaborative psychotherapist: Creating reciprocal relationships with medical professionals.* Washington, DC: American Psychological Association.

World Health Organization. (2006). *Sexual and reproductive health: Defining sexual health.* Retrieved from https://www.who.int/reproductivehealth/topics/sexual_health/sh_definitions/en/

Chapter 3
Treating No-Sex Couples:
Integrating Emotionally Focused Therapy with Sexuality Counseling

Bader, M. (2002). *Arousal: The secret logic of sexual fantasies.* New York: Thomas Dunne Books.

Basson, R. (2001). Human sex response cycles. *Journal of Sex and Marital Therapy, 27*(1), 33–43.

Bowlby, J. (1969). *Attachment and loss: Attachment* (Vol. 1). New York: Basic Books.

Bowlby, J. (1988). *A secure base: Parent-child attachment and healthy human development.* New York: Basic Books.

Eagle, M. (2007). Attachment and sexuality. In D. Diamond, S. J. Blatt, & J. D. Lichtenberg (Eds.), *Attachment and sexuality.* New York: Taylor & Francis Group.

Goldner, V. (2004). Review essay: Attachment and eros: Opposed or synergistic? *Psychoanalytic Dialogues, 14*(3), 381–396.

Greenberg, L., & Johnson, S. (1988). *Emotionally focused therapy for couples.* New York: Guilford Press.

Iasenza, S. (2006). Low sexual desire in gay, lesbian and heterosexual peer marriages. In J. S. Scharff & D. E. Scharff (Eds.), *New paradigms for treating relationships* (pp. 375–383). New York: Jason Aronson.

Iasenza, S. (2010). What is queer about sex? Expanding sexual frames in theory and practice. *Family Process, 49*(3), 291–308.

Johnson, S. (2004). *The practice of emotionally focused couple therapy: Creating connection.* New York: Brunner Routledge.

Johnson, S., Simakodskya, Z., & Moran, M. (2018). Addressing issues of sexuality in couples therapy: Emotionally focused therapy meets sex therapy. *Current Sexual Health Reports, 10*(3), 65–71.

Kleinplatz, P. J. (2003). Optimal erotic intimacy: Lessons from great lovers. In S. B. Levine & S. E. Althof (Eds.), *Handbook of clinical sexuality for mental health professions* (3rd ed., pp. 310–317). New York: Routledge.

Kleinplatz, P. J. (2012). *New directions in sex therapy: Innovations and alternatives* (2nd ed.). New York: Routledge.

Kleinplatz, P. J., Menard, A. D., Paquet, M. P., Paradis, N., Campbell, M., Zuccarini, D., & Mehak, L. (2009). The components of optimal sexuality: A portrait of "great sex." *Canadian Journal of Human Sexuality, 18*(1–2), 1–13.

Masters, W. H., & Johnson, V. E. (1966). *Human sexual response.* New York: Bantam Books.

Morin, J. (1995). *The erotic mind.* New York: HarperPerennial.

Mitchell, S. A. (2002). *Can love last? The fate of romance over time.* New York: W. W. Norton.

Perel, E. (2006). *Mating in captivity: Unlocking erotic intelligence.* New York: Harper Collins.

Schwartz, P. (1994). *Peer marriage: How love between equals really works.* New York: Simon & Schuster.

Weiner, L., & Avery-Clark, C. (2017). *Sensate focus in sex therapy.* New York: Routledge.

Chapter 4
Sex and Imago Relationship Therapy

American Psychiatric Association. (2013). *Diagnostic and statistical manual of mental disorders* (5th ed.). Arlington, VA: Author.

Bader, J. (2002). *Arousal: The secret logic of sexual fantasies.* New York: Thomas Dunne Books.

Hendrix, H. (1988). *Getting the love you want.* New York: Holt Paperbacks.

Masters, W. H., Johnson, V. E., & Kolodny, R. C. (1982). *On sex and human loving.* New York: Little, Brown and Company.

Nelson, T. (2008). *Getting the sex you want: Shed your inhibitions and reach new heights of passion together.* Rockport, MA: Fairwinds Press.

Rosenfeld, S., & Slade, S. (2019). *Finding the sex you lost.* Training sponsored by the American Association of Sexuality Educators, Counselors and Therapists, Original Material.

Chapter 5
Internal Family Systems and Sex Therapy

Berne, E. (1964). *Games people play: The psychology of human relationships*. New York: Groves Press.

Herbine-Blank, T. (2015). *Intimacy from the inside out*. New York: Routledge.

Jung, C. G. (1970). *The structure and dynamics of the psyche* (Collected Works, Vol. 8). Princeton, NJ: Princeton University Press.

McCarthy, B., & Metz, M. (2004). *Coping with premature ejaculation: How to overcome PE, please your partner, & and have great sex*. Oakland, CA: New Harbinger Publications.

Rowan, J. (1990). *Subpersonalities: The people inside us*. London, UK: Routledge.

Schwartz, R. C. (1997). *Internal family systems therapy*. New York: Guilford Press.

Schwartz, R. C. (2001). *Introduction to the internal family systems model*. Oak Park, IL: Trailhead Publishing.

Chapter 6
Healing Sexual Trauma with Couples Therapy in Groups

Brotto, L. A. (2018). *Better sex through mindfulness: How women can cultivate desire*. Berkeley, CA: Greystone Books.

Buchele, B. J. (2000). Group psychotherapy for survivors of sexual and physical abuse. In R. H. Klein & V. L. Schermer (Eds.), *Group psychotherapy for psychological trauma* (pp. 170–187). New York: Guilford Press.

Shapiro, F. (2001). *Eye movement desensitization and reprocessing: Basic principles, protocols and procedures* (2nd ed.). New York: Guilford Press.

Solomon, M. F. (2003). Connection, disruption, repair: Treating the effects of attachment trauma on intimate relationships. In M. F. Solomon & D. J. Siegel (Eds.), *Healing trauma: Attachment, mind, body and brain* (pp. 322–346). New York: Norton.

Yalom, I. D. (1995). *The theory and practice of group psychotherapy*. New York: Basic Books.

Chapter 7
Intersectionality 101 for Sex and Couples Therapists

Adams, D. M., & Lott, E. H. (2019). Black women: Then and now. *Women & Therapy, 42*(3–4), 1–20.

Arrendondo, P. (1994). Multicultural training: A response. *The Counseling Psychologist, 22*, 308–314.

Carastathis, A. (2014). The concept of intersectionality in feminist theory. *Philosophy Compass, 9*(5), 304–314.

Cayleff, S. E. (1986). Ethical issues in counseling gender, race, and culturally distinct groups. *Journal of Counseling and Development, 64*, 345–347.

Collins, P. H., & Bilge, S. (2016). *Intersectionality*. New York: John Wiley & Sons.

Crenshaw, K. (1991). Mapping the margins: Intersectionality, identity politics and violence against women of color. *Stanford Law Review, 43*, 1241–1299.

Helmeke, K., & Sprenkle, D. (2000). Clients' perceptions of pivotal moments in couples therapy: A qualitative study of change in therapy. *Journal of Marital and Family Therapy, 26*, 469–483.

Hooks, B. (1989). *Talking back: Thinking feminist, thinking black*. Toronto: Between the Lines.

McIntosh, P. (1990). White privilege: Unpacking the invisible knapsack. *Independent School, 49*, 31–39.

Mbilishaka, A. M. (2018). Strands of intimacy: Black women's narratives of hair and intimate relationships with men. *Journal of Black Sexuality and Relationships, 5*(1), 43–61.

Nouwen, H. (1972). *The wounded healer*. New York: Doubleday.

Parker, L. (2009). Disrupting power and privilege in couples therapy. *Clinical Social Work Journal, 37*(3), 248–255.

Roberson, Q. M. (2013). *The oxford handbook of diversity and work*. New York: Oxford University Press.

Ryabov, I. (2019). How much does physical attractiveness matter for blacks? Linking skin color, physical attractiveness, and black status attainment. *Race and Social Problems, 11*(1), 68–79.

Sue, D. (2015). Therapeutic harm and cultural oppression. *The Counseling Psychologist, 43*(3), 359–369.

Sue, D. W., Ivey, A. E., & Pedersen, P. B. (Eds.). (1996). *A theory of multicultural counseling and therapy*. Belmont, CA: Thomson Brooks/Cole Publishing.

Williams, N. A., & Ware, C. (2019). A tale of two "halfs": Being black, while being biracial. *International Journal of Qualitative Studies in Education, 32*(1), 85–106.

Wohl, J. (1995). Traditional individual psychotherapy and ethnic minorities. In J. F. Aponte, R. Young Rivers, & J. Wohl (Eds.), *Psychological interventions and cultural diversity* (pp. 74–91). Boston: Allyn & Bacon.

Chapter 8
Relationship Counseling and Sex Therapy with Kinky Clients

Blow, A. J., Sprenkle, D. H., & Davis, S. D. (2007). Is who delivers the therapy more important than the treatment itself? The role of the therapist in common factors. *Journal of Marital and Family Therapy, 33*(3), 298–317.

Cannon, N. (2011, April). *Lost libido: Effective & creative interventions for treating couples with low libido and gaps in sexual desire*. Workshop given for members of the

American Association of Sexuality Educators, Counselors, and Therapists (AASECT), Denver, CO.

Kolmes, K., Stock, W., & Moser, C. (2006). Investigating bias in psychotherapy with BDSM clients. *Journal of Homosexuality, 50*(2/3), 301–324.

Meyer, I. (2003). Prejudice, social stress, and mental health in lesbian, gay, and bisexual populations: Conceptual issues and research evidence. *Psychological Bulletin, 129*(5), 674–697.

Nagoski, E. (2015). *Come as you are: The surprising new science that will transform your sex life*. New York: Simon & Schuster.

Pillai-Friedman, S., Pollitt, J. L., & Castaldo, A. (2015). Becoming kink-aware—a necessity for sexuality professionals. *Sexual and Relationship Therapy, 30*(2), 196–210.

Richters, J., de Visser, R. O., Rissel, C. E., Grulich, A. E., & Smith, A. M. (2008). Demographic and psychosocial features of participants in bondage and discipline, "sadomasochism," or dominance and submission (BDSM): Data from a national survey. *The Journal of Sexual Medicine, 5*(7), 1660–1668.

Rogers, C. R. (2007). The necessary and sufficient conditions of therapeutic personality change. *Psychotherapy: Theory, Research, Practice, Training, 44*(3), 240–248.

Sprott, R. A., Randall, A., Davison, K., Cannon, N., & Witherspoon, R. G. (2017). Alternative or nontraditional sexualities and therapy: A case report. *Journal of Clinical Psychology, 73*(8), 929–937.

Zamboni, B. D. (2017). A qualitative exploration of adult baby/diaper lover behavior from an online community sample. *The Journal of Sex Research, 56*(2), 191–202.

Chapter 9
The Mind-Body Connection: Couples, Sex, and Somatic Therapy

Fosha, D. (2000). *The transforming power of affect: A model for accelerated change*. New York: Basic Books.

Kurtz, R. (1990). *Body-centered psychotherapy: The Hakomi method*. Mendocino, CA: LifeRhythm.

Levine, P. (2010). *In an unspoken voice: How the body releases trauma and restores goodness*. Berkeley, CA: North Atlantic Books.

Ogden, P., & Fisher, J. (2015). *Sensorimotor psychotherapy: Interventions for trauma and attachment*. New York: W. W. Norton.

Porges, S. W. (2011). *The polyvagal theory: Neurophysiological foundations of emotions, attachment, communication, and self-regulation*. New York: W. W. Norton.

Rothschild, B. (2000). *The body remembers*. New York: W. W. Norton.

van der Kolk, B. (2014). *The body keeps the score*. New York: Penguin Books.

Chapter 10
The Nutri-Sexual Health Model

Aarseth, H., & Olsen, B. M. (2008). Food and masculinity in dual-career couples. *Journal of Gender Studies, 17*(4), 277–287.

Bergeron, S., Merwin, K., Dubé, J., & Rosen, N. (2018). Couples sex therapy versus group therapy for women with genito-pelvic pain. *Current Sexual Health Reports, 10*(3), 79–87.

Betchen, S. J. (2009). Premature ejaculation: An integrative, intersystems approach for couples. *Journal of Family Psychotherapy, 20*(2/3), 241–260.

Bove, C. F., & Sobal, J. (2006). Foodwork in newly married couples: Making family meals. *Food, Culture & Society, 9*(1), 69–89.

Di Francesco, S., & Tenaglia, R. L. (2017). Mediterranean diet and erectile dysfunction: A current perspective. *Central European Journal of Urology, 70*(2), 185–187.

Eddy, K. T., Novotny, C. M., & Westen, D. (2004). Sexuality, personality, and eating disorders. *Eating Disorders, 12*(3), 191–208.

Esposito, K., Giugliano, F., Maiorino, M. I., & Giugliano, D. (2010). Dietary factors, Mediterranean diet and erectile dysfunction. *The Journal of Sexual Medicine, 7*(7), 2338–2345.

Gehring, D. (2003). Couples therapy for low sexual desire: A systemic approach. *Journal of Sex & Marital Therapy, 29*(1), 25–38.

Germer, C., & Neff, K. (2013). Self-compassion in clinical practice. *Journal of Clinical Psychology, 69*(8), 856–867.

Giugliano, F., Maiorino, M. I., Di Palo, C., Autorino, R., De Sio, M., Giugliano, D., & Esposito, K. (2010). Women's sexual health: Adherence to Mediterranean diet and sexual function in women with type 2 diabetes. *The Journal of Sexual Medicine, 7*(5), 1883–1890.

Höijer, K., Hjälmeskog, K., & Fjellström, C. (2014). The role of food selection in Swedish home economics: The educational visions and cultural meaning. *Ecology of Food and Nutrition, 53*(5), 484–502.

Johnson, S., Simakhodskaya, Z., & Moran, M. (2018). Addressing issues of sexuality in couples therapy: Emotionally focused therapy meets sex therapy. *Current Sexual Health Reports, 10*(2), 65–71.

Lange, D., Corbett, J., Lippke, S., Knoll, N., & Schwarzer, R. (2015). The interplay of intention, autonomy, and sex with dietary planning: A conditional process model to predict fruit and vegetable intake. *British Journal of Health Psychology, 20*(4), 859–876.

Leach, M. (2005). Rapport: A key to treatment success. *Complementary Therapies in Clinical Practice, 11*(4), 262–265.

Maiorino, M. I., Bellastella, G., Chiodini, P., Romano, O., Scappaticcio, L., Giugliano, D., & Esposito, K. (2016). Primary prevention of sexual dysfunction with

Mediterranean diet in type 2 diabetes: The MÈDITA randomized trial. *Diabetes Care,* *39*(9), e143–e144.

McCarthy, B. W., Ginsberg, R. L., & Fucito, L. M. (2006). Resilient sexual desire in heterosexual couples. *The Family Journal, 14*(1), 59–64.

Neault, R. A., & Pickerell, D. A. (2005). Dual-career couples: The juggling act. *Canadian Journal of Counselling and Psychotherapy/Revue Canadienne de Counseling et de Psychothérapie, 39*(3), 187–198.

Rosen, R., Leiblum, S., & Spector, I. (1994). Psychologically based treatment for male erectile disorder: A cognitive-interpersonal model. *Journal of Sex & Marital Therapy, 20*(2), 67–85.

Salyer, J., Schubert, C., & Chiaranai, C. (2012). Supportive relationships, self-care confidence, and heart failure self-care. *The Journal of Cardiovascular Nursing, 27*(5), 384–393.

Tahan, H., & Sminkey, P. (2012). Motivational interviewing. *Professional Case Management, 17*(4), 164–172.

Tye, M. (2013). *Sexuality and our diversity.* New York: FlatWorld Knowledge.

Weiner, L., & Avery-Clark, C. (2017). *Sensate focus in sex therapy.* New York: Routledge.

Chapter 11
Art Therapy and Sex Therapy:
Infusing Couples Work with Creative Tools

Barth, R. J., & Kinder, B. N. (1985). The use of art therapy in marital and sex therapy. *Journal of Marital and Sex Therapy, 11*(3), 192–198.

Bat Or, M., Ishai, R., & Levi, N. (2015). The symbolic content in adults' PPAT as related to attachment styles and achievement motivation. *The Arts in Psychotherapy, 43*, 49–60.

Chapman, L. (2014). *Neurobiologically informed trauma therapy with children and adolescents: Understanding mechanisms of change.* New York: W. W. Norton.

Dailey, D. (1981). Sexual expression and aging. In F. Berghorn & D. Schafer (Eds.), *The dynamics of aging: Original essays on the processes and experiences of growing old* (pp. 311–330). Boulder, CO: Westview Press.

Dissanayake, E. (2012). *Art and intimacy: How the arts began.* Seattle, WA: University of Washington Press.

Goldner, L., Gazit, O., & Scharf, M. (2017). Separateness and closeness as expressed in bird's nest drawings: Relationships with partners and with the unborn child among expectant parents. *The Arts in Psychotherapy, 53*, 1–11.

Gottman, J. (2004). *The seven principles for making marriage work.* New York: Three Rivers.

Greenman, P. S., & Johnson, S. M. (2013). Process research on emotionally focused therapy (EFT) for couples: Linking theory to practice. *Family Process, 52*(1), 46–61.

Harriss, M., & Landgarten, H. (1973). Art therapy as an innovative approach to conjoint treatment: A case study. *Art Psychotherapy, 1*(3–4), 221–228.

Hinkle, M. S., Radomski, J. G., & Decker, K. M. (2015). Creative experiential interventions to heighten emotion and process in emotionally focused couples therapy. *The Family Journal, 23*(3), 239–246.

Johnson, S. M., Makinen, J. A., & Millikin, J. W. (2001). Attachment injuries in couple relationships: A new perspective on impasses in couples therapy. *Journal of Marital and Family Therapy, 27*(2), 145–155.

Kaiser, D. H. (1996). Indications of attachment security in a drawing task. *The Arts in Psychotherapy, 23*(4), 333–340.

Kaplan, F. F. (1983). Drawing together. *American Journal of Art Therapy, 22,* 79–85.

Kwiatkowska, H. Y. (1978). *Family therapy and evaluation through art.* Springfield, IL: C.C. Thomas.

Lubbers, D. (2017). *Bodymap protocol: Integrating art therapy and focusing in the treatment of adults with trauma* (Doctoral dissertation). Available from Dissertation Abstracts International. (Publication No. 10830077)

Metzl, E. S. (2009). The role of creative thinking in resilience after hurricane Katrina. *Psychology of Aesthetics, Creativity, and the Arts, 3*(2), 112–123.

Metzl, E. S. (2016). *When art therapy meets sex therapy: Creative explorations of sexuality, gender and relationships.* New York: Routledge.

Sarrel, P. M., Sarrel, L. J., & Berman, S. (1981). Using the Draw-a-Person Test in sex therapy. *Journal of Sex and Marital Therapy, 7,* 163–183.

Snir, S., & Wiseman, H. (2010). Attachment in romantic couples and perceptions of a joint drawing session. *The Family Journal, 18*(2), 116–126.

Snir, S., & Wiseman, H. (2013). Relationship patterns of connectedness and individuality in couples as expressed in the couple joint drawing method. *The Arts in Psychotherapy, 40*(5), 501–508.

Snir, S., & Wiseman, H. (2016). Couples' joint drawing patterns: Associations with self-report measures of interpersonal patterns and attachment styles. *The Arts in Psychotherapy, 48,* 28–37.

Wadeson, H. (1972). Conjoint marital art therapy techniques. *Psychiatry, 35,* 89–98.

Zoldbrod, A. P. (1998). *SexSmart: How your childhood shaped your sexual life and what to do with it.* Oakland, CA: New Harbinger Publications.

Chapter 12
Working with LGB(Trans)QIA Couples Using an Intersectional, Psychodynamic, and Gender-Affirmative Approach

American Psychiatric Association. (2013). *Diagnostic and statistical manual of mental disorders* (5th ed). Arlington, VA: Author.

Bancroft, J. (2009). *Human sexuality and its problems* (3rd ed.). Edinburgh, UK: Elsevier.

Bigner, J. J., & Wetchler, J. L. (2012). *Handbook of LGBT-affirmative couple and family therapy*. New York: Routledge.

Blumer, M. L. C., Green, M. S., Knowles, S. J., & Williams, A. (2012). Shedding light on thirteen years of darkness: Content analysis of articles pertaining to transgender issues in marriage/couple family therapy journals. *Journal of Marital and Family Therapy, 38,* 244–256.

Chang, S., Singh, A., & Dickey, I. (2018). *A clinician's guide to gender-affirming care.* Oakland, CA: New Harbinger.

Clark, W., & Serovich, J. M. (1997). Twenty years and still in the dark? Content analysis of articles pertaining to gay, lesbian, and bisexual issues in marriage and family therapy journals. *Journal of Marital and Family Therapy, 23,* 239–253.

Crenshaw, K. (1989). Demarginalizing the intersection of race and sex: A black feminist critique of antidiscrimination doctrine, feminist theory and antiracist politics. *University of Chicago Legal Forum, 1*(8), 139–167.

Erickson-Schroth, L., & Boylan, J. F. (2014). *Trans bodies, trans selves: A resource for the transgender community.* New York: Oxford University Press.

Hartwell, E. E., Serovich, J. M., Grafsky, E. L., & Kerr, Z. Y. (2012). Coming out of the dark: Content analysis of articles pertaining to gay, lesbian, and bisexual issues in couple and family therapy journals. *Journal of Marital and Family Therapy, 38,* 227–243.

Langer, S. J. (2019). *Theorizing transgender identity for clinical practice: A new model for understanding gender.* Philadelphia, PA: Jessica Kingsley Publishers.

Masters, W. H., & Johnson, V. E. (1966). *Human sexual response.* New York: Bantam Books.

Oliver, M. (1996). *Understanding disability: From theory to practice.* London, UK: Palgrave MacMillan.

Wallin, J. (2007). *Attachment in psychotherapy.* New York: Guilford Press.

Chapter 13
Integrative Alternative Mindfulness and Sexuality

Avery-Clark, C., & Weiner, L. (2018, July). *Sensate focus: The alchemy of touch, mindfulness & somatic therapy.* Training sponsored by The Integrative Sex Therapy Institute, Training Program, Washington, DC.

Brotto, L. (2018). *Better sex through mindfulness: How women can cultivate desire.* Berkeley, CA: Greystone Books.

Brotto, L. A., & Basson, R. (2014). Group mindfulness-based therapy significantly improves sexual desire in women. *Behaviour Research and Therapy, 57,* 43–54.

Brotto, L. A., Basson, R., Smith, K. B., Driscoll, M., & Sadownik, L. (2015). Mindfulness-based group therapy for women with provoked vestibulodynia. *Mindfulness, 6*(3), 417–432.

Brotto, L. A., & Heiman, J. R. (2007). Mindfulness in sex therapy: Applications for women with sexual difficulties following gynecologic cancer. *Sexual and Relationship Therapy, 22*(1), 3–11.

Brotto, L. A., Heiman, J. R., Goff, B., Greer, B., Lentz, G. M., Swisher, E., & van Blaricom, A. (2008). A psychoeducational intervention for sexual dysfunction in women with gynecologic cancer. *Archives of Sexual Behavior, 37*(2), 317–329.

Brotto, L. A., Krychman, M., & Jacobson, P. (2008). Eastern approaches for enhancing women's sexuality: Mindfulness, acupuncture, and yoga. *Journal of Sexual Medicine, 5,* 2741–2748.

Kabat-Zinn, J. (1990). *Full catastrophe living: Using the wisdom of your body and mind to face stress, pain, and illness.* New York: Delacorte Press.

Kerner, I. (2004). *She comes first: The thinking man's guide to pleasuring a woman.* New York: HarperCollins.

Kerner, I. (2006). *He comes next: The thinking woman's guide to pleasuring a man.* New York: HarperCollins.

Kleinplatz, P. J., Ménard, A. D., Paquet, M. P., Paradis, N., Campbell, M., Zuccarino, D., & Mehak, L. (2009). The components of optimal sexuality: A portrait of "great sex." *Canadian Journal of Human Sexuality, 18*(1–2), 1–13.

Nelson, T. (2014). *Six weeks of erotic dates & a protocol for erotic recovery.* Retrieved from https://drtammynelson.com/product/ebook-six-weeks-of-erotic-dates-a-protocol-for-erotic-recovery/

Weiner, L., & Avery-Clark, C. (2017). *Sensate focus in sex therapy.* New York: Routledge.

Chapter 14
The Future of Sex:
What Do Polyamory and Technology Mean for Monogamy?

Bennett, J. (2009, July 28). Polyamory: The next sexual revolution? *Newsweek.* Retrieved from https://www.newsweek.com/polyamory-next-sexual-revolution-82053

Fisher, H. (1992). *Anatomy of love: A natural history of mating, marriage, and why we stray.* New York: Random House.

Nelson, T. (2012). *The new monogamy: Redefining your relationship after infidelity.* Oakland, CA: New Harbinger.

Rubin, J. D., Moors, A. C., Matsick, J. L., Ziegler, A., & Conley, T. D. (2014). On the margins: Considering diversity among consensually non-monogamous relationships. [Special Issue on Polyamory]. *Journal für Psychologie, 22*(1), 19–37.

Schmitt, D. P., & Buss, D. M. (2001). Human mate poaching: Tactics and temptations for infiltrating existing mateships. *Journal of Personality and Social Psychology, 80,* 894–917.

Tafoya, M. A., & Spitzberg, B. H. (2007). The dark side of infidelity: Its nature, prevalence, and communicative functions. In B. H. Spitzberg & W. R. Cupach (Eds.), *The dark side of interpersonal communication* (2nd ed., pp. 201–242). Mahwah, NJ: Lawrence Erlbaum Associates.

Vaughan, P. (2003). *The monogamy myth: A personal handbook for recovering from affairs* (3rd ed.). New York: William Morrow Paperbacks.

Index

Made in the USA
Columbia, SC
13 March 2021